THE
HUDSON

By
Benson J. Lossing

Foreword by
Pete Seeger

BLACK·DOME
1011 Route 296
Hensonville, New York 12439
Tel: (518) 734-6357
Fax: (518) 734-5802
www.blackdomepress.com

Published by

Black Dome Press Corp.
1011 Route 296
Hensonville, New York 12439
Tel: (518) 734-6357
Fax: (518) 734-5802
blackdomepress.com

The Hudson, from the Wilderness to the Sea was originally published in 1866 by H.B.
Nims & Co., Troy, New York.

ISBN 1-883789-26-5

Library of Congress Cataloging-in-Publication Data:

Lossing, Benson John, 1813-1891
    The Hudson, from the wilderness to the sea / by Benson J. Lossing; introduction by
Pete Seeger.
        p. cm.
    Originally published: Troy, N.Y. : H.B. Nims & Co., 1866. With new introd.
    ISBN 1-883789-26-5 (trade paper)
    1. Hudson River Valley (N.Y. and N.J.)—Description and travel. 2. Hudson River
Valley (N.Y. and N.J.)—History—19th century. 3. Hudson River Valley (N.Y. and
N.J.)—Pictorial works. 4. Hudson River (N.Y. and N.J.)—Description and travel. 5.
Lossing, Benson John, 1813-1891—Journeys—Hudson River Valley (N.Y. and N.J.) I.
Title.

F127.H8 L8 2000
974.7'3-dc21

                                                                                    00-033663

Cover design by Carol Clement, Artemisia, Inc.
Printed in the USA

Foreword

Lucky is the person who holds a copy of this book in her/his hands. Written a century and a half ago as a series of articles in *The London Art Journal*, it keeps getting reprinted. Let's hope it never goes out of print again.

Lossing, usually accompanied by his wife, took horse and carriage to visit different parts of the river over a couple of years. Staying in local inns, he looked up local historians and story-tellers. With sketchbook always in hand, he captured scenes impossible to find now. Three hundred miles, from Lake Tear in the Adirondacks to the Atlantic Ocean, he recorded winter as well as summer scenes. From his Dutchess County home, it was "clip-clop, clip-clop" for hundreds of hours, and often many hours drying wet clothing in front of an open fire or cleaning mud off boots, then drying them and putting on another coat of oil to waterproof them.

New York City was pushing 300,000 population then. Two newly invented miracles, railroad and telegraph, came to the east shore in 1847. Four hundred sloops still carried bricks and other cargoes then, at speeds between one and ten miles an hour, but steamboats and rail had taken the passenger business. Every inch of the valley not mountainous was farmland or pastureland. The term "suburb" had not yet been invented. Fifteen years before Lossing took on this job, the "Down Rent Wars" enabled tens of thousands of upstate farmers to own their farms at last. Mormons left for the west. Determined women met at Seneca Falls. The temperance movement, the union movement, the abolitionist movement, all picked up speed. Now the nation trembled on the brink of a bloody civil war.

Lossing concentrated on the story of a river. He was not unaware of new ideas. He was on the founding Board of Trustees got together by brewer Matthew Vassar for his new "Vassar Female College." A friend chided him, "Benson, why use the word 'Female'? We don't say 'Yale Male College'." Lossing agreed, and brought the suggestion to the next trustees meeting. The rest agreed and the word was dropped.

Today, as the world trembles on the brink of a population explosion, threatened by scientific inventions that we don't know how to handle, it's worth dipping into this old-time world and contemplating how it has changed-but in some ways has not. The human heart still behaves much the same. The sun, moon and stars still attend their rounds, and birds and flowers, through threatened, still survive in some places. If we know better what has gone before, we can better plan for what we hope is to come, for what should come. Thank you, Benson Lossing, for your unforgettable stories and pictures.

Peter Seeger
April, 2000

LIST OF ILLUSTRATIONS.

PREFACE.

———◆———

HE pen and pencil sketches of the Hudson River and its associations contained in this Volume, were made by the writer a few years ago, and were published in a series of numbers of the London *Art-Journal* (for which they were originally prepared) during the years 1860 and 1861. They have been revised by the writer for publication in the present form, changes in persons and things requiring such revision.

It is impossible to give in pictures so necessarily small as are those which illustrate this Volume, an adequate idea of the beauty and grandeur of the scenery of the Hudson River; so, in the choice of subjects, the judgment was governed more by considerations of utility than of mere artistic taste. Only such objects have been delineated and described as bore relations to the history, traditions, and business life of the river here celebrated, whose course, from the Wilderness to the Sea, measures a distance of full three hundred miles.

The reader will bear in mind that when the present tense is used, allusion is made to the beginning of the year 1866, at which time the revision of these sketches was made.

B. J. L.

POUGHKEEPSIE, N.Y., *March*, 1866.

THE HUDSON,

FROM THE WILDERNESS TO THE SEA.

CHAPTER I.

IT is proposed to present, in a series of sketches with pen and pencil, pictures of the Hudson River, from its birth , among the mountains to its marriage with the ocean. It is by far the most interesting river in America, considering the beauty and magnificence of its scenery, its natural, political, and social history, the agricultural and mineral treasures of its vicinage, the commercial wealth hourly floating upon its bosom, and the relations of its geography and topography to some of the most important events in the history of the Western hemisphere.

High upon the walls of the governor's room in the New York City Hall is a dingy painting of a broad-headed, short-haired, sparsely-bearded man, with an enormous ruffle about his neck, and bearing the impress of an intellectual, courtly gentleman of the days of King James the First of England. By whom it was painted nobody knows, but conjecture shrewdly guesses that . it was delineated by the hand of Paul Van Someren, the skilful Flemish artist who painted the portraits of many persons of distinction in Amsterdam and London, in the reign of James, and died in the British capital four years before that monarch. We are

Albany, was little known to white men, excepting hunters and trappers, and a few isolated settlers; and the knowledge of its sources among lofty alpine ranges is one of the revelations made to the present century, and even to the present generation. And now very few, excepting the hunters of that region, have personal knowledge of the beauty and wild grandeur of lake, and forest, and mountain, out of which spring the fountains of the river we are about to describe. To these fountains and their forest courses I made a pilgrimage toward the close of the summer of 1859, accompanied by Mrs. Lossing and Mr. S. M. Buckingham, an American gentleman, formerly engaged in mercantile business in Manchester, England, and who has travelled extensively in the East.

Our little company, composed of the minimum in the old prescription for a dinner-party—not more than the Muses nor less than the Graces—left our homes, in the pleasant rural city of Poughkeepsie, on the Hudson, for the wildernesss of northern New York, by a route which we are satisfied, by experience and observation, to be the best for the tourist or sportsman bound for the head waters of that river, or the high plateau northward and westward of them, where lie in solitary beauty a multitude of lakes filled with delicious fish, and embosomed in primeval forests abounding with deer and other game. We travelled by railway about one hundred and fifty miles to Whitehall, a small village in a rocky gorge, where Wood Creek leaps in cascades into the head of Lake Champlain. There we tarried until the following morning, and at ten o'clock embarked upon a steamboat for Port Kent—our point of departure for the wild interior, far down the lake on its western border. The day was fine, and the shores of the lake, clustered with historical associations, presented a series of beautiful pictures; for they were rich with forest verdure, the harvests of a fruitful seed-time, and thrifty villages and farmhóuses. Behind these, on the east, arose the lofty ranges of the Green Mountains, in Vermont; and on the west were the Adirondacks of New York, whither we were journeying, their clustering peaks, distant and shadowy, bathed in the golden light of a summer afternoon.

Lake Champlain is deep and narrow, and one hundred and forty mile in length. It received its present name from its discoverer, the eminent French navigator, Samuel Champlain, who was upon its waters the same year when Hudson sailed up the river which bears his name. Champlain came from the north, and Hudson from the south ; and they penetrated the wilderness to points within a hundred miles of each other. Long before, the Indians had given it the significant title of *Can-i-a-de-ri Gua-run-te*, the Door of the Country. The appropriateness of this name will be illustrated hereafter.

It was evening when we arrived at Port Kent. We remained until morning with a friend (Winslow C. Watson, Esq., a descendant of Governor Winslow, who came to New England in the *Mayflower*), whose personal explorations and general knowledge of the region we were about to visit, enabled him to give us information of much value in our subsequent course. With himself and family we visited the walled banks of the Great Au Sable, near Keeseville, and stood with wonder and awe at the bottom of a terrific gorge in sandstone, rent by an earthquake's power, and a foaming river rushing at our feet. The gorge, for more than a mile, is from thirty to forty feet in width, and over one hundred in depth. This was our first experience of the wild scenery of the north. The tourist should never pass it unnoticed.

Our direct route from Keeseville lay along the picturesque valley of the Great Au Sable River, a stream broken along its entire course into cascades, draining about seven hundred square miles of mountain country, and falling four thousand six hundred feet in its passage from its springs to Lake Champlain, a distance of only about forty miles. We made a *détour* of a few miles at Keeseville for a special purpose, entered the valley at twilight, and passed along the margin of the rushing waters of the Au Sable six miles to the Forks, where we remained until morning. The day dawned gloomily, and for four hours we rode over the mountains toward the Saranac River in a drenching rain, for which we were too well prepared to experience any inconvenience. At Franklin Falls, on the Saranac, in the midst of the wildest mountain scenery, where a few years before a forest village had been destroyed by fire, we dined upon trout and venison, the common food of the wilderness, and then rode on toward the Lower Saranac Lake, at the foot of which we were destined to leave roads, and horses, and industrial pursuits behind, and live upon the solitary lake and river, and in the almost unbroken woods.

The clouds were scattered early in the afternoon, but lay in heavy masses upon the summits of the deep blue mountains, and deprived us of the pleasure to be derived from distant views in the amphitheatre of everlasting hills through which we were journeying. Our road was over a high rolling country, fertile, and in process of rapid clearing. The log-houses of the settlers, and the cabins of the charcoal burners, were frequently seen ; and in a beautiful valley, watered by a branch of the Saranac, we passed through a pleasant village called Bloomingdale. Toward evening we reached the sluggish outlet of the Saranac Lakes, and at a little before sunset our postilion reined up at Baker's Inn, two miles from the Lower Lake, and fifty-one from Port Kent. To the lover and student of nature, the artist and the philosopher, the country through which we had passed, and to which only brief allusion may here be made, is among the most inviting spots upon the globe, for magnificent and picturesque scenery, mineral wealth, and geological wonders, abound on every side.

At Baker's Inn every comfort for a reasonable man was found. There we procured guides, boats, and provisions for the wilderness ; and at a little past noon on the following day we were fairly beyond the sounds of the settlements, upon a placid lake studded with islands, the sun shining in unclouded splendour, and the blue peaks of distant mountains looming above the dense forests that lay in gloomy grandeur between us and their rugged acclivities.

Our party now consisted of five, two guides having been added to it. One of them was a son of Mr. Baker, the other a pure-blooded Penobscot Indian from the state of Maine. Each had a light boat—so light that he might carry it upon his shoulders at portages, or the intervals between the navigable portions of streams or lakes. In one of these was borne our luggage, provisions, and Mr. Buckingham, and in the other Mrs. Lossing and myself.

The Saranac Lakes are three in number, and lie on the south-eastern borders of Franklin County, north of Mount Seward. They are known as the Upper, Round, and Lower. The latter, over which we first voyaged, is six miles in length. From its head we passed along a winding and narrow river, fringed with rushes, lilies, and moose-head plants, almost to the central or Round Lake, where we made a portage of a few rods, and dined beneath a towering pine-tree. While there, two deer-hounds, whose voices we had heard in the forest a few minutes before, came dashing up, dripping with the lake water through which they had been swimming, and, after snuffing the scent of our food wistfully for a moment, disappeared as suddenly. We crossed Round Lake, three and a half miles, and went up a narrow river about a mile, to the falls

A LODGE IN THE WILDERNESS.

at the outlet of the Upper Saranac. Here, twelve miles from our embarkation, was a place of entertainment for tourists and sportsmen, in the midst of a small clearing. A portage of an eighth of a mile, over which the boats and luggage were carried upon a waggon, brought us to the foot of the Upper Lake. On this dark, wild sheet of water, thirteen miles in length, we embarked toward the close of the day, and just before sunset reached the lodge of Corey, a hunter and guide well known in all that region. It stood near the gravelly shore of a beautiful bay with a large island in its bosom, heavily wooded with evergreens. It was Saturday evening, and here, in this rude house of logs, where we had evening, presaging a storm, and the night fell intensely dark. The burning hill above us presented a magnificent appearance in the gloom. The fire was in broken points over a surface of half a mile, near the summit, and the appearance was like a city upon the lofty slope, brilliantly illuminated. It was sad to see the fire sweeping away whole acres of fine timber. But such scenes are frequent in that region, and every bald and blackened hill-top in the ranges is the record of a conflagration.

We were detained at Houghton's the following day by a heavy rain. On the morning after, the clouds drifted away early, and with our new and excellent guides, Mitchell Sabattis and William Preston, we went

HENDRICK SPRING.

down the lake eight miles, and landed at a " carry "—as the portages are called—on its eastern shore, within half a mile of Hendrick Spring (so named in honour of Hendrick Hudson), the most remote source of the extreme western branch of our noble river. To reach water navigable with our boats, we were compelled to walk through forest and swamp about two miles. That was our first really fatiguing journey on foot, for to facilitate the passage, we each carried as much luggage as possible.

We found Hendrick Spring in the edge of a swamp—cold, shallow, about five feet in diameter, shaded by trees, shrubbery, and vines, and fringed with the delicate brake and fern. Its waters, rising within half a mile of Long Lake, and upon the same summit level, flow southward to the Atlantic more than three hundred miles; while those of the latter flow to the St. Lawrence, and reach the same Atlantic a thousand miles away to the far north-east. A few years ago, Professor G. W. Benedict (who was connected with the State Geological Survey) attempted to unite these waters by a canal, for lumbering purposes, but the enterprise was abandoned. We followed the ditch that he had cut through the swamp nearly half a mile, among tall raspberry bushes, laden with delicious fruit, and for another half mile we made our way over the most difficult ground imaginable. Dead trees were lying in every direction, some charred, others prone with black ragged roots, and all entangled in shrubbery and vines. Through this labyrinth our guides carried their

SWAMP TRAVEL.

boats, and we quite heavy packs, but all were compelled to rest every few minutes, for the sun was shining hotly upon us. We were nearly an hour travelling that half mile. Thoroughly wearied, we entered one of the boats at the first navigable point on Spring Brook, that flows from the Hendrick source, and rowed leisurely down to Fountain Lake, while our guides returned for the remainder of the luggage and provisions. The passage of that portage consumed four hours.

Fountain Lake is the first collection of the waters of the west branch of the Hudson. It is about two miles in circumference, with highly picturesque shores. It empties into Catlin Lake through a shallow, stony outlet. From both of these we had fine views of the near Santanoni Mountains, and the more distant ranges of Mount Seward, on the east. At the foot of Fountain Lake is another "carry" of a mile. A few rods down its outlet, where we crossed, we found the remains of a dam and

CATLIN LAKE.

sluice, erected by Professor Benedict, to raise the waters so as to flow through his canal into Long Lake, and for another purpose, which will be explained presently. The sun went down while we were crossing this portage, and finding a good place for a camp on the margin of a cold mountain stream in the deep forest, we concluded to remain there during the night. Our guides soon constructed a shelter with an inverted boat, poles, and boughs, and we all slept soundly, after a day of excessive toil.

In the morning we embarked upon the beautiful Catlin Lake, and rowed to its outlet—three miles. After walking a few rods over boulders, while our guides dragged the boats through a narrow channel between them, we re-embarked upon Narrow Lake, and passed through it and Lilypad Pond—a mile and a half—to another "carry" of three-fourths of a mile, which brought us to the junction of the Hudson and Fishing Brook. This was a dreary region, and yet highly picturesque. It was now about noon. Sabattis informed us that, a little way up the Fishing Brook, were a clearing and a saw-mill—the first on the Hudson.

FIRST CLEARING ON THE HUDSON.

We walked about half a mile through the woods to see them. Emerging from the forest, we came to a field filled with boulders and blackened stumps, and, from the summit of a hill, we overlooked an extensive rolling valley, heavily timbered, stretching westward to the Windfall Mountains, and at our feet were the Clearing and the Saw-mill. The latter stood at the head of a deep rocky gorge, down which great logs are sent at high water. The clearing was too recent to allow much fruit of tillage, but preparations were made for farming, in the erection of a good frame dwelling and outhouses. The head waters of this considerable tributary of the Upper Hudson is Pickwaket Pond, four miles above the mill.

A short distance below the confluence of the Hudson and Fishing Brook, we entered Rich's Lake, an irregular sheet of water, about two miles and a half in length, with surroundings more picturesque, in some

FIRST SAW-MILL ON THE HUDSON.

respects, than any we had visited. From its southern shore Goodenow Mountain rises to an altitude of about fifteen hundred feet, crowned by a rocky knob. Near the foot of the lake is a wooded peninsula, whose low isthmus, being covered at high water, leaves it an island. It is called Elephant Island, because of the singular resemblance of some of the lime-

stone formation that composes its bold shore to portions of that animal.
The whole rock is perforated into singularly-formed caves. This, and

ELEPHANT ISLAND.

another similar shore a few miles below, were the only deposits of limestone that we saw in all that region.

At the outlet of Rich's Lake were the ruins of a dam and lumber

LUMBER DAM AND SLUICE,

sluice, similar in construction and intended use to that of Professor
Benedict at Fountain Lake. The object of such structures, which occur

The rapids at the head of Harris's Lake are very picturesque. Looking up from them, Goodenow Mountain is seen in the distance, and still more remote are glimpses of the Windfall range. We passed the rapids upon boulders, and then voyaged down to the confluence of the two streams just mentioned. From a rough rocky bluff a mile below that point, we obtained a distant view of three of the higher peaks of the Adirondacks—Tahawus or Mount Marcy, Mount Colden, and Mount M'Intyre. We returned at evening beneath a canopy of magnificent clouds; and that night was made strangely luminous by one of the most

RAPIDS AT THE HEAD OF HARRIS'S LAKE.

splendid displays of the Aurora Borealis ever seen upon the continent. It was observed as far south as Charleston, in South Carolina.

Sabattis is an active Methodist, and at his request (their minister not having arrived) Mr. Buckingham read the beautiful liturgy of the Church of England on Sunday morning to a congregation of thirty or forty people, in the school-house on our guide's farm. In the afternoon we attended a prayer-meeting at the same place; and early the next morning, while a storm of wind and heavy mist was sweeping over the country, started with our two guides, in a lumber waggon, for the Adirondack Mountains. We now left our boats, in which and on foot we had travelled, from the

lower Saranac to Harris's Lake, more than seventy miles. It was a
tedious journey of twenty-six miles, most of the way over a "corduroy"
road—a causeway of logs. On the way we passed the confluence of Lake
Delia with the Adirondack branch of the Hudson, reached M'Intyre's Inn
(Tahawus House, at the foot of Sandford Lake) toward noon, and at two
o'clock were at the little deserted village at the Adirondack Iron Works,
between Sandford and Henderson Lakes. We passed near the margin of
the former a large portion of the way. It is a beautiful body of water,
nine miles long, with several little islands. From the road along its

SANDFORD LAKE.

shores we had a fine view of the three great mountain peaks just
mentioned, and of the Wall-face Mountain at the Indian Pass. At the
house of Mr. Hunter, the only inhabitant of the deserted village, we
dined, and then prepared to ascend the Great TAHAWUS, or Sky-piercer.

The little deserted village of Adirondack, or M'Intyre, nestled in a
rocky valley upon the Upper Hudson, at the foot of the principal mountain barrier which rises between its sources and those of the Au Sable,
and in the bosom of an almost unbroken forest, appeared cheerful to us
weary wanderers, although smoke was to be seen from only a solitary

chimney. The hamlet—consisting of sixteen dwelling-houses, furnaces, and other edifices, and a building with a cupola, used for a school and public worship—was the offspring of enterprise and capital, which many years before had combined to develop the mineral wealth of that region. That wealth was still there, and almost untouched—for enterprise and capital, compelled to contend with geographical and topographical impediments, have abandoned their unprofitable application of labour, and left the rich iron ores, apparently exhaustless in quantity, to be quarried and transformed in the not far-off future.

The ores of that vicinity had never been revealed to the eye of civilised man until the year 1826, when David Henderson, a young Scotchman, of Jersey City, opposite New York, while standing near the iron-works of his father-in-law, Archibald M'Intyre, at North Elba, in Essex County, was approached by a St. Francis Indian, known in all that region as a brave and skilful hunter—honest, intelligent, and, like all his race, taciturn. The Indian took from beneath his blanket a piece of iron ore, and handed it to Henderson, saying, "You want to see 'um ore? Me fine plenty—all same." When asked where it came from, he pointed toward the south-west, and said, "Me hunt beaver all 'lone, and fine 'um where water run over iron-dam." An exploring party was immediately formed, and followed the Indian into the deep forest. They slept that night at the base of the towering cliff of the Indian Pass. The next day they reached the head of a beautiful lake, which they named "Henderson," and followed its outlet to the site of Adirondack village. There, in a deep-shaded valley, they beheld with wonder the "iron dam," or dyke of iron ore, stretched across a stream, which was afterward found to be one of the main branches of the Upper Hudson. They at once explored the vicinity, and discovered that this dyke was connected with vast deposits of ore, which formed rocky ledges on the sides of the narrow valley, and presented beds of metal adequate, apparently, to the supply of the world's demand for centuries. It is believed that the revealer of this wealth was Peter Sabattis, the father of our Indian guide.

The explorers perceived that all around that vast deposit of wealth in the earth was an abundant supply of hard wood, and other necessary ingredients for the manufacture of iron ; and, notwithstanding it was thirty miles from any highway on land or water, with an uninterrupted sweep of forest between, and more than a hundred miles from any market, the entire mineral region—comprising more than a whole township—was purchased, and preparations were soon made to develop its resources. A partnership was formed between Archibald M'Intyre, Archibald Robert-

THE IRON DAM.

son, and David Henderson, all related by marriage ; and with slight aid from the State, they constructed a road through the wilderness, from the Scarron [Schroon] Valley, near Lake Champlain, to the foot of Sandford Lake, halfway between the head of which and the beautiful Henderson Lake was the "iron dam." There a settlement was commenced in 1834. A timber dam was constructed upon the iron one, to increase the fall of water, and an experimental furnace was built. Rare and most valuable iron was produced, equal to any from the best Swedish furnaces; and it was afterward found to be capable of being wrought into steel equal to the best imported from England.

The proprietors procured an act of incorporation, under the title of the "Adirondack Iron and Steel Company," with a capital, at first, of $1,000,000 (£200,000), afterward increased to $3,000,000 (£600,000), and constructed another furnace, a forge, stamping-mill, saw and grist mill, machine-shops, powder-house, dwellings, boarding-house, school-house, barns, sheds, and kilns for the manufacture of charcoal. At the foot of Sandford Lake, eleven miles south from Adirondack village, they also commenced a settlement, and named it Tahawus, where they erected

ADIRONDACK VILLAGE.

a dam seventeen hundred feet in length, a saw-mill, warehouses, dwellings for workmen, &c. And in 1854 they completed a blast furnace near the upper village, at the head of Sandford Lake, at an expense of $43,000 (£8,600), capable of producing fourteen tons of iron a-day. They also built six heavy boats upon Sandford Lake, for the transportation of freight, and roads at an expense of $10,000 (£2,000). Altogether the proprietors spent nearly half a million of dollars, or £100,000.

Meanwhile the project of a railway from Saratoga to Sackett's Harbour, on Lake Ontario, to bisect the great wilderness, was conceived. A company was formed, and forty miles of the road were put under contract, and actually graded. It would pass within a few miles of the Adirondack

Works, and it was estimated that, with a connecting branch road, the iron might be conveyed to Albany for two dollars a ton, and compete profitably with other iron in the market. A plank road was also projected from Adirondack village to Preston Ponds, and down the Cold River to the Raquette, at the foot of Long Lake.

But the labour on the road was suspended, the iron interest of the United States became depressed, the Adirondack Works were rendered not only unprofitable, but the source of heavy losses to the owners, and for five years their fires had been extinguished. In August, 1856, heavy rains in the mountains sent roaring floods down the ravines, and the Hudson, only a brook when we were there, was swelled to a mighty river. An upper dam at Adirondack gave way, and a new channel for the stream was cut, and the great dam at Tahawus, with the saw-mill, was demolished by the rushing waters. All was left a desolation. Over scores of acres at the head and foot of Sandford Lake (overflowed when the dam was constructed) we saw white skeletons of trees which had been killed by the flood, standing thickly, and heightening the dreary aspect of the scene. The workmen had all departed from Adirondack, and only Robert Hunter and his family, who had charge of the property, remained. The original proprietors were all dead, and the property, intrinsically valuable but immediately unproductive, was in the possession of their respective families. But the projected railway will yet be constructed, because it is needful for the development and use of that immense mineral and timber region, and again that forest village will be vivified, and the echoes of the deep breathings of its furnaces will be heard in the neighbouring mountains.

At Mr. Hunter's we prepared for the rougher travel on foot through the mountain forests to Tahawus, ten miles distant. Here we may properly instruct the expectant tourist in this region in regard to such preparation. Every arrangement should be as simple as possible. A man needs only a stout flannel hunting shirt, coarse and trustworthy trousers, woollen stockings, large heavy boots well saturated with a composition of beeswax and tallow, a soft felt hat or a cap, and strong buckskin gloves. A woman needs a stout flannel dress, over shortened crinoline, of short dimensions, with loops and buttons to adjust its length;

a hood and cape of the same materials, made so as to envelop the head and bust, and leave the arms free, woollen stockings, stout calfskin boots that cover the legs to the knee, well saturated with beeswax and tallow, and an india-rubber satchel for necessary toilet materials. Provisions, also, should be simple. The hunters live chiefly on bread or crackers,

DEPARTURE FOR TAHAWUS.

and maple sugar. The usual preparation is a sufficient stock of Boston crackers, pilot-bread, or common loaf-bread, butter, tea or coffee, pepper and salt, an ample quantity of maple sugar,* and some salted pork, to use in frying or broiling fish, birds, and game. The utensils for cooking are a short-handled frying-pan, a broad and shallow tin pan, tin tea or coffee-

---

* The hard, or Sugar Maple (*Acer saccharinum*), abounds in all parts of the State of New York. It is a beautiful tree, often found from fifty to eighty feet in height, and the trunk from two to three feet in diameter. From the sap, which flows abundantly in the spring, delicious syrup and excellent sugar are made. In the Upper Hudson region, the sap is procured by making a small incision with an axe, or a hole with an augur, into the body of the tree, into which a small tube or gutter is fastened. From thence the sap flows, and is caught in rough troughs, dug out of small logs. [See the initial letter at the head of Chapter III.] It is collected into tubs, and boiled in caldron kettles. The syrup remains in buckets from twelve to twenty-four hours, and settles before straining. To make sugar it is boiled carefully over a slow fire. To cleanse it, the white of one egg, and one gill of milk, are used for every 30 lbs. or 40 lbs. of sugar. Some settlers manufacture a considerable quantity of sugar every year, as much as from 300 lbs. to 600 lbs.

pot, tin plates and cups, knives, forks, and spoons. These, with shawls or overcoats, and india-rubber capes to keep off the rain, the guides will carry, with gun, axe, and fishing-tackle. Sportsmen who expect to camp out some time, should take with them a light tent. The guides will fish, hunt, work, build "camps," and do all other necessary service, for a moderate compensation and their food. It is proper here to remark that the tourist should never enter this wilderness earlier than the middle of August. Then the flies and mosquitoes, the intolerable pests of the forests, are rapidly disappearing, and fine weather may be expected. The sportsman must go in June or July for trout, and in October for deer.

Well prepared with all necessaries excepting flannel over-shirts, we set out from Adirondack on the afternoon of the 30th of August, our guides

FIRST BRIDGE OVER THE HUDSON.

with their packs leading the way. The morning had been misty, but the atmosphere was then clear and cool. We crossed the Hudson three-fourths of a mile below Henderson Lake, upon a rude bridge, made our way through a clearing tangled with tall raspberry shrubs full of fruit, for nearly half a mile, and then entered the deep and solemn forest, composed of birch, maple, cedar, hemlock, spruce, and tall pine trees. Our way was over a level for three-fourths of a mile, to the outlet of Calamity Pond. We crossed it at a beautiful cascade, and then commenced ascending by a sinuous mountain path, across which many a huge tree had been cast by the wind. It was a weary journey of almost four miles (notwith-standing it lay along the track of a lane cut through the forest a few years ago for a special purpose, of which we shall presently speak), for in many places the soil was hidden by boulders covered with thick moss, over which we were compelled to climb. Towards sunset we reached a pleasant little lake, embosomed in the dense forest, its low wet margin fringed with brilliant yellow flowers, beautiful in form but without perfume. At the head of that little lake, where the inlet comes flowing

BARK CABIN AT CALAMITY POND.

sluggishly from a dark ravine scooped from the mountain slope, we built a bark cabin, and encamped for the night.

That tiny lake is called Calamity Pond, in commemoration of a sad circumstance that occurred near the spot where we erected our cabin, in September, 1845. Mr. Henderson, of the Adirondack Iron Company, already mentioned, was there with his son and other attendants. Near the margin of the inlet is a flat rock. On this, as he landed from a scow, Mr. Henderson attempted to lay his pistol, holding the muzzle in his hand. It discharged, and the contents entering his body, wounded him mortally: he lived only half-an-hour. A rude bier was constructed of boughs, on which his body was carried to Adirondack village. It was taken down Sandford Lake in a boat to Tahawus, and from thence again carried on a bier through the wilderness, fifteen miles to the western termination of the road from Scarron valley, then in process of construction. From thence it was conveyed to his home at Jersey City, and a few years afterward his family erected an elegant monument upon the rock where he lost his life. It is of the light New Jersey sandstone, eight feet in height, and bears the following inscription :—" This monument was erected by filial affection to the memory of DAVID HENDERSON, who lost

HENDERSON'S MONUMENT.

his life on this spot, 3rd September, 1845." Beneath the inscription, in high relief, is a chalice, book, and anchor.

The lane through the woods just mentioned was cut for the purpose of allowing the transportation of this monument upon a sledge in winter, drawn by oxen. All the way the road was made passable by packing the snow between the boulders, and in this labour several days were consumed. The monument weighs a ton.

While Preston and myself were building the bark cabin, in a manner similar to the bush one already described, and Mrs. Lossing was preparing a place upon the clean grass near the fire for our supper, Mr. Buckingham and Sabattis went out upon the lake on a rough raft, and caught over two

dozen trout. Upon these we supped and breakfasted. The night was
cold, and at early dawn we found the hoar-frost lying upon every leaf and
blade around us. Beautiful, indeed, was that dawning of the last day of
summer. From the south-west came a gentle breeze, bearing upon its
wings light vapour, that flecked the whole sky, and became roseate in hue
when the sun touched with purple light the summit of the hills westward
of us. These towered in grandeur more than a thousand feet above the
surface of the lake, from which, in the kindling morning light, went up,
in myriads of spiral threads, a mist, softly as a spirit, and melted in the
first sunbeam.

At eight o'clock we resumed our journey over a much rougher way than
we had yet travelled, for there was nothing but a dim and obstructed
hunter's trail to follow. This we pursued nearly two miles, when we
struck the outlet of Lake Colden, at its confluence with the Opalescent
River, that comes rushing down in continuous rapids and cascades from
the foot of Tahawus. The lake was only a few rods distant. Intending
to visit it on our return, we contented ourselves with brief glimpses of it
through the trees, and of tall Mount Colden, or Mount M'Martin, that
rises in magnificence from its eastern shore.

The drought that still prevailed over northern New York and New
England had so diminished the volume of the Opalescent River, that
we walked more than four miles in the bed of the stream upon boulders
which fill it. We crossed it a hundred times or more, picking our way,
and sometimes compelled to go into the woods in passing a cascade. The
stream is broken into falls and swift rapids the whole distance that we
followed it, and, when full, it must present a grand spectacle. At one
place the river had assumed the bed of a displaced trap dyke, by which
the rock has been intersected. The walls are perpendicular, and only a
few feet apart—so near that the branches of the trees on the summits
interlace. Through this the water rushes for several rods, and then
leaps into a dark chasm, full fifty feet perpendicular, and emerges
among a mass of immense boulders. The Indians called this cascade
She-gwi-en-dawkwe, or the Hanging Spear. A short distance above is a
wild rapid, which they called *Kas-kong-shadi,* or Broken Water.

The stones in this river vary in size, from tiny pebbles to boulders of a thousand tons; the smaller ones made smooth by rolling, the larger ones, yet angular and massive, persistently defying the rushing torrent in its maddest career. They are composed chiefly of the beautiful labradorite, or opalescent feldspar, which form the great mass of the

Aganus-chion, or Black Mountain range, as the Indians called this Adirondack group, because of the dark aspect which their sombre cedars, and spruce, and cliffs present at a distance. The bed of the stream is full of that exquisitely beautiful mineral. We saw it glittering in splendour, in pebbles and large boulders, when the sunlight fell full upon the shallow water. A rich blue is the predominant colour, sometimes mingled with a brilliant green. Gold and bronze-coloured specimens have been discovered, and, occasionally, a completely iridescent piece may be found. It is to the abundance of these stones that the river is indebted for its beautiful name. It is one of the main sources of the Hudson, and falls into Sandford Lake, a few miles below Adirondack village.

We followed the Opalescent River to the foot of the Peak of Tahawus, on the borders of the high valley

FALL IN THE OPALESCENT RIVER.

which separates that mountain from Mount Colden, at an elevation nine hundred feet above the highest peaks of the Cattskill range on the Lower Hudson. There the water is very cold, the forest trees are somewhat stunted and thickly planted, and the solitude complete. The silence was almost oppressive. Game-birds and beasts of the chase are there almost unknown. The wild cat and wolverine alone prowl over that lofty valley, where rises one of the chief fountains of the Hudson, and we heard the voice of no living creature excepting the hoarse croak of the raven.

It was noon when we reached this point of departure for the summit of Tahawus. We had been four hours travelling six miles, and yet in that pure mountain air we felt very little fatigue. There we found an excellent bark " camp," and traces of recent occupation. Among them

CLIMBING TAHAWUS.

was part of a metropolitan newspaper, and light ashes. We dined upon bread and butter and maple sugar, in a sunny spot in front of the cabin, and then commenced the ascent, leaving our provisions and other things at the camp, where we intended to repose for the night. The journey upward was two miles, at an angle of forty-five degrees to the base of the rocky pinnacle. We had no path to follow. The guides " blazed " the larger trees (striking off chips with their axes), that they might with more ease find their way back to the camp. Almost the entire surface was covered with boulders, shrouded in the most beautiful alpine mosses. From among these shot up dwarfing pines and spruces, which diminished in height at every step. Through their thick horizontal branches it was difficult to pass. Here and there among the rocks was a free spot, where the bright trifoliolate oxalis, or wood-sorrel, flourished, and the shrub of the wild currant, and gooseberry, and the tree-cranberry appeared. At length we reached the foot of the open rocky pinnacle, where only thick mosses, lichens, a few alpine plants, and little groves of dwarfed balsam, are seen. The latter trees, not more than five feet in height, are, most of them, centenarians. Their stems, not larger than a strong man's wrist,

exhibited, when cut, over one hundred concentric rings, each of which indicates the growth of a year. Our journey now became still more difficult, at the same time more interesting, for, as we emerged from the forest, the magnificent panorama of mountains that lay around us burst upon the vision. Along steep rocky slopes and ledges, and around and beneath huge stones a thousand tons in weight, some of them apparently poised, as if ready for a sweep down the mountain, we made our way cautiously, having at times no other support than the strong moss, and occasionally a gnarled shrub that

SPRING ON THE PEAK OF TAHAWUS.

sprung from the infrequent fissures. We rested upon small terraces, where the dwarf balsams grow. Upon one of these, within a hundred feet of the summit, we found a spring of very cold water, and near it quite thick ice. This spring is one of the remote sources of the Hudson. It bubbles from the base of a huge mass of loose rocks (which, like all the other portions of the peak, are composed of the beautiful labradorite), and sends down a little stream into the Opalescent River, from whose bed we had just ascended. Mr. Buckingham had now gained

the summit, and waved his hat, in token of triumph, and a few minutes
later we were at his side, forgetful, in the exhilaration of the moment,
of every fatigue and danger that we had encountered.   Indeed it was a
triumph for us all, for few persons have ever attempted the ascent of that
mountain, lying in a deep wilderness, hard to penetrate, the nearest point
of even a bridle path, on the side of our approach, being ten miles from
the base of its peak.   Especially difficult is it for the feet of woman to
reach the lofty summit of the *Sky-piercer*—almost six thousand feet
above the sea—for her skirts form great impediments.   Mrs. Lossing, we
were afterwards informed by the oldest hunter and guide in all that

HOSPICE ON THE PEAK OF TAHAWUS.

region (John Cheney), is only the third woman who has ever accomplished
the difficult feat.

The summit of Tahawus is bare rock, about four hundred feet in length
and one hundred in breadth, with an elevation of ten or twelve feet at
the south-western end, that may be compared to the heel of an upturned
boot, the remainder of the surface forming the sole.   In a nook on the
southern side of this heel, was a small hut, made of loose stones gathered
from the summit, and covered with moss.   It was erected the previous
year by persons from New York, and had been occupied by others a fort-

night before our visit. Within the hut we found a piece of paper, on which was written :—" This hospice, erected by a party from New York, August 19, 1858, is intended for the use and comfort of visitors to Tahawus.—F. S. P.—M. C.—F. M. N." Under this was written :— " This hospice was occupied over night of August 14, 1859, by A. G. C. and T. R. D. Sun rose fourteen minutes to five." Under this :— " Tahawus House Register, August 14, 1859, Alfred G. Compton, and Theodore R. Davis, New York. August 16, Charles Newman, Stamford, Connecticut; Charles Bedfield, Elizabeth Town, New York." To these we added our own names, and those of the guides.

Our view from the summit of Tahawus will ever form one of the most remarkable pictures in memory; and yet it may not properly be called a *picture*. It is a topographical map, exhibiting a surface diversified by mountains, lakes, and valleys. The day was very pleasant, yet a cold north-westerly wind was sweeping over the summit of the mountain. A few clouds, sufficient to cast fine shadows upon the earth, were floating not far above us, and on the east, when we approached the summit at three o'clock, an iridescent mist was slightly veiling a group of mountains, from their thick wooded bases in the valleys, to their bold rocky summits. Our stand-point being the highest in all that region, there was nothing to obstruct the view. *To-war-loon-dah*, or Hill of Storms (Mount Emmons), *Ou-kor-lah*, or Big Eye (Mount Seward), *Wah-o-par-te-nie*, or White-face Mountain, and the Giant of the Valley—all rose peerless above the other hills around us, excepting Colden and M'Intyre, that stood apparently within trumpet-call of Tahawus, as fitting companions, but over whose summits, likewise, we could look away to the dark forests of Franklin and St. Lawrence Counties, in the far north-west. Northward we could see the hills melting into the great St. Lawrence level, out of which arose the Royal Mountain back of the city of Montreal. Eastward, full sixty miles distant, lay the magnificent Green Mountains, that give name to the state of Vermont, and through a depression of that range, we saw distinctly the great Mount Washington among the White Hills of New Hampshire, one hundred and fifty miles distant. Southward the view was bounded by the higher peaks of the Cattskills, or Katzbergs, and westward by the mountain ranges in Hamilton and Herkimer

Counties. At our feet reposed the great wilderness of northern New York, full a hundred miles in length, and eighty in breadth, lying in parts of seven counties, and equal in area to several separate smaller States of the Union. On every side bright lakes were gleaming, some nestling in unbroken forests, and others with their shores sparsely dotted with clearings, from which arose the smoke from the settler's cabin. We counted twenty-seven lakes, including Champlain—the Indian *Can-i-a-de-ri Gua-run-te*, or Door of the Country—which stretched along the eastern view one hundred and forty miles, and at a distance of about fifty miles at the nearest point. We could see the sails of water-craft like white specks upon its bosom, and, with our telescope, could distinctly discern the houses in Burlington, on the eastern shore of the lake.

From our point of view we could comprehend the emphatic significance of the Indian idea of Lake Champlain—the *Door of the Country*. It fills the bottom of an immense valley, that stretches southward between the great mountain ranges of New York and New England, from the St. Lawrence level toward the valley of the Hudson, from which it is separated by a slightly elevated ridge.* To the fierce Huron of Canada, who loved to make war upon the more southern Iroquois, this lake was a wide open door for his passage. Through it many brave men, aborigines and Europeans, have gone to the war-paths of New York and New England, never to return.

Standing upon Tahawus, it required very little exercise of the imagination to behold the stately procession of historic men and events, passing through that open door. First in dim shadows were the dusky warriors

---

* In the introduction to his published sermon, preached at Plymouth, in New England, in the year 1621 (and the first ever preached there), the Rev. Robert Cushman, speaking of that country, says:— " So far as we can find, it is an island, and near about the quantity of England, being cut out from the mainland in America, as England is from the main of Europe, by a great arm of the sea [Hudson's River], which entereth in forty degrees, and runneth up north-west and by west, and goeth out, either into the South Sea [Pacific Ocean], or else into the Bay of Canada [the Gulf of St. Lawrence]." The old divine was nearly right in his conjecture that New England was an island. It is a peninsula, connected to the main by a very narrow isthmus, the extremities of which are at the villages of Whitehall, on Lake Champlain, and Fort Edward, on the Hudson, about twenty-five miles apart. The lowest portion of that isthmus is not more than fifty feet above Lake Champlain, whose waters are only ninety above the sea. This isthmus is made still narrower by the waters of Wood Creek, which flow into Lake Champlain, and of Fort Edward Creek, which empty into the Hudson. These are navigable for light canoes, at some seasons of the year, to within a mile and a-half of each other. The canal, which now connects the Hudson and Lake Champlain, really makes New England an island.

of the ante-Columbian period, darting swiftly through in their bark canoes, intent upon blood and plunder. Then came Champlain and his men [1609], with guns and sabres, to aid the Hurons in contests with the Adirondacks and other Iroquois at Crown Point and Ticonderoga. Then came French and Indian allies, led by Marin [1745], passing swiftly through that door, and sweeping with terrible force down the Hudson valley to Saratoga, to smite the Dutch and English settlers there. Again French and Indian warriors came, led by Montcalm, Dieskau, and others [1755-1759], to drive the English from that door, and secure it for the house of Bourbon. A little later came troops of several nationalities, with Burgoyne at their head [1777], rushing through that door with power, driving American republicans southward, like chaff before the wind, and sweeping victoriously down the valley of the Hudson to Saratoga and beyond. And, lastly, came another British force, with Sir George Prevost at their head [1814], to take possession of that door, but were turned back at the northern threshold with discomfiture. In the peaceful present that door stands wide open, and people of all nations may pass through it unquestioned. But the Indian is seldom seen at the portal.

CHAPTER III.

T HE cold increased every moment as the sun declined, and, after remaining on the summit of Tahawus only an hour, we descended to the Opalescent River, where we encamped for the night. Toward morning there was a rain-shower, and the water came trickling upon us through the light bark roof of our " camp." But the clouds broke at sunrise, and, excepting a copious shower of small hail, and one or two of light rain, we had pleasant weather the remainder of the day. We descended the Opalescent in its rocky bed, as we went up, and at noon dined on the margin of Lake Colden, just after a slight shower had passed by.

We were now at an elevation of almost three thousand feet above tide water. In lakes Colden and Avalanche, which lie close to each other, there are no fishes. Only lizards and leeches occupy their cold waters. All is silent and solitary there. The bald eagle sweeps over them occasionally, or perches upon a lofty pine, but the mournful voice of the Great Loon, or Diver (*Colymbus glacialis*), heard over all the waters of northern New York and Canada, never awakens the echoes of these solitary lakes.* These waters lie in a high basin between the Mount Colden and Mount M'Intyre ranges, and have experienced great changes. Avalanche Lake, evidently once a part of Lake Colden, is about eighty feet higher than the latter, and more than two miles from it. They have been separated by, perhaps, a series of avalanches, or mountain slides, which still occur in that region. From

---

* The water view in the picture of the Loon is a scene on Harris's Lake, with Goodenow Mountain in the distance.

the top of Tahawus we saw the white glare of several, striping the sides of mountain cones.

At three o'clock we reached our camp at Calamity Pond, and just before sunset emerged from the forest into the open fields near Adirondack village, where we regaled ourselves with the bountiful fruitage of the raspberry shrub. At Mr. Hunter's we found kind and generous entertainment, and at an early hour the next morning we started for the great Indian Pass, four miles distant.

Half a mile from Henderson Lake we crossed its outlet upon a picturesque bridge, and following a causeway another half a mile through a

THE LOON.

clearing, we penetrated the forest, and struck one of the chief branches of the Upper Hudson, that comes from the rocky chasms of that Pass. Our journey was much more difficult than to Tahawus. The undergrowth of the forest was more dense, and trees more frequently lay athwart the dim trail. We crossed the stream several times, and, as we ascended, the valley narrowed until we entered the rocky gorge between the steep slopes of Mount M'Intyre and the cliffs of Wall-face Mountain. There we encountered enormous masses of rocks, some worn by the abrasion of the elements, some angular, some bare, and some covered with moss, and many of them bearing large trees, whose roots, clasping them on all sides, strike into the earth for sustenance. One of the masses presented a singular appearance; it is of cubic form, its summit full thirty feet from its base, and upon it was quite a grove of hemlock and cedar trees. Around and partly under this and others lying loosely, apparently kept from rolling by roots and vines, we were compelled to clamber a long distance, when we reached a point more than one hundred

LAKE COLDEN.

feet above the bottom of the gorge, where we could see the famous pass in all its wild grandeur. Before us arose a perpendicular cliff, nearly twelve hundred feet from base to summit, as raw in appearance as if cleft only yesterday. Above us sloped M'Intyre, still more lofty than the cliff of Wall-face, and in the gorge lay huge piles of rock, chaotic in position, grand in dimensions, and awful in general aspect. They appear to have been cast in there by some terrible convulsion not very remote. Within the memory of Sabattis, this region has been shaken by an earthquake, and no doubt its power, and the lightning, and the frost, have hurled these masses from that impending cliff. Through these the waters of this branch of the Hudson, bubbling from a spring not far distant (close by a fountain of the Au Sable), find their way. Here the head-waters of this river commingle in the Spring season, and when they separate they find their way to the Atlantic Ocean, as we have observed,

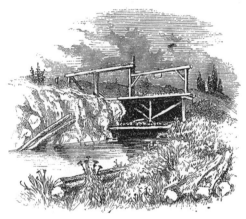

OUTLET OF HENDERSON LAKE.

at points a thousand miles apart. The margin of the stream is too rugged and cavernous in the Pass for human footsteps to follow.

Just at the lower entrance to the gorge, on the margin of the little brook, we dined, and then retraced our steps to the village, stopping on the way to view the dreary swamp at the head of Henderson Lake, where the Hudson, flowing from the Pass, enters it. Water, and not fire, has blasted the trees, and their erect stems and prostrate branches, white and ghost-like in appearance, make a tangled covering over many acres.

That night we slept soundly again at Mr. Hunter's, and in the morning left in a waggon for the valley of the Scarron. During the past four days we had travelled thirty miles on foot in the tangled forest, camped out two nights, and seen some of nature's wildest and grandest lineaments. These mountain and lake districts, which form the wilderness of northern New York, give to the tourist most exquisite sensations, and the physical system appears to take in health at every pore. Invalids go in with hardly strength enough to reach some quiet log-house in a clearing, and come out with strong quick pulse and elastic muscles. Every year the number of tourists and sportsmen who go there rapidly increases, and women begin to find more pleasure and health in that wilderness than at fashionable watering-places. No wild country in the world can offer

TREES ON BOULDERS.

more solid attractions to those who desire to spend a few weeks of leisure away from the haunts of men. Pure air and water, and game in abundance, may there be found, while in all that region not a venomous reptile or poisonous plant may be seen, and the beasts of prey are too few and shy to cause the least alarm to the most timid. The climate is delightful, and there are fertile valleys among those rugged hills that will yet smile in beauty under the cultivator's hand. It has been called by the uninformed the "Siberia of New York;" it may more properly be called the "Switzerland of the United States."

The wind came from among the mountains in fitful gusts, thick mists were sweeping around the peaks and through the gorges, and there were frequent dashes of rain, sometimes falling like showers of gold, in the sunlight that gleamed through the broken clouds, on the morning when we left Adirondack village. We had hired a strong waggon, with three spring seats, and a team of experienced horses, to convey us from the heart of the wilderness to the Scarron valley, thirty miles distant, and after breakfast we left the kind family of Mr. Hunter, accompanied by Sabattis and Preston, who rode with us most of the way for ten miles, in

ADIRONDACK, OR INDIAN PASS.

the direction of their homes. Our driver was the owner of the team—a careful, intelligent, good-natured man, who lived near Tahawus, at the foot of Sandford Lake. But in all our experience in travelling, we never endured such a journey. The highway, for at least twenty-four of the thirty miles, is what is technically called *corduroy*—a sort of corrugated stripe of logs ten feet wide, laid through the woods, and dignified with the title of "The State road." It gives to a waggon the jolting motion of the "dyspeptic chair," and in that way we were "exercised" all day long, except when dining at the Tahawus House, on some wild pigeons

shot by Sabattis on the way. That inn was upon the road, near the site
of Tahawus village, at the foot of Sandford Lake, and was a half-way
house between Long Lake and Root's Inn in the Scarron valley, toward
which we were travelling. There we parted with our excellent guides,
after giving them a sincere assurance that we should recommend all
tourists and hunters, who may visit the head waters of the Hudson, to
procure their services, if possible.

About a mile on our way from the Tahawus House, we came to the
dwelling and farm of John Cheney, the oldest and most famous hunter

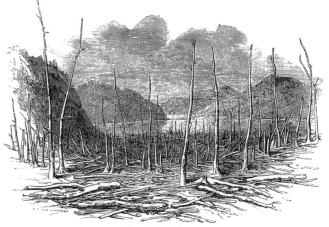

HENDERSON'S LAKE.

and guide in all that region. He then seldom went far into the woods,
for he was beginning to feel the effects of age and a laborious life. We
called to pay our respects to one so widely known, and yet so isolated,
and were disappointed. He was away on a short hunting excursion, for
he loves the forest and the chase with all the enthusiasm of his young
manhood. He is a slightly-built man, about sixty years of age. He
was the guide for the scientific corps, who made a geological reconnoissance
of that region many years before, and for a quarter of a century he had
there battled the elements and the beasts with a strong arm and unflinching will. Many of the tales of his experience are full of the wildest

romance, and we hoped to hear the narrative of some adventure from his own lips.

For many years John carried no other weapons than a huge jack-knife and a pistol. One of the most stirring of his thousand adventures in the woods is connected with the history of that pistol. It has been related by an acquaintance of the writer, a man of rare genius, and who, for many years, has been an inmate of an asylum for the insane, in a neighbouring State. John Cheney was his guide more than twenty years before our visit. The time of the adventure alluded to was winter, and the snow lay four feet deep in the woods. John went out upon snowshoes, with his rifle and dogs. He wandered far from the settlement, and made his bed at night in the deep snow. One morning he arose to examine his traps, near which he would lie encamped for weeks in complete solitude. When hovering around one of them, he discovered a famished wolf, who, unappalled by the hunter, retired only a few steps, and then, turning round, stood watching his movements. "I ought, by rights," said John, "to have waited for my two dogs, who could not have been far off, but the cretur looked so sassy, standing there, that though I had not a bullet to spare, I could not help letting into him with my rifle." John missed his aim, and the animal gave a spring, as he was in the act of firing, and turned instantly upon him before he could reload his piece. So effective was the unexpected attack of the wolf, that his fore-paws were upon Cheney's snow-shoes before he could rally for the fight. The forester became entangled in the deep drift, and sank upon his back, keeping the wolf at bay only by striking at him with his clubbed rifle. The stock of it was broken into pieces in a few moments, and it would have fared ill with the stark woodsman if the wolf, instead of making at his enemy's throat when he had him thus at disadvantage, had not, with blind fury, seized the barrel of the gun in his jaws. Still the fight was unequal, as John, half buried in the snow, could make use of but one of his hands. He shouted to his dogs, but one of them only, a young, untrained hound, made his appearance. Emerging from a thicket he caught sight of his master, lying apparently at the mercy of the ravenous beast, uttered a yell of fear, and fled howling to the woods again. "Had I had one shot left," said Cheney, "I would have given

it to that dog instead of dispatching the wolf with it." In the exaspe-
ration of the moment John might have extended his contempt to the
whole canine race, if a stauncher. friend had not, at the moment, interposed to vindicate their character for courage and fidelity. All this
had passed in a moment; the wolf was still grinding the iron gun-barrel
in his teeth—he had even once wrenched it from the hand of the hunter
—when, dashing like a thunderbolt between the combatants, the other
hound sprang over his master's body, and seized the wolf by the throat.
"There was no let go about that dog when he once took hold," said John.
"If the barrel had been red hot the wolf couldn't have dropped it
quicker, and it would have done you good, I tell you, to see that old dog
drag the cretur's head down in the snow, while I, just at my leisure,
drove the iron into his skull. One good, fair blow, though, with a heavy
rifle barrel, on the back of the head, finished him. The fellow gave a
kind o' quiver, stretched out his hind legs, and then he was done for. I
had the rifle stocked afterwards, but she would never shoot straight since
that fight, so I got me this pistol, which, being light and handy, enables
me more conveniently to carry an axe upon my long tramps, and make
myself comfortable in the woods."

Many a deer has John since killed with that pistol. "It is curious,"
said the narrator, "to see him draw it from the left pocket of his grey
shooting-jacket, and bring down a partridge. I have myself witnessed
several of his successful shots with this unpretending shooting-iron, and
once saw him knock the feathers from a wild duck at fifty yards."

Most of our journey toward the Scarron was quite easy for the horses,
for we were descending the great Champlain slope. The roughness of the
road compelled us to allow the team to walk most of the way. The
country was exceedingly picturesque. For miles our track lay through
the solitary forest, its silence disturbed only by the sound of a mountain
brook, or the voices of the wind among the hills. The winding road was
closely hemmed by trees and shrubs, and sentineled by lofty pines, and
birches, and tamaracks, many of them dead, and ready to fall at the touch
of the next strong wind. Miles apart were the rude cabins of the settlers,
until we came out upon a high, rolling valley, surrounded by a magnificent
amphitheatre of hills. Through that valley, from a little lake toward

the sources of the Au Sable, flows the cold and rapid Boreas River, one of the chief tributaries of the Upper Hudson. The view was now grand : all around us stood the great hills, wooded to their summits, and over-looking deep valleys, wherein the primeval forest had never been touched by axe or fire ; and on the right, through tall trees, we had glimpses of an irregular little lake, called Cheney Pond. For three or four miles after passing the Boreas we went over a most dreary " clearing," dotted with blackened stumps and boulders as thick as hail, a cold north-west wind driving at our backs. In the midst of it is Wolf Pond, a dark

OUT OF THE WILDERNESS.

water fringed with a tangled growth of alders, shrubs, and creepers, and made doubly gloomy by hundreds of dead trees, that shoot up from the *chapparal.*

This was the " darkness just before daylight," for we soon struck a branch of the Scarron, rushing in cascades through a rocky ravine, along whose banks we found an excellent road. The surrounding country was very rugged in appearance. The rocky hills had been denuded by fire, and everything in nature presented a strong contrast to the scene that burst upon the vision at sunset, when, from the brow of a hill, we saw the beautiful Scarron valley smiling before us. In a few minutes we crossed the Scarron River over a covered bridge, and found ourselves fairly out of the wilderness, at a new and spacious inn, kept by Russell Root, a small, active, and obliging man, well known all over that northern country. His house was the point of departure and arrival for those who take what may be called the lower route to and from the hunting and fishing grounds of the Upper Hudson, and the group of lakes beyond. Over his door a pair of enormous moose horns formed an appropriate sign-board, for he was both quarter-master and commissary of sportsmen in

MOOSE HORNS.

that region. At his house everything necessary for the woods and waters might be obtained.

The Scarron, or Schroon River, is the eastern branch of the Hudson. It rises in the heart of Essex County, and flowing southward into Warren county, receiving in its course the waters of Paradox and Scarron, or Schroon Lake, and a large group of ponds, forms a confluence, near Warrensburg, with the main waters of the Hudson, that come down from the Adirondack region. The name of Schroon for this branch is fixed in the popular mind, appears in books and on maps, and is heard upon every lip. It is a corruption of Scarron, the name given to the lake by French officers, who were stationed at Fort St. Frederick, on Crown Point, at the middle of the last century. In their rambles in the wilderness on the western shore of Lake Champlain, they discovered a beautiful lake, and named it in gallant homage to the memory of the widow of the poet Scarron, who, as Madame de Maintenon, became the queen of Louis XIV. of France. The name was afterwards applied to the river, and the modern corrupt orthography and pronunciation were unknown before the present century, at the beginning of which settlements were first commenced in that region. In the face of legal documents, common speech, and maps, we may rightfully call it Scarron; for the antiquity and respectability of an error are not valid excuses for perpetuating it.

From Root's we rode down the valley to the pleasant little village on the western shore of Scarron Lake. We turned aside to visit the beautiful Paradox Lake, nestled among wooded hills a short distance from the river. It is separated from Scarron Lake by a low alluvial drift, and is so nearly

OUTLET OF PARADOX LAKE.

on a level with the river into which it empties, that when torrents from the hills swell the waters of that stream, a current flows back into Paradox Lake, making its *out*let an *in*let for the time. From this circumstance it received its name. We rode far up its high southern shore to enjoy many fine views of the lake and its surroundings, and returning, lunched in the shadows of trees at a rustic bridge that spans its outlet a few rods below the lake.

Scarron Lake is a beautiful sheet of water, ten miles in length, and about a mile in average width. It is ninety miles north of Albany, and lies partly in Essex and partly in Warren County. Its aspect is interest-

ing from every point of view.   The gentle slopes on-its western shore are
well cultivated and thickly inhabited, the result of sixty years' settlement,
but on its eastern shore are precipitous and rugged hills, which extend in
wild and picturesque succession to Lake Champlain, fifteen or twenty
miles distant.   In the bosom of these hills, and several hundred feet
above the Scarron, lies Lake Pharaoh, a body of cold water surrounded
by dark mountains, and near it is a large cluster of ponds, all of which
find a receiving reservoir in Scarron Lake, and make its outlet a large
stream.

In the lake directly in front of Scarron village is an elliptical island,

ISOLA BELLA.

containing about one hundred acres.   It was purchased a few years ago
by Colonel A. L. Ireland, a wealthy gentleman of New York, who went
there in search of health, and who spent large sums of money in subduing
the savage features of the island, erecting a pleasant summer mansion
upon it, and in changing the rough and forbidding aspect of the whole
domain into one of beauty and attractiveness.   Taste and labour had
wrought wonderful changes there, and its appearance justified the title it
bore of Isola Bella—the Indian *Cay-wa-noot*.   The mansion was cruciform,

and delightfully situated. In front of it were tastefully ornamented grounds, with vistas through the forest trees, that afforded glimpses of charming lake, landscape, and distant mountain scenery. Within were evidences of elegant refinement—a valuable library, statuary, bronzes, and some rare paintings. Among other sketches was a picture of Hale Hall, in Lancashire, England—the ancestral dwelling of Colonel Ireland, who is a lineal descendant of Sir John de Ireland, a Norman baron who accompanied William the Conqueror to England, was at the battle of Hastings, and received from the monarch a large domain, upon which he built a castle. On the site of that castle, Hale Hall was erected by Sir Gilbert Ireland, who was a member of parliament, and lord-lieutenant of his county. Hale Hall remains in possession of the family.

We were conveyed to Isola Bella in a skiff, rowed by two watermen, in the face of a stiff breeze that ruffled the lake, and it was almost sunset when we returned to the village of Scarron Lake. It was Saturday evening, and we remained at the village until Monday morning, and then rode down the pleasant valley to Warrensburg, near the junction of the Scarron and the west branch of the Hudson, a distance of almost thirty miles. It was a very delightful ride, notwithstanding we were menaced by a storm. Our road lay first along the cultivated western margin of the lake, and thence through a rolling valley, from which we caught occasional glimpses of the river, sometimes near and sometimes distant. The journey occupied a greater portion of the day. We passed two quiet villages, named respectively Pottersville and Chester. The latter, the larger of the two, is at the outlet of Loon and Friendship Lakes— good fishing places, a few miles distant. Both villages are points upon the State road, from which sportsmen depart for the adjacent woods and waters. An hour's ride from either place will put them within the borders of the great wilderness, and beyond the sounds of the settlements.

Warrensburg is situated partly upon a high plain and partly upon a slope that stoops to a bend of the Scarron, about two miles above its confluence with the west branch of the Hudson. It was a village of about seven hundred inhabitants, in the midst of rugged mountain scenery, the hills abounding with iron ore. As we approached it we came to a wide plain, over which lay—in greater perfection than any we had yet seen—stump fences, which are peculiar to the Upper Hudson country. They are composed of the stumps of large pine-trees, drawn from the soil by machines made for the purpose, and they are so disposed in rows, their roots interlocking, as to form an effectual barrier to the passage of any animal on whose account fences are made. The stumps are full of sap (turpentine), and we were assured, with all the confidence of experience, that these fences would last a thousand years, the turpentine preserving the woody fibre. One of the stump-machines stood in a field near the road. It was a simple derrick, with a large wooden screw hanging from the apex, where its heavy matrix was fastened. In the lower end of the screw was a large iron bolt, and at the upper end, or head, a strong lever

STUMP-MACHINE.

was fastened. The derrick is placed over a stump, and heavy chains are wound round and under the stump and over the iron bolt in the screw. A horse attached to the lever works the screw in such a manner as to draw the stump and its roots clean from the ground. The stump fences formed quite a picturesque feature in the landscape, and at a distance have the appearance of masses of deer horns.

It was toward evening when we arrived at Warrensburg, but before sunset we had strolled over the most interesting portions of the village, along the river and its immediate vicinity. Here, as elsewhere, the prevailing drought had diminished the streams, and the Scarron, usually a

wild, rushing river, from the village to its confluence with the Hudson
proper, was a comparatively gentle creek, with many of the rocks in its
bed quite bare, and timber lodged among them. The buildings of a large
manufactory of leather skirted one side of the rapids, and at their head
was a large dam and some mills. That region abounded with establishments for making leather, the hemlock-tree, whose bark is used for
tanning, being very abundant upon the mountains.

We passed the night at Warrensburg, and early in the morning rode to
the confluence of the Scarron and Hudson rivers, in a charming little

VIEW AT WARRENSBURG.

valley which formed the Indian pass of *Teo-ho-Ken* in the olden time,
between the Thunder's Nest and other high hills. The point where the
waters met was a lovely spot, shaded by elms and other spreading trees,
and forming a picture of beauty and repose in strong contrast with the
rugged hills around. On the north side of the valley rises the Thunder's
Nest (which appears in our little sketch), a lofty pile of rocks full eight
hundred feet in height; and from the great bridge, three hundred feet
long, which spanned the Hudson just below the confluence, there was a
view of a fine amphitheatre of hills.

From the broad colonnade of the hotel the eye takes in the lake and its shores to the Narrows, about fifteen miles, and includes a theatre of great historic interest. Over those waters came the Hurons to fight the Mohawks, and during the Seven Years' war, when French dominion in America was crushed by the united powers of England and her American colonies, those hills often echoed the voice of the trumpet, the beat of the drum, the roar of cannon, the crack of musketry, the savage yell, and the shout of victory. At the head of the lake, British and Gallic warriors fought desperately, early in September, 1755; and history has recorded the results of many battle-fields in that vicinity during the last century, before and after the colonists and the mother-country came to blows, after a long and bitter quarrel. At the head of Lake George, where another fort had been erected near the ruins of William Henry, the republicans, in the old War for Independence, had a military depôt; and until the surrender of Sir John Burgoyne, at Saratoga, on the Hudson, in 1777, that lake was a minor theatre of war, where the respective adherents of the "Continental" and "Ministerial" parties came into frequent collisions. Since then a profound peace has reigned over all that region, and at the Fort William Henry House and its neighbours are gathered every summer the wise and the wealthy, the noble, gay, and beautiful of many lands, seeking and finding health in recreation.

CHAPTER IV.

WE started for Luzerne after an early dinner, crossing on our way the "French field," whereon Dieskau disposed his troops for action. We then entered the woods, and our route of eleven miles lay through a highly picturesque country, partially culti- vated, among the hills, and following the old Indian war-path from the Sacandaga to Lake George. As we approached Luzerne, the country spread into a high plain, as at Warrensburg, on the southern margin of which, overlooked by lofty hills, lies Luzerne Lake. We passed it on our left, and then went down quite a steep and winding way into the village, on the bank of the Hudson, and found an excellent home at Rockwell's spacious inn. We have seldom seen a village more picturesquely situated than this. It is about seventy miles from the Adirondack village, and on the borders of the great wilderness, where game and fish abound, and for a quiet place of summer resort, can hardly be surpassed. It lies at the foot of a high bluff, down which flows in cascades the outlet of Luzerne Lake, and leaps into the Hudson, which here makes a magnificent sweep before rushing, in narrow channel and foaming rapids between high rocky banks, to receive the equally turbulent waters of the Sacandaga, just below. That place the Indians called *Tio-sa-ron-da*, the "Meeting of the Waters." Twenty years ago, there were several mills at the head of these falls: a flood swept them away, and they have never been rebuilt.

The rapids at Luzerne, which form a fall of about eighteen feet, bear the name of Jesup's Little Falls, to distinguish them from Jesup's Great

Falls, five miles below, both being included in patents granted to Ebenezer
Jesup, who, with a family of Fairchilds, settled there before the Revolution, when Luzerne was called Westfield.   These settlers espoused the
cause of the king, and because of their depredations upon their Whig
neighbours, became very obnoxious.   They held intercourse with the
loyal Scotch Highlanders, who were under the influence of the Johnsons
and other royalists in the Mohawk valley, and acted as spies and
informants for the enemies of republicanism.   In the summer of 1777,

FALLS AT LUZERNE.

while Burgoyne was making his way toward Albany, Colonel St. Leger
penetrated the upper Mohawk valley, and laid siege to Fort Schuyler.
On one occasion he sent Indian messengers to the Fairchilds, who took
the old trail through the Sacandaga valley, by way of the Fish House,
owned by Sir William Johnson.   When they approached *Tio-sd-ron-da*
(Luzerne), they were discovered and pursued by a party of republicans,
and one of them, close pressed, leaped the Hudson, at the foot of Jesup's
Little Falls, the high wooded banks then approaching within twenty-five
feet of each other.   He escaped, took the trail to Lake George, and pushed
on to Skenesborough (now Whitehall), where he found Burgoyne.   Soon after

this a small party of republican troops, sent by General Gates, not succeeding in capturing these royalists at Westfield, laid waste the settlement.

Luzerne Lake, lying many feet above the village, is a beautiful little sheet of water, with a single small island upon its bosom. It is the larger of a series of four lakes, extending back to within five miles of Lake George. It abounds with fine fish, the largest and most delicious being the *Masque alonge*, a species of pike or pickerel, which is also found in the Upper Hudson, and all over northern New York. One was caught

MASQUE ALONGE.

in the lake, and brought to Rockwell's, on the morning of our departure, which weighed between five and six pounds.*

On the northern shore of Luzerne Lake, where the villas of Benjamin C. Butler and J. Leati, Esqs. (seen in the picture), stood, was the ancient gathering place of the Indians in council. Here was the fork of the great Sacandaga and Oneida trail, one branch extending to Lake George and the northern country, and the other to Fort Edward and the more southern country. All around the lake and village are ranges of lofty hills, filled with iron ore. On the west is the Kayaderosseros range, extending from Ballston to the Adirondacks, and on the east of the

---

* The *Masque alonge* (*Esor estor*) derived its name from the peculiar formation of its mouth and head. The French called it *Masque alonge*, or Long-face. It is the largest of the pickerel species. Some have been caught among the Thousand Islands in the St. Lawrence, in the vicinity of Alexandria Bay, on its southern shore, weighing fifty pounds, and measuring five feet in length. It is the most voracious of fresh-water fish.

Luzerne range, stretching from Saratoga Springs to the western shores of
Lake George.   Four miles north of the village is a hemispherical moun-

LUZERNE LAKE.

tain, eight hundred feet in height, rocky and bald, which the Indians
called *Se-non-ge-wah*, the Great Upturned Pot.

CONFLUENCE OF THE HUDSON AND SACANDAGA.

The Sacandaga is the largest tributary of the Mohawk, and comes down
seventy-five miles from the north-west, out of lakes and ponds in the

wilderness of Hamilton County. Its confluence with its receptacle is at the head of a very beautiful valley, that terminates at Luzerne. It comes sweeping around the bases of high hills with a rapid current, and rushes swiftly into the Hudson, where the latter has become deep and sluggish after its commotion at the falls above. Down that valley we rode, with the river in view all the way to the village of Corinth, at the head of the long rapids above Jesup's Great Falls, the *Kah-che-bon-cook* of the Indians. These were formerly known as the Hadley Falls. They were afterward called Palmer's Falls, the land on each side of the river

KAH-CHE-BON-COOK, OR JESUP'S GREAT FALLS

being in possession of Beriah Palmer and others, who there constructed extensive works for manufacturing purposes. The water-power there, even at the very low stage of the river, as when we visited it, has been estimated to be equal to fifteen thousand horse-power. They had laid out a village, with a public square and fountain, and were preparing for industrial operations far greater than at any point so far up the Hudson. It is only sixteen miles north of Saratoga Springs.

We followed a path down the margin of the roaring stream some distance, and, returning, took a rough road which led to the foot of the

Great Fall. From Jesup's landing to this point, a distance of more than a mile, the river descends about one hundred and twenty feet, in some places rushing wildly through rocky gorges from eighty to one hundred feet in depth. The perpendicular fall is seventy-five feet. We did not see it in its grandeur, the river was so low. From its course back, some distance, the stream was choked with thousands of logs that had come down from the wilderness and lodged there. They lay in a mass, in every conceivable position, to the depth of many feet, and so filled the river as to form a safe, though rough bridge, for us to cross. Between this point and Glen's Falls, thirteen miles distant by the nearest road, the Hudson makes a grand sweep among lofty and rugged hills of the Luzerne range, and flows into a sandy plain a few miles above the latter village. We did not follow its course, but took that nearest road, for the day was waning. Over mountains and through valleys, catching glimpses of the river here and there, we travelled that bright afternoon in early autumn, our eyes resting only upon near objects most of the time, until we reached the summit of a lofty hill, nine miles from Glen's Falls. There a revelation of beauty, not easily described, burst upon the vision. Looking over and beyond the minor hills through an opening in the Luzerne range, we saw the Green Mountains of Vermont in the far distance, bathed in shadowy splendour, and all the intervening country, with its villages and farm-houses, lay before us. The spires and white houses of Glen's Falls appeared so near, that we anticipated a speedy end to our day's journey. That vision was enjoyed but for a few moments, for we were soon again among the tangled hills. But another appeared to charm us. We had just commenced the descent of a mountain, along whose brow lies the dividing line between the towns of Luzerne and Queensbury, when a sudden turn in the road revealed a deep, narrow valley far below us, with the Hudson sweeping through it with rapid current. The sun's last rays had left that valley, and the shadows were deepening along the waters as we descended to their margin. Twilight was drawing its delicate veil over the face of nature when we reached the plain just mentioned, and the night had closed in when we arrived at the village of Glen's Falls. We had hoped to reach there in time to visit the State Dam and the

Great Boom, which span the Hudson at separate points, a few miles above the falls, but were compelled to forego that pleasure until morning.

We were now fairly out of the wilderness in which the Hudson rises, and through which it flows for a hundred miles; and here our little party was broken by the departure of Mr. Buckingham for home. Mrs. Lossing and myself lingered at Glen's Falls and at Fort Edward, five miles below, a day or two longer, for the purpose of visiting objects of interest in their vicinity, a description of which will be given as we proceed with our

THE HUDSON NEAR THE QUEENSBURY LINE.

notes. A brief notice of the State Dam and Great Boom, just mentioned, seems necessary.

The dam was about two and a-half miles above Glen's Falls. It had been constructed about fifteen years before, to furnish water for the feeder of the canal which connects the Hudson river and Lake Champlain. It was sixteen hundred feet in length; and the mills near it have attracted a population sufficient to constitute quite a village, named State Dam. About two miles above this dyke was the Great Boom, thrown across the river for the purpose of catching all the logs that come floating from above. It was made of heavy, hewn timbers, four of them bolted together raft-wise. The ends of the groups were connected by chains, which worked over friction rollers, to allow the boom to accommodate itself to the motion of the water. Each end of the boom was secured to a heavy abutment by chains; and above it were strong triangular structures to break the ice, to serve as anchors for the boom, and to operate as shields to prevent the logs striking the boom with the full speed of the current. At times, immense numbers of logs were collected above this boom, filling the river for two or three miles. In the spring of 1859, at least half a million of logs were collected there, ready to be taken into small side-

THE GREAT BOOM.

booms, assorted by the owners according to their private marks, and sent down to Glen's Falls, Sandy Hill, or Fort Edward, to be sawed into boards at the former places, or made into rafts at the latter, for a voyage down the river. Heavy rains and melting snows filled the river to over-flowing. The great boom snapped asunder, and the half million of logs went rushing down the stream, defying every barrier. The country below was flooded by the swollen river; and we saw thousands of the logs scattered over the valley of the Hudson from Fort Edward to Troy, a distance of about forty miles.

We have taken leave of the wilderness. Henceforth our path will be where the Hudson flows through cultivated plains, along the margins of gentle slopes, of rocky headlands, and of lofty hills; by the cottages of the humble, and the mansions of the wealthy; by pleasant hamlets, through thriving villages, ambitious cities, and the marts of trade and commerce.

Unlike the rivers of the elder world, famous in the history of men, the Hudson presents no grey and crumbling monuments of the ruder civilisations of the past, or even of the barbaric life so recently dwelling upon its borders. It can boast of no rude tower or mouldering wall, clustered with historical associations that have been gathering around them for centuries. It has no fine old castles, in glory or in ruins, with visions of romance pictured in their dim shadows; no splendid abbeys or cathedrals, in grandeur or decay, from which emanate an aura of religious memories. Nor can it boast of mansions or ancestral halls wherein a line of heroes have been born, or illustrious families have lived and died, generation after generation. Upon its banks not a vestige of feudal power may be seen, because no citadel of great wrongs ever rested there. The dead PAST has left scarcely a record upon its shores. It is full of the living PRESENT, illustrating by its general aspect the free thought and free action which are giving strength and solidity to the young and vigorous nation within whose bosom its bright waters flow.

Yet the Hudson is not without a history—a history brilliant in some respects, and in all interesting, not only to the American, but to the whole civilised world. From the spot where we now stand—the turbulent Glen's Falls—to the sea, the banks of the beautiful river have voices innumerable for the ear of the patient listener; telling of joy and woe, of love and beauty, of noble heroism, and more noble fortitude, of glory, and high renown, worthy of the sweetest cadences of the minstrel, the glowing numbers of the poet, the deepest investigations of the philosopher, and the gravest records of the historian. Let us listen to those voices.

Glen's Falls consist of a series of rapids and cascades, along a descent of about eighty feet, the water flowing over ragged masses of black marble, which here form the bed and banks of the river. Hawk-eye, in Cooper's "Last of the Mohicans," has given an admirable description of these falls, as they appeared before the works of man changed their features. He is

of that section of the State.*   The water-power there is very great, and
is used extensively for flouring and lumber mills.   The surplus water
supplies a navigable feeder to the Champlain Canal, that connects Lake
Champlain with the Hudson.   There are also several mills for slabbing
the fine black marble of that locality for the construction of chimney-
pieces, and for other uses.   These various mills mar the natural beauty of
the scene, but their uncouth and irregular forms give picturesqueness to
the view.   The bridge crosses just at the foot of the falls.   It rests upon
abutments of strong masonry at each end, and a pier in the middle, which

BELOW THE BRIDGE AT GLEN'S FALLS.

is seated upon the caverned rock, just mentioned, which was once in the
bed of the stream.   The channel on the southern side has been closed by
an abutment, and one of the chambers of the cavern, made memorable by
Cooper, is completely shut.   When we were there, huge logs nearly filled
the upper entrance to it.   Below the bridge the shores are black marble,
beautifully stratified, perpendicular, and, in some places, seventy feet in

---

* Not long after our visit here mentioned, a greater portion of the village was destroyed by fire, but
it was soon rebuilt.

height. Between these walls the water runs with a swift current for nearly a mile, and finally, at Sandy Hill, three miles below, is broken into rapids.

At Sandy Hill the Hudson makes a magnificent sweep, in a curve, when changing its course from an easterly to a southerly direction; and a little below that village it is broken into wild cascades, which have been named Baker's Falls. Sandy Hill, like the borough of Glen's Falls, stands upon a high plain, and is a very beautiful village, of about thirteen hundred inhabitants. In its centre is a shaded green, which tradition points to as the spot where a tragedy was enacted more than a century ago, some incidents of which remind us of the romantic but truthful story of Captain Smith and Pocahontas, in Virginia. The time of the tragedy was during the old French war, and the chief actor was a young Albanian, son of Sybrant Quackenboss, one of the sturdy Dutch burghers of that old city. The young man was betrothed to a maiden of the same city; the marriage day was fixed, and preparations for the nuptials were nearly completed, when he was impressed into the military service as a waggoner, and required to convey a load of provisions from Albany to Fort William Henry, at the head of Lake George. He had passed Fort Edward with an escort of sixteen men, under Lieutenant McGinnis, of New Hampshire, and was making his way through the gloomy forest at the bend of the Hudson, when they were attacked, overpowered, and disarmed by a party of French Indians, under the famous partizan Marin. The prisoners were taken to the trunk of a fallen tree, and seated upon it in a row. The captors then started toward Fort Edward, leaving the helpless captives strongly bound with green withes, in charge of two or three stalwart warriors, and their *squaws*, or wives. In the course of an hour the party returned. Young Quackenboss was seated at one end of the log, and Lieutenant McGinnis next him. The savages held a brief consultation, and then one of them, with a glittering tomahawk, went to the end of the log opposite Quackenboss, and deliberately sank his weapon in the brain of the nearest soldier. He fell dead upon the ground. The second shared a like fate, then a third, and so on until all were slain but McGinnis and Quackenboss. The tomahawk was raised to cleave the skull of the former, when he threw himself suddenly backward from the

Raccoon Skin, in Lieu and Steade of all other Rents, Services, Dues, Dutyes, and Demands whatsoever for the said Tract of Land, and Islands, and Premises." Governor Bellomont soon succeeded Fletcher, and, through his influence, the legislature of the province annulled this and other similar grants. That body, exercising ecclesiastical as well as civil functions, also passed a resolution, suspending Dellius from the ministry, for " deluding the Maquaas (Mohawk) Indians, and illegal and surreptitious obtaining of said grant." Dellius denied the authority of the legislature, and, after contesting his claim for a while, he returned to Holland. There he transferred his title to the domain to the Rev. John Lydius, who became Dellius's successor in the ministry at Albany, in 1703. Lydius soon afterward built a stone trading-house upon the site of Fort Edward. Its door and windows were strongly barred, and near the roof the walls were pierced for musketry. It was erected upon a high mound, and palisaded, as a defence against enemies.

In 1709 an expedition was prepared for the conquest of Canada. The commander of the division to attack Montreal was Francis Nicholson, who had been lieutenant-governor of the province of New York. Under his direction a military road, forty miles in length, was opened from Saratoga, on the east side of the Hudson, to White Hall, on Lake Champlain. Along this route three forts were erected. The upper one was named Fort Anne, in honour of the Queen of England; the middle one, of which Lydius's house formed a part, was called Fort Nicholson, in

GROUND-PLAN OF FORT EDWARD.

honour of the commander; and the lower one, just below the mouth of the Batten-Kill, was named Fort Saratoga. Almost fifty years later, when a provincial army, under General Johnson, of the Mohawk valley, and General Lyman, of Connecticut, was moving forward to drive the French from Lake Champlain, a strong irregular quadrangular fort was erected by the latter officer, upon the site of Fort Nicholson, and the fortification was called Fort Lyman, in his honour. It was not fairly completed when a successful battle was fought with the French and Indians under the Baron Dieskau, at the head of Lake George, the honours of which were more greatly due to Lyman than Johnson. But the latter was chief commander. His king, as we have seen, gave him the honours of knighthood and £4,000. With a mean spirit of jealousy, Johnson not only omitted to mention General Lyman in his despatches, but changed the name of the fort which he had erected, to *Edward*, in honour of one of the royal family of England.

Fort Edward was an important military post during the whole of the French and Indian war,—that Seven Years' War which cost England more than a hundred millions of pounds sterling, and laid one of the broadest of the foundation-stones of her immense national debt. There, on one occasion, Israel Putnam, a bold provincial partizan, and afterward a major-general in the American revolutionary army, performed a most daring exploit. It was winter, and the whole country was covered with deep snow. Early in the morning of a mild day, one of the rows of wooden barracks in the fort took fire; the flames had progressed extensively before they were discovered. The garrison was summoned to duty, but all efforts to subdue the fire were in vain. Putnam, who was stationed upon Roger's Island, opposite the fort, crossed the river upon the ice with some of his men, to assist the garrison. The fire was then rapidly approaching the building containing the powder-magazine. The danger was becoming every moment more imminent and frightful, for an explosion of the powder would destroy the whole fort and many lives. The water-gate was thrown open, and soldiers were ordered to bring filled buckets from the river. Putnam mounted to the roof of the building next to the magazine, and, by means of a ladder, he was supplied with water. Still the fire raged, and the commandant of the fort, perceiving Putnam's danger, ordered him down. The unflinching major begged permission to remain a little longer. It was granted, and he did not leave his post until he felt the roof beneath him giving way. It fell, and only a few feet from the blazing mass was the magazine building, its sides already charred with the heat. Unmindful of the peril, Putnam placed himself between the fire and the sleeping power in the menaced building, which a spark might arouse to destructive activity. Under a shower of cinders, he hurled bucket-full after bucket-full of water upon the kindling magazine, with ultimate success. The flames were subdued, the magazine and remainder of the fort were saved, and the intrepid

Putnam retired from the terrible conflict amidst the huzzas of his companions in arms. He was severely wounded in the contest. His mittens were burned from his hands, and his legs, thighs, arms, and face were dreadfully blistered. For a month he was a suffering invalid in the hospital.

Fort Edward was strengthened by the republicans, and properly garrisoned, when the revolution broke out in 1775. When General Burgoyne, with his invading army of British regulars, hired Germans, French, Canadians, and Indians, appeared at the foot of Lake Champlain, General Philip Schuyler was the commander-in-chief of the republican army in the Northern Department. His head-quarters were at Fort Anne, and General St. Clair commanded the important post of Ticonderoga. In July, Burgoyne came sweeping down the lake triumphantly. St. Clair fled from Ticonderoga, and his army was scattered and sorely smitten in the retreat. When the British advanced to Skenesborough, at the head of the lake, Schuyler retreated to Fort Edward, felling trees across the old military road, demolishing the causeways over the great Kingsbury marshes, and destroying the bridges, to obstruct the invader's progress. With great labour and perseverance Burgoyne moved forward, and on the 29th of July he encamped upon the high bank of the Hudson, at the great bend where the village of Sandy Hill now stands.

At this time a tragedy occurred near Fort Edward, which produced a great sensation throughout the country, and has been a theme for history, poetry, romance, and song. It was the death of Jenny M'Crea, the daughter of a Scotch Presbyterian clergyman, who is described as lovely in disposition, graceful in manners, and so intelligent and winning in all her ways, that she was a favourite of all who knew her. She was visiting a Tory friend at Fort Edward at this time, and was betrothed to a young man of the neighbourhood, who was a subaltern in Burgoyne's army. On the approach of the invaders, her brother, who lived near, fled, with his family, down the river, and desired Jenny to accompany them. She preferred to stay under the protection of her Tory friend, who was a widow, and a cousin of General Fraser, of Burgoyne's army.

Burgoyne had found it difficult to restrain the cruelty of his Indians. To secure their co-operation he had offered them a bounty for prisoners and scalps, at the same time forbidding them to kill any person not in arms for the sake of scalps. The offer of bounties stimulated the savages to seek captives other than those in the field, and they went out in small parties for the purpose. One of these prowled around Fort Edward early on the morning after Burgoyne arrived at Sandy Hill, and, entering the house where Jenny was staying, carried away the young lady and her

THE JENNY M'CREA TREE.

friend. A negro boy alarmed the garrison, and a detachment was sent after the Indians, who were fleeing with their prisoners toward the camp. They had caught two horses, and on one of them Jenny was already placed by them, when the detachment assailed them with a volley of musketry. The savages were unharmed, but one of the bullets mortally wounded their fair captive. She fell and expired, as tradition relates, near a pine-tree, which remained as a memorial of the tragedy until a few years ago. Having lost their prisoner, they secured her scalp, and, with her black tresses wet with her warm blood, they hastened to the camp. The friend of Jenny had just arrived, and the locks of the maiden, which were of great length and beauty, were recognised by her. She charged the Indians with her murder, which they denied, and told the story substantially as it is here related.

This appears, from corroborating circumstances, to be the simple truth of a story which, as it went from lip to lip, became magnified into a tale of darkest horror, and produced wide-spread indignation. General Gates, who had just superseded General Schuyler in the command of the northern army, took advantage of the excitement which it produced, to increase the hatred of the British in the hearts of the people, and he charged Burgoyne with crimes utterly foreign to that gentleman's nature. In a published letter, he accused him of hiring savages to "scalp Europeans and the descendants of Europeans;" spoke of Jenny as having been "dressed to meet her promised husband, but met her murderers," employed by Burgoyne; asserted that she, with several women and children, had been taken "from the house into the woods, and there scalped and mangled in a most shocking manner;" and alleged that he had "paid the price of blood!" This letter, so untruthful and ungenerous, was condemned by Gates's friends in the army. But it had the desired effect; and the sad story of Jenny's death was used with power against the ministry by the opposition in the British parliament.

The lover of Jenny left the army, and settled in Canada, where he lived to be an old man. He was naturally gay and garrulous, but after that event he was ever sad and taciturn. He never married, and avoided society. When the anniversary of the tragedy approached, he would shut himself in his room, and refuse to see his most intimate acquaintances; and at all times his friends avoided speaking of the American revolution in his presence. The body of Jenny was buried on her brother's land: it was re-interred at Fort Edward in 1826, with imposing ceremonies; and again in 1852, her remains found a new resting-place in a beautiful cemetery, half-way between Fort Edward and Sandy Hill. Her grave is near the entrance; and upon a plain white marble stone, six feet in height, standing at its head, is the following inscription:—

"Here rest the remains of Jane M'Crea, aged 17; made captive and murdered by a band of Indians, while on a visit to a relative in the neighbourhood, A.D. 1777. To commemorate one of the most thrilling incidents in the annals of the American revolution, to do justice to the fame of the gallant British officer to whom she was affianced, and as a simple tribute

BALM-OF-GILEAD TREE.

to the memory of the departed, this stone is erected by her niece, Sarah Hanna Payne, A.D. 1852."

No relic of the olden time now remains at Fort Edward, excepting a few logs of the fort on the edge of the river, some faint traces of the embankments, and a magnificent Balm-of-Gilead tree, which stood, a sapling, at the water-gate, when Putnam saved the magazine. It has three huge trunks, springing from the roots. One of them is more than half decayed, having been twice riven by lightning within a few years. Upon Rogers's Island, in front of the town, where armies were encamped, and a large block-house stood, Indian arrow-heads, bullets, and occasionally a piece of " cob-money," * are sometimes upturned by the plough.

A picture of the village of Fort Edward, in 1820, shows only six houses and a church; now, as we have observed, it was a busy town with two

VIEW AT FORT EDWARD.

thousand inhabitants. Its chief industrial establishment was an extensive blast-furnace for converting iron ore into the pure metal. Upon rising ground, and overlooking the village and surrounding country, was a colossal educational establishment, called the Fort Edward Institute.

" COB-MONEY."

* The old silver coins occasionally found at Fort Edward are called " cob-money" by the people. I could not ascertain the derivation of the name. The picture represents both sides of two pieces in my possession, the proper size. The larger one is a cross-pistareen, of the value of about sixteen cents; the other is a quarter fraction of the same. They are irregular in form, and the devices and dates, respectively 1741 and 1743, are imperfect. These Spanish coins formed the bulk of the specie circulated among the French in Canada a hundred years ago.

The building was erected, and its affairs were controlled, by the Methodist denomination, and it was widely known as one of the most flourishing institutions of its kind in the country. The building was five stories in height, and was surrounded by pleasant grounds. It is seen in our view at Fort Edward, which was taken from the end of the bridge that connects Rogers's Island with the western shore of the Hudson. The blast-furnace, and a portion of the Fort Edward dam, built by the State for the use of the Champlain Canal, is also seen in the picture.

A carriage-ride from Fort Edward down the valley of the Hudson,

FORT MILLER RAPIDS.

especially on its western side, affords exquisite enjoyment to the lover of beautiful scenery and the displays of careful cultivation. The public road follows the river-bank nearly all the way to Troy, a distance of forty miles, and the traveller seldom loses sight of the noble stream, which is frequently divided by islands, some cultivated, and others heavily wooded. The most important of these, between Fort Edward and Schuylerville, are Munro's, Bell's, Taylor's, Galusha's, and Payne's; the third one containing seventy acres. The shores of the river are everywhere fringed with beautiful shade-trees and shrubbery, and fertile lands spread out on every side.

Seven miles below Fort Edward, on the western shore, is the site of Fort Miller, erected during the French and Indian war; and opposite, at the head of foaming rapids, which afford fine water-power for mills, is the village of Fort Miller, then containing between two and three hundred inhabitants. Not a vestige of the fort remains. The river here rushes over a rough rocky bed, and falls fifteen or twenty feet in the course of eighty rods. Here was the scene of another of Putnam's adventures during the old war. He was out with a scouting party, and was lying alone in a batteau on the east side of the river, when he was surprised by some Indians; he could not cross the river swiftly enough to escape the balls of their rifles, and there was no alternative but to go down the foaming rapids. He did not hesitate a moment. To the astonishment of the savages, he steered directly down the current, amid whirling eddies and over ragged and shelving rocks, and in a few moments his vessel had cleared the rushing waters, and was gliding upon the tranquil river below, far out of reach of their weapons. The Indians dared not make the perilous voyage: they regarded Putnam as God-protected, and believed that it would be an affront to the Great Spirit to make further attempts to kill him with powder and ball.

CHAPTER V.

FOR the twofold purpose of affording water-power for mills, and providing still water for the boats of the Champlain Canal to cross, the Saratoga Dam is constructed at Fort Miller, three miles below the rapids. The dam forms an elbow in the middle of the stream, and is about 1,400 feet in length. Below it are considerable rapids; just above it is a bridge, which has a carriage-way for the public use, and a narrower passage for the horses that draw the canal boats. These vessels float safely on the usually still water of the river, but sometimes, when the stream is very full, the passage is attended with some difficulty, if not danger, on account of the strong though sluggish current. When we visited the spot, a large-class boat lay wrecked in the rapids below, having gone over the dam the day before.

The country in this vicinity is beautiful: the valley is narrow, and the hills, on the eastern side especially, rise one above the other in the landscape, until the view is bounded by a broken mountain range beyond. Here we crossed the river upon the canal bridge, and rode down to the mouth of the Batten-Kill, near where it enters the Hudson, to visit the spot —on the plain just above its mouth—where the army of Burgoyne lay encamped, before he crossed the Hudson to engage in those conflicts at Bemis's Heights, which resulted in his discomfiture and captivity. There he established a slaughter-yard; and it is said that the fertility imparted to the soil by the blood and offal left there was visible in its effects upon the crops raised thereon for more than sixty years afterwards.

The Batten-Kill is a shallow and rapid stream, and one of the largest of the tributaries of the Hudson, flowing in from the eastward. It rises cannonade upon it, and all the inmates took refuge in the cellar. "The ladies of the army who were with me," says the Baroness, "were Mrs. Harnage, a Mrs. Kennels, the widow of a lieutenant who was killed, and the lady of the commissary. Major Harnage, his wife, and Mrs. Kennels, made a little room in a corner, with curtains to it, and wished to do the same for me, but I preferred being near the door, in case

DI-ON-ON-DEH-O-WA, OR GREAT FALLS OF THE BATTEN-KILL.

of fire. Not far off my women slept, and opposite to me three English officers, who, though wounded, were determined not to be left behind: one of them was Captain Green, an aide-de-camp to Major-General Phillips, a very valuable officer and most agreeable man. They each made me a most sacred promise not to leave me behind, and, in case of sudden retreat, that they would each of them take one of my children on his horse; and for myself one of my husband's was in constant readiness. . . . . . The want of water distressed us much; at length we found a soldier's wife

THE REIDESEL HOUSE.

who had courage enough to fetch us some from the river—an office nobody else would undertake, as the Americans shot at every person who approached it, but out of respect for her sex they never molested her."

CELLAR OF REIDESEL HOUSE.

Six days these ladies and their companions remained in that cellar, when hostilities ceased, and the British army surrendered to the Americans.

The village of Schuylerville is pleasantly situated upon a slope on the western margin of the Upper Hudson valley, on the north bank of the Fish Creek (the outlet of Saratoga Lake), which there leaps to the plain in a series of beautiful cascades, after being released from the labour of turning several mill-wheels. These cascades or rapids commence at the bridge where the public road crosses the creek, and continue for many rods, until a culvert under the Champlain Canal is passed. Viewed from the grounds around the Schuyler mansion, at almost every point, they

RAPIDS OF THE FISH CREEK, AT SCHUYLERVILLE.

present very perfect specimens of a picturesque water-course, having considerable strength and volume.

The village, containing about twelve hundred inhabitants, occupies the site of General Burgoyne's intrenched camp, at the time when he surrendered to General Gates, in the autumn of 1777. It was named in honour of General Philip Schuyler, upon whose broad domain of Saratoga, and in whose presence, the last scenes in that memorable campaign were performed, and who, for forty years, was a conspicuous actor in civil and military life in his native State of New York.

Upon one of the conical hills on the opposite side of the valley, just below the Batten-Kill, was old Fort Saratoga, written Sarahtogue in the old records. It was a stockade, weakly garrisoned, and, with the scattered village of thirty families, of the same name, upon the plain below, was destroyed in the autumn of 1745, by a horde of Frenchmen and Indians, under the noted partisan Marin, whose followers, as we have seen, performed a sanguinary tragedy at Sandy Hill ten years later. They had left Montreal for the purpose of making a foray upon some English settlements on the Connecticut river. It was late in the season, and at Crown Point, on Lake Champlain, the Indians refused to go eastward, because of their lack of preparations for the rigour of winter. On the suggestion of Father Piquet, the French Prefect Apostolique of Canada, who met the expedition at Crown Point, Marin led his white and red savages southward, towards Orange, as Albany was then called by the French, to cut off the advancing English settlements, and bear away what plunder they might obtain. Father Piquet accompanied them, and the invaders fell upon the inhabitants when they were asleep. They burnt the fort and most of the houses, murdered some who resisted, and carried away captive over one hundred men, women, and children.

Upon the south side of the Fish Creek, on the margin of the rapids, stood a brick mansion, pierced near the roof for musketry, and owned and occupied by a kinsman of General Schuyler, bearing the same name. His house was attacked, and in an attempt to defend it he was shot. His body was consumed, with other persons who had escaped to the cellar, when, after plundering the house, the savages set it on fire. That Saratoga estate was bequeathed by the murdered owner to his nephew Philip (the General), who built a country mansion, elegant for the times, near the site of the old one, and occupied it when Burgoyne invaded the valley in 1777. During that invasion the general's house and mills were burned by Burgoyne's orders. It was an act which the British general afterwards lamented, for he soon learned to honour Schuyler as one of the noblest men he had ever met. The mansion was rebuilt immediately after the campaign was over, a few rods from the site of the old one, but in a style much inferior in beauty and expense. It was the general's country-seat (his town residence being in Albany) until his death in 1804, and was still preserved in its original form at the time of our visit, and surrounded by beautiful shady trees, many of which were planted by the master's own hand. It was then the residence of George Strover, Esq., who took pleasure in preserving it as General Schuyler left it. Even some ancient lilac shrubs, now quite lofty trees, gnarled and unsightly, that were in the garden of the old mansion, were cherished as precious mementoes of the past.

An outline sketch of events to which allusion has just been made is

THE SCHUYLER MANSION.

necessary to a full comprehension of the isolated historical facts with which this portion of our subject abounds. We will trace it with rapid pencil, and leave the completion of the picture to the careful historian.

The campaigns of 1775 and 1776, against the rebellious Americans, were fruitless of any satisfactory results. The British cabinet, supported by heavy majorities in both Houses of Parliament, resolved to open the campaign of 1777 with such vigour, and to give to the service in America such material, as should not fail to put down the rebellion by midsummer.

So long as the Republicans remained united, so long as there existed a free communication between Massachusetts and Virginia, or, in other words, between the Eastern and the Middle and Southern States, permanent success of the British arms in America seemed questionable. The rebellion was hydra-headed, springing into new life and vigour suddenly and powerfully, from the inherent energies of union, in places where it seemed to be subdued or destroyed. To sever that union, and to paralyse the vitality dependent thereon, was a paramount consideration of the British Government when planning the campaign of 1777.

General Sir William Howe was then in quiet possession of the city of New York, at the mouth of the Hudson river. A strong British force occupied Rhode Island, and kept watch over the whole eastern coast of New England. Republicans who had invaded Canada had been driven back by Governor Carleton; and nothing remained to complete the separation of the two sections of the American States, but to march an invading army from Canada, secure the strongholds upon Lakes George and Champlain, press forward to Albany, and there form a junction with Howe, whose troops, meanwhile, should have taken possession of the Hudson Highlands, and every place of importance upon that river.

The leadership of that invasion from the North was intrusted to Lieutenant-General Sir John Burgoyne, who had won military laurels in Portugal, had held a seat in the king's council, and was then a member of Parliament. He arrived at Quebec in March, 1777, and in June had collected a large force of English and German troops, Canadians, and Indians, at the foot of Lake Champlain. At the beginning of July he invested Ticonderoga with ten thousand men, drove the Americans from that old fortress and its dependencies, and, as we have observed, swept victoriously up the lake to Skenesborough, and advanced to Fort Edward. From that point he sent a detachment to Bennington, in Vermont, to seize cattle and provisions for the use of the army. The expedition was defeated by militia, under Stark, and thereby Burgoyne received a blow from which he did not recover. Yet he moved forward, crossed the Hudson a little above Schuylerville, and pitched his tents, and formed a fortified camp upon the site of that village. He had stated at Fort Edward that he should eat his Christmas dinner in Albany, a laurelled conqueror, with the great objects of the campaign perfectly accomplished; but now he began to doubt.

General Schuyler had been the commander of the troops opposed to Burgoyne until the 19th of August, when he surrendered his charge to General Gates, a conceited officer, very much his inferior in every particular. This supersedure had been accomplished by political intrigue.

When Burgoyne crossed the Hudson, Gates, then at the mouth of the Mohawk, advanced with his troops to Bemis's Height, about twelve miles below the halting British army, and there established a fortified camp. Perceiving the necessity of immediate hostile action—because the Republican army was hourly augmenting (volunteers flocking in from all quarters, and particularly from New England)—Burgoyne crossed the Fish Creek, burned the mills and mansion of General Schuyler, and advanced upon Gates.

A severe but indecisive battle was fought at Bemis's Heights on the 19th of September; Burgoyne fell back a few miles toward his intrenched camp, and resolved there to await the expected approach of Sir Henry Clinton, with a large force, up the lower Hudson. Clinton was tardy, perils were thickening, and Burgoyne resolved to make another attack upon Gates. After a severe battle fought on the 7th of October, upon almost the same ground occupied in the engagement on the 19th of September, he was again compelled to fall back. He finally retreated to his intrenched camp beyond the Fish Creek.

Burgoyne's force was now hourly diminishing, the Canadians and Indians deserting him in great numbers, while volunteers were swelling the ranks of Gates. The latter now advanced upon Burgoyne, and, on the 17th of October, that general surrendered his army of almost six thousand men, and all its appointments, into the hands of the Republicans. The forts upon Lakes George and Champlain were immediately abandoned by the British, and the Republicans held an unobstructed passage from the Hudson Highlands to St. John, on the Sorel, in Canada.

The spot where Burgoyne's army laid down their arms is upon the plain in front of Schuylerville, near the site of old Fort Hardy, a little north of the highway leading from the village across the Hudson, over the long bridge already mentioned. Our view is taken from one of the canal bridges, looking north-east. The Hudson is seen beyond the place of surrender, and in the more remote distance may be observed the conical hills which, on the previous day, had swarmed with American volunteers.

With the delicate courtesy of a gentleman, General Gates ordered all his army within his camp, that the vanquished might not be submitted to the mortification of their gaze at the moment of the great humiliation. The two generals had not yet seen each other. As soon as the troops had laid down their arms, Burgoyne and his officers proceeded towards Gates's

SCENE OF BURGOYNE'S SURRENDER.

camp, to be introduced. They crossed the Fish Creek at the head of the rapids, and proceeded towards the republican general's quarters, about a mile and a-half down the river. Burgoyne led the way, with Kingston (his adjutant-general), and his aides-de-camp, Captain Lord Petersham and Lieutenant Wilford, followed by Generals Phillips, Reidesel, and Hamilton, and other officers, according to rank. General Gates, informed of the approach of Burgoyne, went out with his staff to meet him at the head of his camp. Burgoyne was dressed in a rich uniform of scarlet and gold, and Gates in a plain blue frock coat. When within about a sword's length of each other, they reined up their horses, and halted. Colonel Wilkinson, Gates's aide-de-camp, then introduced the two generals. Both dismounted, and Burgoyne, raising his hat gracefully, said — "The fortune of war, General Gates, has made me your prisoner." The victor promptly replied—"I shall always be ready to bear testimony that it has not been through any fault of your excellency." The other officers were then introduced in turn, and the whole party repaired to Gates's head-quarters, where the best dinner that could be procured was served.

The plain farmhouse in which that remarkable dinner-party was

GATES'S HEAD-QUARTERS.

assembled remained unaltered externally when we visited it, excepting such changes as have been effected by necessary repairs. It stood about eighty rods from the Hudson, on the western margin of the plain; and between it and the river the Champlain Canal passed. Our sketch was made from the highway, and includes glimpses of the canal, the river, and the hills on the eastern side of the plain.

The Baroness Reidesel, in her narrative of these events, says: " I was, I confess, afraid to go over to the enemy, as it was quite a new situation to me. When I drew near the tents, a handsome man approached and met me, took my children from the *caléche*, and hugged and kissed them, which affected me almost to tears. 'You tremble,' said he, addressing himself to me; 'be not afraid.' 'No,' I answered, 'you seem so kind and tender to my children, it inspires me with courage.' He now led me to the tent of General Gates, where I found Generals Burgoyne and Phillips, who were on a friendly footing with the former.

"All the generals remained to dine with General Gates. The same gentleman who received me so kindly, now came and said to me, 'You will be very much embarrassed to eat with all those gentlemen; come with your children to my tent, where I will prepare for you a frugal dinner, and give it with a free will.' I said, 'You are certainly a husband and a father, you have shown me so much kindness.' I now found that he was GENERAL SCHUYLER. He treated me with excellent smoked tongue, beef-steaks, potatoes, and good bread and butter. Never could I have wished to eat a better dinner. I was content; I saw all around me were so likewise. When we had dined, he told me his residence was at Albany, and that General Burgoyne intended to honour him as his guest, and invited myself and children to do so likewise. I asked my husband how I should act; he told me to accept the invitation." General Schuyler's house at Albany yet remains, and there we shall hereafter meet the Baroness and Burgoyne, as guests of that truly noble republican.

The Hudson, from Schuylerville to Stillwater, a distance of about thirteen miles, flows through a rich plain, and its course is unbroken by island, rapid, or bridge. Between it and the western margin of the plain is the Champlain Canal, bearing upon its quiet bosom the wealth of a large internal commerce, extending from New York and Albany to Canada. It was spanned, for the convenience of the farmers through whose land it passes, with numerous bridges, stiff and ungraceful in appearance, and all of the same model. A picture of one of them is given at the head of this chapter. The river was also crossed in several places by means of rope ferries. These, at times, presented quite picturesque scenes, when men and women, teams, live stock, and merchandize, happen to constitute the freight at one time. The vehicle was a large scow or batteau, which was pushed by means of long poles, that reached to the bottom of the river;

and it was kept in its course, in defiance of the current, by ropes fore and aft, attached by friction rollers to a stout cable stretched across the stream. There were several of these ferries between Fort Edward and Stillwater, the one most used being that at Bemis's Heights, of which we give a drawing.

Three miles below Schuylerville, on the same side of the river, is the hamlet of Coveville, formerly called Do-ve-gat, or Van Vechten's Cove. It is a pretty, quiet little place, and sheltered by hills in the rear; the

ROPE FERRY.

inhabitants are chiefly agriculturists, and the families of those employed in canal navigation. Here Burgoyne halted, and encamped for two days, after leaving his intrenched camp to confront Gates, while a working party repaired the roads and bridges in advance to Wilbur's Basin, three miles below. He then advanced, and pitched his tents at the latter place, upon the narrow plain between the river and the hills, and upon the slopes. Here he also encamped on the morning after the first battle at Bemis's Heights, the opening of a cloudy, dull, and cheerless day, that harmonised with the feelings of the British commander. He felt convinced that, without the aid of General Clinton's co-operation in drawing off a part of the republican army to the defence of the country below, he should not be able to advance. Yet he wrought diligently in strengthening his position. He erected four redoubts, one upon each of four hills, two above and two below Wilbur's Basin, and made lines of intrenchments from them to the river, covering each with a battery. From this camp he marched to battle on the 7th of October, and in that engagement lost

BURGOYNE'S ENCAMPMENT (from a print published in London, in 1779).

his gallant friend, General Simon Fraser, who, at the head of five hundred picked men, was the directing spirit of the British troops in action. This was perceived by the American commanders, for Fraser's skill and courage were everywhere conspicuous. When the lines gave way, he brought order out of confusion; when regiments began to waver, he infused courage into them by voice and example. He was mounted upon a splendid iron-grey gelding, and dressed in the full uniform of a field officer. He was thus made a conspicuous object for the mark of the Americans.

It was evident that the fate of the battle depended upon General Fraser, and this the keen eye and quick judgment of Colonel Morgan, commander of a rifle corps from the south, perceived. A thought flashed through his brain, and in an instant he prepared to execute a deadly purpose. Calling a file of his best men around him, he said, as he pointed toward the British right wing, which was making its way victoriously,—"That gallant officer is General Fraser; I admire and honour him, but it is necessary he should die; victory for the enemy depends upon him. Take your stations in that clump of bushes, and do your duty." Within five minutes after this order was given, General Fraser fell, and was carried

HOUSE IN WHICH GENERAL FRASER DIED.

from the field by two grenadiers. His aide-de-camp had just observed that the general was a particular mark for the enemy, and said,—"Would it not be prudent for you to retire from this place?" Fraser replied, "My duty forbids me to fly from danger," and the next moment he fell.

About half way between Wilbur's Basin and Bemis's, stood, until within twenty years, a rude building, the upper half somewhat projecting, and every side of it battered and pierced by bullets. It was used by Burgoyne as his quarters when he first moved forward to attack Gates, and there the Baron Reidesel had his quarters at the time of the battle of the 7th of October. Thither the wounded Fraser was conveyed by his grenadiers, and consigned to the care of the wife of the Brunswick general.

"About four o'clock in the afternoon," says the baroness, "instead of the guests [Burgoyne and Phillips] whom I expected to dinner, General Fraser was brought on a litter mortally wounded. The table, which was already set, was instantly removed, and a bed placed in its stead for the wounded general. He said to the surgeon, 'Tell me if my wound is

FRASER'S BURIAL-PLACE.

mortal; do not flatter me.' The ball had passed through his body, and, unhappily for the general, he had eaten a very hearty breakfast, by which the stomach was distended, and the ball, as the surgeon said, had passed through it. I often heard him exclaim, with a sigh, 'O fatal ambition! Poor General Burgoyne! O my dear wife!' He was asked if he had any request to make, to which he replied, that, if General Burgoyne would permit it, he should like to be buried at six o'clock in the evening, on the top of a mount, in a redoubt which had been built there."

General Fraser died at eight o'clock the following morning, and was buried in the redoubt upon the hill at six o'clock that evening, according to his desire.* It was just at sunset, on a mild October evening, when the funeral procession moved slowly up the hill, bearing the body of the gallant dead. It was composed of only the members of his own military family, the commanding generals, and Mr. Brudenell, the chaplain; yet the eyes of hundreds of both armies gazed upon the scene. The Americans,

NEILSON'S HOUSE, BEMIS'S HEIGHTS.

ignorant of the true character of the procession, kept up a constant cannonade upon the redoubt, toward which it was moving. Undismayed, the companions of Fraser buried him just as the evening shadows came on: Before the impressive burial services of the Anglican Church were ended, the irregular firing ceased, and the solemn voice of a single canon, at measured intervals, boomed along the valley, and awakened responses from the hills. It was a minute-gun, fired by the Americans in honour

* The redoubt was upon the middle one of the three hills seen in the picture of Burgoyne's encampment.

of the accomplished soldier. When information reached the Republicans that the gathering at the redoubt was a funeral company, fulfilling the wishes of a brave officer, the cannonade with balls instantly ceased.

Other gallant British officers were severely wounded on that day; one of these was the accomplished Major Ackland, of the grenadiers, who was accompanied in the campaign by his charming wife, the Lady Harriet, fifth daughter of Stephen, first Earl of Ilchester, and great-grandmother of the present Earl of Carnarvon. He was shot through both legs, and conveyed to the house of Mr. Neilson, upon Bemis's Heights, within the American lines.

CHAPTER VI.

THE heroic Lady Ackland had listened to the thunder of the battle in which her husband was engaged, and when, on the morning of the 8th, the British fell back in confusion toward Wilbur's Basin, she, with the other women, was obliged to take refuge among the dead and dying, for the tents were all struck, and hardly a shed was left standing. Then she was informed that her husband was wounded and a prisoner. She instantly sought the advice of her friend, the Baroness Reidesel, and resolved to visit the American camp, and implore the privilege of a personal attendance upon her husband. She sent a message by Lord Petersham to Burgoyne, asking his permission to depart. The general was astonished that, after all she had endured from exposure to cold, hunger, and heavy rain, she should be capable of such an undertaking. "The assistance I was enabled to give," he said, "was small indeed. I had not even a cup of wine to offer her; but I was told she had found, from some kind and fortunate hand, a little rum and dirty water. All I could furnish to her was an open boat, and a few lines written upon dirty wet paper, to General Gates, recommending her to his protection." *

Lady Harriet set out in an open boat on the Hudson, accompanied by Chaplain Brudenell, her waiting-maid, and her husband's valet, who had

---

* The following is a copy of Burgoyne's note to Gates:—

SIR,—Lady Harriet Ackland, a lady of the first distinction of family, rank, and personal virtues, is under such concern on account of Major Ackland, her husband, wounded and a prisoner in your hands, that I cannot refuse her request to commit her to your protection. Whatever general impropriety there may be in persons of my situation and yours to solicit favours, I cannot see the uncommon perseverance in every female grace and exaltation of character of this lady, and her very hard fortune, without testifying that your attention to her will lay me under obligations.

I am, Sir, your obedient servant,

J. BURGOYNE.

This note is preserved among Gates's manuscript papers, in the collection of the New York Historical Society.

been severely wounded while searching for his master on the battle-field. They started at sunset, in the midst of a violent storm of wind and rain. It was long after dark when they reached the American outposts, and there they were detained, in a comfortable position, until orders should be received from head-quarters. Early in the morning she received the joyful tidings that her husband was safe. At the same time she was treated with paternal kindness by General Gates, who sent her to her husband at Neilson's house, under a suitable escort. She found him suffering, but well taken care of, in the portion of the house occupied as

ROOM OCCUPIED BY MAJOR ACKLAND.

quarters by General Poor, and there she remained until Major Ackland was removed to Albany, and finally to New York.*

From the house of Mr. Neilson, whose descendants now occupy it, a fine view of the surrounding country may be obtained. On the north and west, beginning at its very doors, lies the entire battle-ground of the 19th of September; and bounding the horizon in the distance beyond, are the Luzerne Mountains (already mentioned), through which flow the waters of the Upper Hudson. On the east rise Willard's Mountain, the heights of Bennington, the Green Mountains, and the famous Mount Tom; and stretching away in the blue distances towards Albany, are seen the gentle hills and beautiful valley of the Hudson. And there the visitor may see

---

* Major Ackland died in November, 1778. On her return to England, a portrait of Lady Harriet, standing in a boat, with a white handkerchief in her hand as a flag of truce, was exhibited at the Royal Academy (London), from which a plate was afterwards engraved. The person of her ladyship was spoken of as "highly graceful and delicate," and her manners "elegantly feminine."

many relics from the battle-field, turned up by the plough, such as cannon-balls, bullets, Indian tomahawks and knives, rusty musket barrels, bayonets, halberds, military buttons, pieces of money, et cætera.

At the foot of Bemis's Heights, where the old tavern of Bemis—famous for good wines and long pipes, a spacious ball-room and a rich larder—once stood, a pleasant hamlet has grown up. It is one of the numerous offsprings of the canal. Two miles below it, at the head of long rapids, is Stillwater, the most pleasing in situation and appearance of all the villages in the valley of the Upper Hudson. It is otherwise remarkable only for a long, gloomy, and unsightly covered toll-bridge, which, resting upon several huge piers, spans the Hudson; and also as

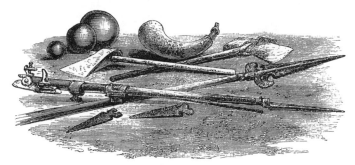

RELICS FROM THE BATTLE-FIELD.

the head-quarters of the republican army, for a short time, in the summer of 1777, after they had retreated down the valley before victorious Burgoyne. The house of Derrick Swart, where General Schuyler had his quarters at that time, was yet standing in the upper part of the village, and awakened in the mind of the historical student recollections of a scene that occurred there at a most gloomy period of the campaign. The army, wretchedly furnished and daily diminishing, had retreated before an exultant foe; food, clothing, and artillery were all wanting. The pecuniary resources and public credit of the continental congress were failing, and all the future seemed dark. At that moment intelligence came that Colonel St. Leger, who had been sent up the St. Lawrence by Burgoyne, with instructions to cross Lake Ontario to Oswego, penetrate the Mohawk valley from that point, form an alliance with the Tories and Indians, and press forward to Albany with destructive energy, had actually appeared before Fort Schuyler, where the village of Rome now stands. The people of the Mohawk valley were wild with consternation, and sent swift messengers to General Schuyler, imploring immediate assistance. The prudent foresight and far-reaching humanity of that officer at once dictated his course. He called a council of officers at his quarters, and proposed sending a detachment immediately to the relief of Fort Schuyler.

DERRICK SWART'S HOUSE AT STILLWATER.

They opposed him with the argument that his whole force was insufficient to stay the progress of Burgoyne. Schuyler persisted in his opinion, and earnestly besought them to second his views. His political enemies had already sown the seeds of distrust concerning his intentions; and as he was pacing the floor in anxious solicitude, he heard from one of his subordinate officers the half-whispered remark, "He means to weaken the army." Never was a thought more unjust and ungenerous! Wheeling suddenly toward the slanderer and those around him, and unconsciously biting into several pieces a pipe that he was smoking, Schuyler indignantly exclaimed, "Gentlemen, I shall take the responsibility upon myself; where is the brigadier that will take command of the relief? I shall beat up for volunteers to-morrow."

The brave and impulsive Arnold, who afterwards became a traitor, at once stepped forward. The next morning, when the drum beat for volunteers, no less than eight hundred strong men offered their services. They were enrolled; Fort Schuyler was saved, and the forces of St. Leger scattered to the winds. In after years the recollection of those burning words of calumny always stirred the spirit of the veteran patriot with violent emotions; for if ever a bosom glowed with true devotion to his country, it was that of Philip Schuyler.

From Stillwater to Troy at the head of free sloop navigation, a distance of about sixteen miles, the Hudson flows in a rapid stream, sometimes turbulent, but generally with a placid current. The valley, maintaining the same average width and general aspect, becomes richer in numerous farm-houses and more careful cultivation as we approach the cluster of large towns whose church spires may be seen soon after leaving Mechanics-ville and Half-Moon, two pleasant little villages on the west bank of the Hudson. These are in the township of Half-Moon, so called in memory of Hendrick Hudson's famous yacht, in which he discovered the river that bears his name. They are a short distance below Stillwater. The Champlain Canal and the Rensselaer and Saratoga Railway pass through them. On the site of the latter village stood "ye ffort of ye Half-Moon, about ye house and barne of Harme Lievese"—a stockade for defence against the Indians. It was removed in the year 1689.

The summer drive upon the public road in this part of the valley is delightful. The plain and slopes have the appearance of a garden; while the hills on both sides present sweet pictures of mingled forest and culti-vated fields, enlivened by small flocks and herds, and dotted with the homes of a thrifty people. But the river appears solitary. Not a boat may be seen upon it, until Waterford is passed, for the current is too swift for navigation. "The water in the river here," wrote Kalm, the Swedish naturalist and traveller, in his journal, more than one hundred years ago, "was very clear, and generally shallow, being only from two to four feet deep, running very violently against us in most places."

Between Mechanicsville and Waterford, near the junction of two railways, the viaduct of the Vermont Central Railroad, twelve hundred feet in length, stretches across the Hudson. It is constructed of square timber, and rests upon heavy stone piers, besides the shore abutments. From that point to Waterford, the river views from the highway are very picturesque, and when within half a mile of that large village upon Half-Moon Point, at a bend in the stream, the traveller obtains a sight of Waterford and Lansingburgh, on opposite sides of the river, with the

VIADUCT OF THE VERMONT CENTRAL RAILWAY.

covered toll-bridge that connects them. The church spires of Troy are also seen, and in dim blue outline, in the extreme southern horizon, appear the higher spurs of the Katzbergs, or Catskill Mountains.

Waterford is a very pleasant town, at the confluence of the Mohawk and Hudson rivers, and had then a little more than three thousand inhabitants. It stands upon the level bank of the Hudson. Most of its streets are fringed with the maple and elm, the favourite shade trees in the northern and eastern villages and cities of the United States. It is a young town, compared with Lansingburgh, its still more pleasant

neighbour across the river, which was dignified with the title of New
City as early as 1788, when its now stately rival, Troy, could not boast
of half-a-dozen houses, and was known only as Vanderheyden, or Ashley's
Ferry. It has outstripped that older town in population, and equals it
in enterprise. Between them the current of the Hudson is strong, yet
vessels laden with merchandise ascend to the wharves of each, with the

WATERFORD AND LANSINGBURGH BRIDGE.

aid of small steam-tugs, which tow them from the draw of the great
bridge at Troy, two miles below.

At Waterford the ear catches the subdued roar of Cohoes Falls * in the
Mohawk river, three-fourths of a mile distant. That stream is the largest
tributary of the Hudson. It flows eastward, with a rapid current most
of the way, from Oneida County, in the interior of the State of New
York, through one of the richest agricultural regions in the world, for
about one hundred and thirty-five miles, and enters the Hudson in four

---

* Cah-hoos, an Iroquois word, according to Brant, the great Mohawk chief, signifying a canoe
falling.

channels, formed by three islands, named respectively, Van Hover's, Van Schaick's, or Cohoes, and Green or Tibbett's Islands. Van Schaick's alone, which is almost inaccessible at many points, because of its high rocky shores, has escaped the transforming hand of improvement. There, in the summer of 1777, General Schuyler cast up some fortifications, with the determination to dispute with Burgoyne the passage of the Mohawk. Faint traces of those intrenchments may yet be seen; and, in the spring of 1860, a large zinc cartridge-box was found in that vicinity, supposed to have been left when General Schuyler moved northward. The banks of Van Schaick's are steep, a forest of evergreens clothes a large portion of its surface, and only a solitary barn indicates its cognizance by man.

Green Island, the larger of the three, stretches along the upper part of Troy, and is a theatre of industry for a busy population, engaged chiefly in manufactures, or in employments connected with railways. There was the immense establishment of Messrs. Eaton, Gilbert, & Co. (afterward destroyed by fire), the most extensive manufacturers of railway carriages, omnibuses, and stage coaches in the United States, if not in the world.

The scenery about the mouth of the Mohawk, particularly in the vicinity of Cohoes Falls, is exceedingly picturesque, and at some points really grand. A highway bridge, nine hundred feet in length, and a railway viaduct still longer, cross the river over the rapids a short distance below the falls. From the former, a fine distant view of the cataract and the rapids below may be obtained; but the best places to observe them in all their beauty and grandeur, are at and near the Cataract House, in the village of Cohoes, which stands upon the summit verge of a precipice one hundred and seventy feet in height. Down a steep slope of that precipice, for about fifty feet, the proprietor has constructed a flight of steps, and upon the top of a broad terrace at their foot he has planted a flower garden, for the enjoyment of visitors. Around its edge, from which may be obtained a view of the entire cataract, is a railing with seats, and there the visitor may contemplate at ease the wild scene on every hand. On his left, as he gazes up the river, rush large streams of water from the top of the precipice above him, in almost perpendicular currents, from the waste-sluices of a canal, which, commencing at a dam almost two miles above the falls, conveys water to numerous mill-wheels in the village. By this means immense hydraulic power is obtained and distributed.*

VIEW AT COHOES FALLS.

The width of the grand cataract of Cohoes is nine hundred feet, and the fall seventy-eight feet, of which about forty are perpendicular.

* The water-power at Cohoes was under the control of a stock company, who rented it to the proprietors of mills and factories. The entire fall of water controlled by the company was one hundred and twenty feet; and the minimum supply of water was one thousand cubic feet each second. The estimated value of the various articles manufactured there at that time, was nearly three millions of dollars per annum.

Below the fall, the water rushes over a rocky bed, in foaming rapids, between high banks, to the plain, where the islands divide it into channels, and through these it flows gently into the Hudson. It was a beautiful afternoon in early spring when we visited the falls. The water was abundant, for the snow upon the hills that border the charming valley of the Mohawk was rapidly melting, and filled the river to the brim. We never saw the cataract in more attractive form, and left it with reluctance when the declining sun admonished us to ride back to Waterford, for we intended to cross the long bridge there, pass through Lansingburgh, and lodge that night in Troy. It was just at sunset when we crossed the bridge and entered the beautiful avenue which leads through Lansingburgh, into the heart of Troy. Through the village it is shaded with stately elms, and along the whole distance of two miles between that "New City" of the past and modern Troas, it follows the bank of the river in a straight line, and affords a most delightful drive in summer.

In the upper suburb of Troy we came to a mass of rock rising a few yards from the avenue to the height of fifty or sixty feet, with a tall, crooked sapling shooting up from its summit, which had been placed there for a flagstaff. The classical taste which gave the name of the city built where the dappled heifer of Ilus lay down, to this modern town, when it was little more than a hamlet, and which dignified the irregular hill that overlooks it with the title of Mount Ida (called Ida Hill by the inhabitants), named this rocky peak Mount Olympus. We saw nothing upon its "awful summit" to remind us of the Thessalian dwelling-place of the gods; and the apparition nearest to that of "Olympian Jove" (whom the artists portrayed in human form) that we saw in the fading twilight, was a ragged boy, with a cigar in his mouth, vainly endeavouring to climb the sapling.

The peak of Olympus was once much higher. It has been carried away from time to time to furnish materials for docks, and in strengthening the dam, twelve hundred feet in length, which the State built across the Hudson at this point to furnish a feeder to the Champlain Canal. The water at the dam has a fall of about twelve feet, and at the east end is a heavy lock, constructed of hewn stone, through which sloops and other

vessels are taken into the river above, and towed by steam-tugs, as we
have observed, up to Lansingburgh and Waterford.   Just above the dam,
and near Waterford, there is a communication between the canal and the
river, and many loaded boats from the former there enter the latter, pass
through the lock, and are towed, some to Troy and Albany, and others to
New York.   The dam also furnishes water power to a number of mills
on the Troy shore below it, into which grain is taken from vessels lying
at the docks, by means of "elevators" worked by the water wheels.
These form a striking feature in the scene below the dam.

From the lock may be obtained an excellent view of the river below,

LOCK AT STATE DAM, TROY.

with the last of the bridges that then spanned the Hudson.   Since then
a railway-bridge has been thrown across it at Albany, six miles below.
Glimpses of Troy, and Watervliet or West Troy opposite, and of the
Katzbergs, thirty miles distant, were obtained from the same point of
view.   The Troy Bridge was sixteen hundred feet in length, and
connected Green Island with the main, having a draw at the eastern end
for vessels to pass through.   It was used as a public highway in crossing
the river, and also as a viaduct of the Rensselaer and Saratoga Railway.
It was built of timber, was closely covered, and rested upon heavy stone
piers.   It crossed where formerly lay a group of beautiful little islands,
when Troy was in its infancy.   They have almost disappeared, except

the larger one, which is bisected by the bridge. Among these islands shad and sturgeon, fish that abound in every part of the river below, were caught in large quantities, but they are seldom seen there now.

Troy, the capital of Rensselaer County, is six miles above Albany, at the head of tide-water, one hundred and fifty-one miles from the city of New York. It is a port of entry, and its commerce is very extensive for an inland town. It is seated upon a plain between the foot of Mount Ida and the river. It has crept up that hill in some places, but very cautiously, because the earth is unstable, and serious avalanches have from time to time occurred. Its site was originally known as Ferry Hook, then Ashley's Ferry,* and finally Vanderheyden, the name of the first proprietor of the soil on which Troy stands, after it was conveyed in fee from the Patroon of Rensslaerwyck, in the year 1720. After the Revolution the spot attracted some attention as an eligible village site. Town lots were laid out there in the summer of 1787, and two years afterward the freeholders of the embryo city, at a meeting in Albany, resolved that "in future it should be called and known by the name of Troy." At the same time, with the prescience of observing men, they said—"It may not be too sanguine to expect, at no very distant period, to see Troy as famous for her trade and navigation as many of our first towns." It was incorporated a village in 1801, and a city in 1816.

From the beginning Troy was a rival of Lansingburgh. It was settled chiefly by enterprising New England people. They perceived the advantages of their location at the head of tide-water and sloop navigation, between two fine streams (Poesten Kill and Wynant's Kill) that flow in wild cascades from Mount Ida and its connections, affording

---

* Stephen Ashley kept the first tavern at the ferry, in the farm-house of Matthias Vanderheyden, on the south-east corner of River and Division Streets. It is the oldest house in Troy, having been built as early as 1752. On the front of the house, between the two windows on the left, was a brick, on which was cut "ᗡ V H. A.D. 1752." The initials stood for Derick (Richard) Vanderheyden. The D was reversed. Between the second window on the left and the door was another brick inscribed "M V H. 1752." These were the initials of Matthias Vanderheyden. South of the window on the right, and a little above it, was another brick inscribed "I V H. 1752." These were the initials of Jacob Vanderheyden. Matthias occupied this, and the other two built houses elsewhere on the plot. Ashley afterward kept an inn at the corner of River and Ferry Streets. On his sign was a portrait of Washington, and the words "Why here's Ashley's."

VANDERHEYDEN HOUSE.

extensive water power. After a hard struggle, Troy was made the county-seat, and the court-house was erected there, and from that time the growth of Lansingburgh was slow, whilst Troy increased with wonderful rapidity. The former had 6,000 inhabitants in 1860, and the latter almost 50,000. It has always been conspicuous for well-directed and associated public spirit, and its institutions of learning are among the best in the land. The most noted of these are the Rensselaer Institute, founded and endowed by the late Stephen Van Rensselaer of the Manor,

RENSSELAER AND SARATOGA RAILWAY BRIDGE.

the Troy Female Seminary, and the Troy University. The latter was established under the auspices of the Methodist denomination, but the funds for the building were liberally subscribed by men of various sects. It stands upon Mount Ida, and is the most conspicuous object in a view of the city seen from any point. In its immediate vicinity are beautiful residences, which command extensive and interesting pictures of town and country. In their chaste and modest style of architecture, they present striking contrasts to the more meretricious "Byzantine style" of the University.

Opposite Troy is the bustling village of West Troy (formerly Watervliet), with a population of about 9,000 in 1860. At the south end of the village, and occupying a front of a quarter of a mile along the west bank of the Hudson, is the United States Military establishment called the Watervliet Arsenal. It was one of the largest of the six principal establishments then belonging to the United States, where, under the direction of the Ordnance Department, were manufactured the arms and munitions of war required for the use of the army and the

VIEW OF TROY FROM MOUNT IDA.

militia before the Civil War. About twelve acres of land were purchased at that point by the United States, in 1813, for arsenal purposes, and the group of buildings seen in the sketch was erected. The grounds comprised about one hundred acres, part covered with necessary buildings and a parade, and the remainder was under cultivation. About two hundred yards west of the highway, the Erie Canal passed through the grounds, and was spanned by a picturesque iron bridge near the officers' quarters. Along the river front was a double row of stately elm trees, whose branches form a leafy arch over the highway in summer. From these the green-sward bank slopes gently toward the river, and affords a delightful promenade on summer afternoons.*

The highway along the plain from West Albany is a fine macadamised

UNITED STATES ARSENAL AT WATERVLIET.

road, with the Erie Canal, the Hudson, and the amphitheatre of the Greenbush heights on the left. The hills on the right are near, and

* I was indebted to the courtesy of Lieutenant George T. Balch, then stationed there, for the following facts:—"As the necessity for greater manufacturing facilities arose, additional lands were purchased, and extensive shops, storehouses, timber-sheds, magazines, barracks and quarters, were erected from time to time, until at the present (1860), the real estate and the improvements are valued at 500,000 dollars, and the military stores and supplies collected, in the various buildings, at 1,500,000. The principal operations carried on are the manufacture of heavy artillery carriages for the sea-coast forts, with all the requisite implements and equipments; carriages for siege trains and field batteries, with their equipments and harness; all machines used in transporting and repairing artillery; ammunition of all kinds for sea-coast, siege, and field guns, and for small arms, and the repair and preservation of the large quantity of material of war in store. The shops comprise all requisite facilities for the various mechanics employed, as well as a conveniently arranged and roomy laboratory. The motive power is water, furnished by the Erie Canal. Under ordinary circumstances from 110 to 150 workmen are employed, but, when the exigencies of the service demand it, 500 to 600 can easily be accommodated. The establishment is under the control of a field officer of the ordnance department, assisted by subalterns of the same, a military storekeeper and paymaster, who is a civilian, and the requisite master, workmen, &c. Forty enlisted Ordnance men are at present stationed at the post, who perform the necessary guard duty and drills, and are at other times variously engaged in out-of-door and mechanical employments. The United States have exclusive control of the grounds included within the arsenal enclosure, the State exercising only concurrent jurisdiction in civil actions and criminal cases."

pleasant mansions and fertile acres are seen on every side. There is a house a mile and a half below the arsenal, scarcely visible from the road because of trees and shrubbery which conceal it, and, when seen, it would not attract special attention, excepting for the extreme plainness and antiquated style of its architecture. A pleasant lane leads to it from the canal, and the margin of the sloping lawn on its river front, over which stately elms cast their shadows, is swept by the Hudson's tide. It is famous in colonial history as the residence of Colonel Peter Schuyler, of.

SCHUYLER HOUSE AT THE FLATS.

the Flats, the first Mayor of Albany, and who, as Indian Commissioner, in after years took four kings or sachems, of the Mohawks, to England, and presented them at the court of Queen Anne. After his death, his son Philip, the well-beloved of the Mohawks, who married his sweet cousin Katrina—the "Aunt Schuyler" immortalised by Mrs. Grant, of Laggan, in her charming pictures of "Albany Society a Hundred Years Ago"—resided there, and with ample resources dispensed hospitality with a bounteous hand. And yet this is not the identical house in which the mayor lived, and his son Philip entertained friends and strangers, but the one built upon its ruins, in the same style, the summer days of which

are so charmingly portrayed by Mrs. Grant.   The old one was consumed
by fire in the summer of 1759, when Philip had been dead eighteen
months, and "Aunt Schuyler," his widow, whose waist he spanned with
his hands when they were married forty years before, had grown to such
enormous dimensions, that a chair was máde for her special use.   In
that chair she was seated, under the cherry-trees in the lane, one hot day
in August, when the eminent Colonel John Bradstreet, riding up, gave
her the first intimation that her house was on fire.   With calmness she
kept her seat, and gave directions to her servants and neighbours how to
check the flames, and to save her most valued articles.   Before evening
the blackened brick walls were all that were left of that pleasant mansion.
Aunt Schuyler had a larger house in Albany, but she took shelter with
her husband's deaf brother Peter, who lived upon the hills near by.

Intelligence of the disaster brought the people from all quarters.   They
testified their love for "Aunt Schuyler" by offering their services.   In a
few days materials for a new house were collected.   Colonel Bradstreet
sent up some of the king's troops then stationed in Albany to assist in
building, and the part of the house seen on the right in the picture, was
completed for use before the winter set in.   Over the yawning cellars of
the late mansion a broad wooden bridge was built, furnished with seats
like a portico.   "This," says Mrs. Grant, "with the high walls of the
ancient house, which were a kind of screen before the new one, gave the
whole the appearance of an ancient ruin." *   Aunt Schuyler removed
to her house in Albany, and leased the homestead ; and, a few years
later, the present house was built.   In it a part of the old walls may be
seen.   It was owned when I visited it by Stephen R. Schuyler, Esq., a
descendant of the mayor.   His brother, John C. Schuyler, living upon
the gentle hills near by, possessed a finely-executed portrait of that
earliest chief magistrate of the city of Albany.

As we approach Albany from the Flats, and reach the boundaries of
" the Colonie;" † the river shores are seen covered with huge piles of
lumber, and lined with vessels of almost every kind.   The ear catches
the distant hum of a large town and the jangle of steamboat bells, while

---

* "Memoirs of an American Lady," by Mrs. Grant, of Laggan.
† So named because it was the seat of the ancient colony of Rensselaerwyck.

the city itself, built upon hills and slopes, is more than half concealed by the lofty trees which surround the manor house of the Van Rensselaer family in the northern part of the city. This is one of the most attractive town residences in the State. The mansion, erected in 1765, and recently somewhat modified in external appearance, stands within a park of many acres, beautified by the hand of taste. It is adorned with flowers and shrubbery, and its pleasant walks are shaded by grand old trees, some of which were, doubtless, planted or were forest saplings, two

VAN RENSSELAER MANOR HOUSE.

hundred years or more ago, when the first *Patroon's* mansion, with its reed-covered roof, was erected there. Through the grounds flows Mill Creek, a clear stream that comes down from the hills on the west, through the once sweet vale of Tivoli, where, until the construction of a railway effaced it, the music of a romantic cascade—the Falls of Tivoli—was heard.

The reader may inquire why the proprietor of this estate was called *the Patroon*, and invested with manorial title and privileges. History furnishes an answer in this wise :—The Dutch West India Company, having made all proper arrangements for colonising New Netherlands, as

New York was then called, passed a charter of privileges and exemptions in 1629, for the encouragement of *Patroons*, or patrons, to make settlements. It was provided that every Patroon, to whom privileges and exemptions should be granted, should, within four years after the establishment of a colony, have there, as permanent residents, at least fifty persons over fifteen years of age, one-fourth of whom should be located within the first year. Such privileges were granted to Killian Van Rensselaer, a pearl merchant of Amsterdam, and one of the directors of the West India Company, and by his direction the commissary and under commissary of Fort Orange, around whose site the city of Albany now stands, purchased of the Indians a tract of land in that vicinity. Another district was afterwards purchased, and Killian Van Rensselaer and three others became the proprietors of a tract of land, twenty-four miles long, upon each side of the Hudson, and forty-eight miles broad, containing over 700,000 acres of land, and comprising the present counties of Albany, Rensselaer, and a part of Columbia. Van Rensselaer held two shares, and the others one share each. They were his equals in privileges and exemptions, except in the title of Patroon, which, with all the feudal honours, was vested in him alone, the partners binding themselves to do fealty and homage for the fief on his demise, in the name and on behalf of his son and heirs. The manor did not become the sole property of the Van Rensselaer family until 1685.

The Patroon was invested with power to administer civil and criminal justice, in person or by deputy, within his domain, and, to some extent, he was a sort of autocrat. These powers were abolished when the English took possession of the province in 1664, and with it fell many of the special privileges, but, by the English law of primogeniture, that princely domain, farmed out to many tenants, remained in the family until the Revolution in 1775, and the title of Patroon was held by the late General Stephen Van Rensselaer, until his death, early in 1840, when it expired. A great portion of the manor has passed out of the hands of the Van Rensselaer family.

CHAPTER VII.

HE grounds around Van Rensselaer Manor House extend from Broadway to the river, and embrace a large garden and conservatory. There in the midst of rural scenery, the sounds of a swift-running brook, and almost the quietude of a sylvan retreat, the "lord of the manor of Rensselaerwyck," the lineal descendant of Killian, the pearl merchant, and first *Patroon*, was living when our sketch was made in elegant but unostentatious style—a simple Republican, without the feudal title of his progenitors, except by courtesy. Within the mansion are collected some exquisite works of Art, and family portraits extending in regular order back to the first Patroon. At the head of the great staircase leading from the spacious hall to the chambers was a portion of the illuminated window which, for one hundred and ninety years, occupied a place in the old Dutch Church that stood in the middle of State Street, at its intersection by Broadway. It bears the arms of the Van Rensselaer family, which were placed in the church by the son of Killian.

·VAN RENSSELAER'S ARMS.

That old church, a sketch of which, with the appearance of the neighbourhood at the time of its demolition in 1805, is seen in our picture, was a curiously arranged place of worship. It was built of stone, in 1715, over a smaller one erected in 1656, in which the congregation continued to worship, until the new one was roofed. There was an interruption in the stated worship for only three Sabbaths. It had a low gallery, and the huge stove used in heating the building was placed upon a platform so high, that the sexton went upon it from the gallery to kindle the fire, implying a belief in those days that heated air descended, instead of ascending, as we are now taught by the philosophers. The pulpit was made of carved oak, octagonal in form, and in front of it was a bracket, on which the minister placed his hour-glass, when he commenced preaching. From the pulpit shone in succession those lights of the Reformed Dutch Church in America, Dominies Schaats, Delius, the land speculator, Lydius, Vandriéssen, Van Schie, Frelinghuysen, Westerlo,

OLD DUTCH CHURCH IN ALBANY.

and Johnson. And from it the Gospel is still preached in Albany. With its bracket, it occupies a place in the North Dutch Church, in that city.

The bell-rope of the old church hung down in the centre of the building, and upon that cord tradition has suspended many a tale of trouble for Mynheer Brower, one of its sextons, who lived in North Pearl Street. He went to the church every night at eight o'clock, pursuant to orders, to ring the "suppawn bell." This was the signal for the inhabitants to eat their "suppawn," or hasty-pudding, and prepare for bed. It was equivalent in its office to the old English curfew bell. On these occasions the wicked boys would sometimes tease the old bell-ringer. They would slip stealthily into the church while he was there with his dim lantern, unlock the side door, hide in some dark corner, and when the old man was fairly seated at home, and had his pipe lighted for a last smoke, they would ring the bell furiously. Down to the old church the sexton would hasten, the boys would slip out at the side door before his arrival, and the old man would return home thoughtfully, musing upon the probability of invisible hands pulling at his bell-rope—those

> " People—ah, the people,
> They that dwell up in the steeple
>   All alone ;
> And who, tolling, tolling, tolling,
>   In that muffled monotone,
>   Feel a glory in so rolling
>   On the human heart a stone ;
> They are neither man nor woman,
> They are neither brute nor human,
>   They are ghouls ! "

Albany wore a quaint aspect until the beginning of the present century, on account of the predominance of steep-roofed houses, with their terraced gables to the street. A fair specimen is given in our Street View in Ancient Albany, which shows the appearance of the town at the intersection of North Pearl and State Streets, sixty years ago. The house at the nearer corner was built as a parsonage for the Rev. Gideon Schaats, who arrived in Albany in 1652. The materials were imported from Holland, —bricks, tiles, iron, and wood-work,—and were brought, with the church bell and pulpit, in 1657. "When I was quite a lad," says a late writer, "I visited the house with my mother, who was acquainted with the father of Balthazar Lydius, the last proprietor of the mansion. To my eyes it appeared like a palace, and I thought the pewter plates in a corner cupboard were solid silver, they glittered so. The partitions were made of mahogany, and the exposed beams were ornamented with carvings in high relief, representing the vine and fruit of the grape. To show the relief more perfectly, the beams were painted white. Balthazar was an eccentric old bachelor, and was the terror of all the boys. Strange stories, almost as dreadful as those which cluster around the name of Bluebeard, were told of his fierceness on some occasions ; and the urchins, when they saw him in the streets, would give him the whole side-walk, for he made them think of the ogre, growling out his

'Fee, fo, fum,
I smell the blood of an Englishman.'

He was a tall, spare Dutchman, with a bullet head, sprinkled with thin white hair in his latter years. He was fond of his pipe and his bottle, and gloried in his celibacy, until his life was 'in the sere and yellow leaf.'

STREET VIEW IN ANCIENT ALBANY.

Then he gave a pint of gin for a squaw (an Indian woman), and calling her his wife, lived with her as such until his death.''

On the opposite corner was seen an elm-tree, yet standing in 1860, but of statelier proportions, which was planted more than a hundred years before by Philip Livingston, one of the signers of the Declaration of Independence, whose dwelling was next to the corner. It was a monument to the planter, more truly valued of the Albanians in the heats of summer, than would be the costliest pile of brass or marble.

Further up the street is seen a large building, with two gables, which was known as the Vanderheyden Palace. It is a good specimen of the external appearance of the better class of houses erected by the Dutch in Albany. It was built in 1725, by Johannes Beekman, one of the old burghers of that city; and was purchased, in 1778, by one of the Vander-heydens of Troy, who, for many years, lived there in the style of the old Dutch aristocracy. On account of its size, it was dignified with the title of palace. It figures in Washington Irving's story of Dolph Heyliger, in "Bracebridge Hall," as the residence of Heer Anthony Vanderheyden;

VANDERHEYDEN PALACE.

and when Mr. Irving transformed the old farmhouse of Van Tassel into his elegant Dutch cottage at "Sunnyside," he made the southern gable an exact imitation of that of the palace in Albany. And the iron vane, in the form of a horse at full speed, that turned for a century upon one of the gables of the Vanderheyden Palace, now occupies the peak of that southern gable at delightful "Sunnyside."

Kalm, the Swedish traveller, who visited Albany in 1748 and 1749, says in his Journal,—" The houses in this town are very neat, and partly built with stones, covered with shingles of the white pine. Some are slated with tiles from Holland. Most of the houses are built in the old way, with the gable-end toward the street; a few excepted, which were lately built in the manner now used. . . . . The gutters on the roofs reach almost to the middle of the street. This preserves the walls from being damaged by the rain, but it is extremely disagreeable in rainy weather for the people in the streets, there being hardly any means for avoiding the water from the gutters. The street doors are generally in the middle of the houses, and on both sides are seats, on which, during fair weather, the people spend almost the whole day, especially on those which are in the shadow of the houses. In the evening these seats are covered with people of both sexes; but this is rather troublesome, as those who pass by are obliged to greet everybody, unless they will shock the politeness of the inhabitants of the town."

Kalm appears to have had some unpleasant experiences in Albany, and in his Journal gave his opinion very freely concerning the inhabitants. "The avarice and selfishness of the inhabitants of Albany," he says, "are very well known throughout all North America. If a Jew, who understands the art of getting forward perfectly well, should settle amongst them, they would not fail to ruin him; for this reason, no one comes to this place without the most pressing necessity." He complains that he "was obliged to pay for everything twice, thrice, and four times as dear as in any other part of North America" which he had passed through. If he wanted any help, he had to pay "exorbitant prices for their services," and yet he says he found some exceptions among them. After due reflection, he came to the following conclusion respecting "the origin of the inhabitants of Albany and its neighbourhood. Whilst the Dutch possessed this country, and intended to people it, the government took up a pack of vagabonds, of which they intended to clear the country, and sent them, along with a number of other settlers, to this province. The vagabonds were sent far from the other colonists, upon the borders toward the Indians and other enemies; and a few honest families were persuaded to go with them, in order to keep them in bounds. I cannot in any other way account for the difference between the inhabitants of Albany and the other descendants of so respectable a nation as the Dutch."

Albany was settled by the Dutch, and is the oldest of the permanent

European settlements in the United States. Hudson passed its site in the *Half-Moon*, in the early autumns of 1609; and the next year Dutch navigators built trading-houses there, to traffic for furs with the Indians. In 1614 they erected a stockade fort on an island near. It was swept away by a spring freshet in 1617. Another was built on the main: it was abandoned in 1623, and a stronger one erected in what is now Broadway, below State Street. This was furnished with eight cannon loaded with stones, and was named Fort Orange, in honour of the then Stadtholder of Holland. Down to the period of the intercolonial wars, the settlement and the city were known as Fort Orange by the French in Canada. Families settled there in 1630, and for awhile the place was called Beverwyck. When James, Duke of York and Albany (brother to

FORT FREDERICK.

Charles II.), came into possession of New Netherland, New Amsterdam was named New York, and Orange, or Beverwyck, was called Albany.

In 1647 a fort, named Williamstadt, was erected upon the hill at the head of State Street, very near the site of the State Capitol, and the city was enclosed by a line of defences in septangular form. In 1683 the little trading post, having grown first to a hamlet and then to a large village, was incorporated a city, and Peter Schuyler, already mentioned (son of the first of that name who came to America), was chosen its first mayor. Out of the manor of Rensselaerwyck a strip of land, a mile wide, extending from the Hudson at the town, thirteen miles back, was granted to the city, but the title to all the remainder of the soil of that broad domain was confirmed to the Patroon. When, toward the middle of the last century, the province was menaced by the French and Indians, a strong quadrangular fort, built of stone, was erected upon the site of that

of Williamstadt. Within the heavy walls, which had strong bastions at
the four corners, was a stone building for the officers and soldiers. It
was named Fort Frederick; but its situation was so insecure, owing to
higher hills in the rear, from which an enemy might attack it, it was not
regarded as of much value by Abercrombie and others during the
campaigns of the Seven Years' War. From that period until the present,
Albany has been growing more and more cosmopolitan in its population,
until now very little of the old Dutch element is distinctly perceived.
The style of its architecture is changed, and very few of the buildings
erected in the last century and before, are remaining.

Among the most interesting of these relics of the past is the mansion
erected by General Philip Schuyler, at about the time when the Van
Rensselaer Manor House was built. It stands in the southern part of the
city, at the head of Schuyler Street, and is a very fine specimen of the
domestic architecture of the country at that period. It is entered at the
front by an octagonal vestibule, richly ornamented within. The rooms
are spacious, with high ceilings, and wainscoted. The chimney-pieces in
some of the rooms are finely wrought, and ornamented with carvings from
mantel to ceiling. The outhouses were spacious, and the grounds around
the mansion, so late as 1860, occupied an entire square within the city.
Its site was well chosen, for even now, surrounded as it is by the city, it
commands a most remarkable prospect of the Hudson and the adjacent
country. Below it are the slopes and plain toward the river, which once
composed the magnificent lawn in front of the general's mansion; further
on is a dense portion of the city; but looking over all the mass of buildings
and shipping, the eyes take in much of the fine county of Rensselaer, on
the opposite side of the river, and a view of the Hudson and its valley
many miles southward.

In that mansion General Schuyler and his family dispensed a princely
hospitality for almost forty years. Every stranger of distinction passing
between New York and Canada, public functionaries of the province and
state visiting Albany, and resident friends and relatives, always found a
hearty welcome to bed and board under its roof. And when the British
army had surrendered to the victorious republicans at Saratoga, in the
autumn of 1777, Sir John Burgoyne, the accomplished commander of the

royal troops, and many of his fellow-captives, were treated as friendly guests at the general's table. To this circumstance we have already alluded.

"We were received by the good General Schuyler, his wife and daughters," says the Baroness Reidesel, "not as enemies, but as kind friends; and they treated us with the most marked attention and politeness, as they did General Burgoyne, who had caused General

GENERAL SCHUYLER'S MANSION IN ALBANY.

Schuyler's beautifully-finished house to be burned. In fact, they behaved like persons of exalted minds, who determined to bury all recollections of their own injuries in the contemplation of our misfortunes. General Burgoyne was struck with General Schuyler's generosity, and said to him, 'You show me great kindness, though I have done you much injury.' 'That was the fate of war,' replied the brave man, 'let us say no more about it.'"

"The British commander was well received by Mrs. Schuyler," says the Marquis De Chastellux, in his "Travels in America," "and lodged in the best apartment in the house. An excellent supper was served him in the evening, the honours of which were done with so much grace that he was affected even to tears, and said, with a deep sigh, ' Indeed, this is doing too much for the man who has ravaged their lands and burned their dwellings ! ' The next morning he was reminded of his misfortunes by an incident that would have amused any one else. His bed was prepared in a large room, but as he had a numerous suite, or family, several mattresses were spread on the floor, for some officers to sleep near him. Schuyler's second son, a little fellow, about seven years old, very arch and forward, but very amiable, was running all the morning about the house. Opening the door of the saloon, he burst out a laughing on seeing all the English collected, and shut it after him, exclaiming, ' You are all my prisoners ! ' This innocent cruelty rendered them more melancholy than before."

Schuyler's mansion was the theatre of a stirring event, in the summer of 1781. The general was then engaged in the civil service of his country, and was at home. The war was at its height, and the person of Schuyler was regarded as a capital prize by his Tory enemies. A plan was conceived to seize him, and carry him a prisoner into Canada. A Tory of his neighbourhood, named Waltemeyer, a colleague of the more notorious Joe Bettys, was employed for the purpose. With a party of his associates, some Canadians and Indians, he prowled in the woods, near Albany, for several days, awaiting a favourable opportunity. From a Dutch labourer, whom he seized, he learned that the general was at home, and kept a body-guard of six men in the house, three of them, in succession, being continually on duty. The Dutchman was compelled to take an oath of secrecy, but appears to have made a mental reservation, for, as soon as possible, he hastened to Schuyler's house, and warned him of his peril.

At the close of a sultry day in August, the general and his family were sitting in the large hall of the mansion; the servants were dispersed about the premises; three of the guard were asleep in the basement, and the other three were lying upon the grass in front of the house. The night had fallen, when a servant announced that a stranger at the back gate wished to speak with the general. His errand was immediately apprehended. The doors and windows were closed and barred, the family were hastily collected in an upper room, and the general ran to his bed-chamber for his arms.   From the window he saw the house surrounded by armed men.   For the purpose of arousing the sentinels upon the grass, and, perhaps, alarm the town, then half a mile distant, he fired a pistol from the window.   At that moment the assailants burst open the doors, and, at the same time, Mrs. Schuyler perceived that, in the confusion and alarm, in their retreat from the hall, her infant child, a few months old,

STAIRCASE IN SCHUYLER'S MANSION.

had been left in a cradle in the nursery below.   She was flying to the rescue of her child, when the general interposed, and prevented her.   But her third daughter (who afterwards became the wife of the last Patroon of Rensselaerwyck) instantly rushed down stairs, snatched the still sleeping infant from the cradle, and bore it off in safety.   One of the Indians hurled a sharp tomahawk at her as she ascended the stairs.   It cut her dress within a few inches of the infant's head, and struck the stair rail at the lower turn, where the scar may be still seen. At that moment, Waltemeyer, supposing her to be a servant, exclaimed, "Wench, wench, where is your master?" With great presence of mind, she replied, "Gone to alarm the town." The general heard her, and, throwing up the window, called out, as if to a multitude, "Come on, my brave fellows! surround the house, and secure the villains!" The marauders were then in the dining-room, plundering the general's plate. With this, and the three guards that were in the house, and were disarmed, they made a precipitate retreat in the direction of Canada.

The infant daughter, who so narrowly escaped death, was the late Mrs. Catherine Van Rensselaer Cochran, of Oswego, New York, who was General Schuyler's youngest and last surviving child. She died toward the close of August, 1857, at the age of seventy-six years.

Albany was made the political metropolis of the State of New York early in the present century, when the Capitol, or State-House, was erected. It stands upon a hill at the heat of broad, steep, busy State Street, one hundred and thirty feet above the Hudson, and commands a fine prospect of the whole surrounding country, especially the rich agricultural district on the east side of the river. In front of the Capitol is a small well-shaded park, or enclosed public square, on the eastern side of which are costly white marble buildings devoted to the official business of the State and city. The Capitol is an unpretending structure, of brown free-stone from the Nyack quarries, below the Highlands. It is two stories in height, and ornamented with a portico, whose roof is supported by four grey marble columns of the Ionic order, tetrastyle. The building is surmounted by a dome supported by several small Ionic columns, and bearing upon its crown a wooden statue of Themis, the goddess of justice and law. Within it are halls for the two branches of the State legislature (Senate and General Assembly), an executive chamber for the official use of the Governor, an apartment for the Adjutant-General, and rooms for the use of the higher state courts.

Immediately in the rear of the Capitol is the building containing the State library, which includes nearly forty thousand volumes, and some valuable manuscripts. It is a free, but not a circulating, library.

Albany contained only about six thousand inhabitants when it was made the State capital, and its progress in business and population was very slow until the successful establishment of steam-boat navigation on the Hudson, and the completion of that stupendous work of internal improvement, the Erie Canal, by which the greatest of the inland seas of the United States (Lake Erie, Huron, Michigan, and Superior) were connected by navigable waters with the Atlantic Ocean, through the

THE STATE CAPITOL.

Hudson River. The idea of such connection had occupied the minds of sagacious men for many years, foremost among whom were Elkanah Watson, General Philip Schuyler, Christopher Colles, and Gouverneur Morris; and thirty years before the great work was commenced, Joel Barlow, one of the early American poets, wrote in his *Vision of Columbus*—

> "He saw as widely spreads the unchannelled plain,
> Where inland realms for ages bloomed in vain,
> *Canals*, long winding, ope a watery flight,
> And distant streams, and seas, and lakes unite.

> "From fair Albania tow'rd the fading sun,
> Back through the midland lengthening channels run;
> Meet the far lakes, their beauteous towns that lave,
> And *Hudson* joined to broad *Ohio's* wave."

The Erie Canal enters the Hudson at Albany. Its western terminus is the city of Buffalo, at the east end of Lake Erie. The length of the canal is 360 miles, and its original width was forty feet, with depth sufficient to bear boats of eighty tons burden. It was completed in the year 1825, at a cost to the State of nearly eight millions of dollars. The business demands upon it warranting an enlargement to seventy feet in width, work with that result in view has been in progress for several years. It flows through the entire length of the beautiful Mohawk valley, crosses

CANAL BASIN AT ALBANY.

the Mohawk River several times, and enters Albany at the north end of the city.

Near where the last aqueduct of the canal crosses the Mohawk River, the rapids above Cohoes Falls commence. The Indians had a touching legend connected with these rapids, that exhibits, in brief sentences, a vivid picture of the workings of the savage mind.

Occuna, a young Seneca warrior, and his affianced were carelessly paddling along the river in a canoe, at the head of the rapids, when they suddenly perceived themselves drawn irresistibly by the current to the middle of, and down, the stream towards the cataract. When they found deliverance to be impossible, the lovers prepared to meet the great Master of Life with composure, and began the melancholy death-song, in responsive sentences. *Occuna* began : " Daughter of a mighty warrior ! the Great Manitore [the Supreme God] calls me hence; he bids me hasten into his presence ; I hear his voice in the stream ; I perceive his Spirit in the moving of the waters. The light of his eyes danceth upon the swift rapids."

The maiden replied : "Art thou not thyself a mighty warrior, O *Occuna*? Hath not thy hatchet been often bathed in the red blood of thine enemies ? Hath the fleet deer ever escaped thy arrow, or the beaver eluded thy pursuit ? Why, then, shouldst thou fear to. go into the presence of Manitore ? "

Occuna responded : " Manitore regardeth the brave —he respecteth the prayer of the mighty ! When I selected thee from the daughters of thy mother, I promised to live and die with thee. The Thunderer hath called us together.

" Welcome, O shade of *Oriska*, great chief of the invincible *Senecas* ! Lo, a warrior and the daughter of a warrior come to join you in the feast of the blessed ! "

Occuna was dashed in pieces among the rocks, but his affianced maiden was preserved to tell the story of her perils. *Occuna*, the Indian said, " was raised high above the regions of the moon, from whence he views with joy the prosperous hunting of the warriors ; he gives pleasant dreams to his friends, and terrifies their enemies with dreadful omens." And when any of his tribe passed this fatal cataract, they halted, and with brief solemn ceremonies commemorated the death of *Occuna*.

A capacious basin, comprising an area of thirty-two acres, was formed for the reception of the vessels and commerce of the canal, and in safe harbour for its boats and the river craft, in winter, by the erection of a pier, a mile in length, upon a shoal in front of the city. It was constructed by a stock company. The basin was originally closed at the upper and lower ends by lock-gates. These were soon removed to allow the tide and currents of the river to flow freely through the basin, for the dispersion of obstructions. When the Western Railway from Boston to

Albany was completed, a passage was made through this pier for ferry-boats, the bridges not being sufficient for the accommodation of travellers and freight. The pier was also soon covered with storehouses; and when the Harlem and Hudson River Railways (the former skirting the western borders of Connecticut, eighteen or twenty miles east of the Hudson, and the latter following the river shore) were finished, and their termini were fixed at the point of that of the Western Railway, the opening in the pier was widened, and ferry-boats made a passage through continually.

These roads, with the great Central Railway extending west from Albany, and others penetrating the country northward, together with the Champlain Canal, have made that city the focus of an immense trade and travel. The amount of property that reaches Albany by canal alone, is between two and three millions of tons annually; of which almost a million of tons, chiefly in the various forms of timber, are the products of the forests. The timber trade of Albany is very extensive, amounting in value to between six or seven millions of dollars annually. Manufacturing is carried on there extensively; and the little town of six thousand inhabitants, when it was made the State capital, about sixty years before, comprised in 1860 almost seventy thousand souls.

It is not within the scope of our plan of illustrating the Hudson to do more than offer a general outline of its various features, as exhibited in the forms of nature and the works of man. We leave to the statistician the task of giving in detail an account of the progress of towns and villages, in their industrial operations and the institutions of learning. We picture to the eye and mind only such prominent features as would naturally engage the observation of the tourist seeking recreation and incidental knowledge. With this remark we leave the consideration of Albany, after saying a few words concerning the Dudley Observatory, an establishment devoted to astronomical science, and ranking in its appropriate appointments with the best of its class of aids to human knowledge.

The Dudley Observatory was projected about eight years ago, and is nearly completed. It is the result of a conference of several scientific gentlemen, who resolved to establish at the State capital an astronomical observatory, that, for completeness, should be second to none in the world.

General Van Rensselaer, the present proprietor of the Manor House, at Albany, presented for the purpose eight acres of land upon an eminence north of the city. This preliminary step was followed by Mrs. Blandina Dudley, widow of a wealthy Albany merchant, who offered twelve thousand dollars towards the cost of erecting a building. Those having the matter in charge resolved to call it the Dudley Observatory, in honour of the generous lady. She subsequently increased her gift for apparatus and endowments to seventy-six thousand dollars. The chief spring of her

THE DUDLEY OBSERVATORY.

generosity was a reverential respect for her husband. With wisdom she chose this instrument of scientific investigation to be his enduring monument. Others made liberal donations, trustees were appointed, a scientific council, to take charge of the establishment, was formed, and the building was commenced in the spring of 1853. A great heliometer, named in honour of Mrs. Dudley, was constructed; and Thomas W. Olcott, of Albany, who took great interest in the enterprise from the beginning, contributed sufficient money to purchase the splendid meridian circle by Pistor and Martin, of Berlin, the finest instrument of the kind in the world.

peaceful pursuits of agriculture have taken the place of the turmoil of the camp, and instead of the music of the shrill fife and the sonorous drum that came up from the river's brink, when battalions marched away for the field, the scream of the steam-whistle, the jingle of bells, and the hoarse breathings of the locomotive are heard—for at Greenbush are concentrated the termini of four railways, that are almost hourly pouring living freight and tons of merchandise upon the vessels of the Albany ferries. Buildings of every description for the use of these railways are there in a cluster, the most conspicuous of which is the immense many-sided engine-house of the Western Road, whose great dome, covered with bright tin, is a conspicuous object on a sunny day for scores of miles around.

The Hudson River Railway is on the east side of the stream, and follows its tortuous banks all the way from Albany to New York, sometimes leading through tunnels or deep rocky gorges at promontories, and at others making tangents across bays and the mouths of tributary streams by means of bridges, trestlework, and causeways. Its length is 143 miles. More than a dozen trains each way pass over portions of the road in the course of twenty-four hours, affording the tourist an opportunity to visit in a short space of time every village on both sides of the river, there being good ferries at each. The shores are hilly and generally well-cultivated; and the diversity of the landscape, whether seen from the cars or a steamer, present to the eye, in rapid succession, ever-varying pictures of life and beauty, comfort and thrift.

CHAPTER VIII.

THE first village below Albany is the pretty one of Castleton, on the Hudson River Railway, about eight miles below Greenbush. Around it is a pleasant agricultural country, and between it and Albany, on the western shore, flows in the romantic Norman's-Kill (the Indian *Tawasentha*, or Place of many Dead), that comes down from the region of the lofty Helderbergs. Upon the island in the Hudson, at the mouth of this stream—a noted place of encampment and trade for the Iroquois—the Dutch built their first fort on the Hudson in 1614, and placed it in command of Captain Christians. The island was named Kasteel, or Castle, and from it the little village just mentioned received its name. The alluvial " flats " in this neighbourhood are wide, and low islands, partly wooded and partly cultivated, divide the river in channels. They stretch parallel with the shores, a considerable distance, and the immense passenger steamers sometimes find it difficult to traverse the sinuous main channel. These, and the tall-masted sloops, have the appearance, from the Castleton shore, of passing through vast meadows, the water that bears them not being visible.

In this vicinity is the famous hidden sand-bar, called Overslagh by the Dutch, so formidable to the navigators of this part of the river, not because of any actual danger, but of tedious detentions caused by running aground. Some improvements have been made. In former years the sight of from twenty to fifty sail of river craft, fast aground on the Overslagh at low tide, was not rare, and the amount of profanity uttered by the vexed sailors was sufficient to demoralise the whole district. This bar is formed by the sand brought in by the Norman's Kill and other streams, and large sums have been expended in damming, dredging, and dyking, without entire success. As early as 1790, the State legislature authorised the proprietors of Mills and Papskni Islands to erect a dam or dyke between them, so as to throw all the water into the main channel, and thus increase its velocity sufficient to carry away the accumulating sand. It abated, but did not cure the difficulty. This bar is a perpetual contradiction to the frequent boast, that the navigation of the Hudson is unobstructed along its entire tide-watercourse. The Overslagh is the only exception, however.

About four miles below Castleton, is the village of Schodack, a deriva-

VIEW NEAR THE OVERSLAGH.

tive from the Mohegan word *is-cho-da,* " a meadow, or fire-plain." This was anciently the seat of the council fire of the Mohegans upon the Hudson. They extended their villages along the eastern bank of the stream, as high as Lansingburgh, and their hunting grounds occupied the entire counties of Columbia and Rensselaer. As the white settlements crowded there, the Mohegans retired eastwardly to the valley of the Housatonnuc, in Massachusetts, where their descendants, known as the Stockbridge Indians, were for a long time religiously instructed by the eminent Jonathan Edwards. They embraced Christianity, abandoned the chase as a means of procuring subsistence, and adopted the arts of civilised life. A small remnant of these once powerful Mohegans is now living, as thriving agriculturists, on the shores of Winnebago Lake, in the far north-west.

About seven miles below Schodack is Stuyvesant Landing, the "port" of Kinderhook (*Kinders Hoeck*), the Dutch name for "children's point, or corner." It is derived, as tradition asserts, from the fact that a Swede, the first settler at the point at Upper Kinderhook Landing, had a numerous progeny. The village, which was settled by Dutch and Swedes at an early period, is upon a plain five miles from the river, with most attractive rural surroundings. There, for more than twenty years after his retirement from public life, the late Honourable Martin Van Buren, a descendant of one of the early settlers, and the eighth president of the United States, resided. His pleasant seat, embowered in lindens, is called "Lindenwold," and there, in delightful quietude, the retired chief magistrate of the republic spent the evening of his days.

The country road from Kinderhook to the Coxsakie station passes through a rich and well-cultivated region, and leads the tourist to points from which the first extensive views of the magnificent range of the Katzbergs may be obtained.

Coxsakie village is upon the west side of the river, partly along the shore for a mile, in three clusters. The more ancient portion, called Coxsakie Street, is upon a beautiful plain a mile from the river. The latter was originally built upon the post road, as most of the old villages along the Hudson were, the river traffic being at that time inconsiderable. The name is the Iroquois word *Kuxakee*, or the Cut Banks, Anglicised. Its appropriateness may be understood by the form of the shore, whose banks have evidently been cut down by the rushing river currents that sweep swiftly along between an island and the main, when the spring freshets occur. From a high rocky bluff at the ferry, on the east side of the river, a fine view of Coxsakie, with the blue Katzbergs as a background, may be obtained. Turning southward, the eye takes in a broad expanse of the river and country, with the city of Hudson in the distance, and northward are seen the little villages of Coeymans and New Baltimore,

on the western shore.   The site of the former bore the Indian name of
Sanago.   It was settled by the Dutch, and received its present name
from one of its earlier inhabitants.

It was in blossoming May, in 1860, when the shad fishers were in
their glory, drawing full nets of treasure from the river in quick
succession, when the "tide served," that I visited this portion of the
Hudson.   On both sides of the river they were pursuing their vocation
with assiduity, for "the season" lasts only about two months.   The

COXSAKIE.

immense reels on which they stretch and dry their nets, the rough,
uncouth costume of the fishermen, appropriate to the water and the slime,
the groups of young people who gather upon the beach to see the
"catch," form interesting and sometimes picturesque foregrounds to
every view on these shores.   The shad* is the most important fish of the
Hudson, being very delicious as food, and caught in such immense

---

* *Alosa præstabilis.* Head and back dark bluish ; sides of the body greenish, with blue and yellowish
changeable metallic reflections ; belly nearly white ; length from one to two feet. It resides in the
northern seas, but comes to us from the south to deposit its spawn. It appears at Charleston in January
or February ; early in March at Norfolk and Baltimore, and at New York at the latter end of March.

numbers, as to make them cheap dishes for the poor man's table. They enter the Hudson in immense numbers towards the close of March or beginning of April, and ascend to the head of tide water to spawn. It is while on their passage up that the greater number and best conditioned are caught, several hundreds being sometimes taken in a single "catch." They generally descend the river at the close of May, when they are

FISHING STATION.—STURGEON, SHAD, BASS.*

called Back Shad, and are so lean and almost worthless, that "thin as a June Shad" is a common epithet applied to lean persons.

The Sturgeon † is also caught from the Hudson in large numbers at most of the fishing stations. The most important of these are in the vicinity of Hyde Park, a few miles above, and Low Point, a few miles below, the city of Poughkeepsie. These fish are sold in such quantities in Albany, that they have been called, in derision, "Albany beef," and

* The largest fish in the picture is the sturgeon, the smallest the striped bass, and the other a shad. The relative sizes and proportions are correct.

† The short-nosed Sturgeon (*Acipenser brevinostris*) is a large agile fish without scales, the smooth skin covered with small spinous asperites scattered equally over it. Its colour is dusky above, with faint traces of oblique bands; belly white, and the fins tinged with reddish colour.

the inhabitants of that ancient town, "Sturgeonites." They vary in size from two to eight feet in length, and in weight from 100 to 450 lbs. The "catch" commences in April, and continues until the latter end of August. The flesh is used for food by some, and the oil that is extracted is considered equal to the best sperm as an illuminator. The voyagers upon the Hudson may frequently see them leap several feet out of water when chasing their prey of smaller fish to the surface, and they have been known to seriously injure small boats, either by striking their bottoms with their snout in rising, or falling into them. Bass and herring are also caught in abundance in almost every part of the river, and numerous smaller fishes reward the angler's patience by their beauty of form, if he be painter or poet, and their delicious flavour, if the table gives him pleasure.

About thirty miles below Albany, lying upon a bold, rocky promontory that juts out from the eastern shore at an elevation of fifty feet, with a beautiful bay on each side, is the city of Hudson, the capital of Columbia County, a port of entry, and one of the most delightfully situated towns on the river. It was founded in 1784 by thirty proprietors, chiefly Quakers from New England. Never in the history of the rapid growth of cities in America has there been a more remarkable example than that of Hudson. Within three years from the time when the farm on which it stands was purchased, and only a solitary storehouse stood upon the bank of the river at the foot of the bluff, one hundred and fifty dwellings, with wharves, storehouses, workshops, barns, &c., were erected, and a population of over fifteen hundred souls had settled there, and become possessed of a city charter.

The principal street of the city of Hudson extends from the slopes of a lofty eminence called Prospect Hill, nearly a mile, to the brow of the promontory fronting the river, where a pleasant public promenade was laid out more than fifty years ago. It is adorned with trees and shrubbery, and gravelled walks, and affords charming views up and down the river of the beautiful country westward, and the entire range of the Katzbergs, lying ten or twelve miles distant. In the north-west, the Helderberg range looms up beyond an agricultural district dotted with villages and farmhouses. Southward the prospect is bounded by Mount

Merino high and near, over the bay, which is cultivated to its summit, and from whose crown the Highlands in the south, the Luzerne Mountains, near Lake George, in the north, the Katzbergs in the west, and the Green Mountains eastward, may be seen, blue and shadowy, and bounding the horizon with a grand and mysterious line, while at the feet of the observer, the city of Hudson lies like a picture spread upon a table. Directly opposite the city is Athens, a thriving little village, lying upon the river slope, and having a connection with its more stately sister by

VIEW FROM THE PROMENADE, HUDSON.

means of a steam ferry-boat. It was first named Lunenberg, then Esperanza, and finally was incorporated under its present title. Behind it spreads out a beautiful country, inhabited by a population consisting chiefly of descendants of the Dutch. All through that region, from Coxsakie to Kingston, the Dutch language is still used in many families.

The country around Hudson is hilly and very picturesque, every turn in the road affording pleasant changes in landscape and agreeable surprises. A little northward, Claverack (*Het Klauver Rack*, the Clover Reach) Creek comes down from the hills in falls and cascades, and

of worship, consisting chiefly in singing and dancing; their quaint costume, their simple manners, their industry and frugality, the perfection of all their industrial operations, their chaste and exemplary lives, and the unsurpassed beauty and picturesqueness of the country in which they are seated, render a visit to the Shakers of Lebanon a long-to-be-remembered event in one's life.

About six miles below Hudson is the Oak-Hill Station, opposite the Katz-Kill (Cats-Kill) landing, at the mouth of the Katz-Kill, a clear and beautiful stream that flows down from the hill country of Schoharie County for almost forty miles. It was near here that the *Half Moon* anchored on the 20th September, 1609, and was detained all the next day on account of the great number of natives who came on board, and had a merry time. Master Juet, one of Hudson's companions, says, in his journal,—" Our master and his mate determined to trie some of the chiefe men of the countrey, whether they had any treacherie in them. So they tooke them downe into the cabbin, and gave them so much wine and *aqua vitæ* that they were all merrie, and one of them had his wife with him, which sate so modestly, as any of our countrey women would doe in a strange place. In the end, one of them was drunke, which had been aboord of our ship all the time that we had beene there : and that was strange to them, for they could not tell how to take it. The canoes and folke went all on shoare, but some of them came againe, and brought stropes of beades [wampum, made of the clam-shell] ; some had sixe, seven, eight, nine, ten, and gave him. So he slept all night quietly." The savages did not venture on board until noon the next day, when they were glad to find their old companion that was so drunk quite well again. They then brought on board tobacco, and more beads, which they gave to Hudson, " and made an Oration," and afterward sent for venison, which was brought on board.

At the Oak Hill station the tourist upon the railway will leave it for a trip to the Katzbergs before him, upon which may be seen, at the distance of eight miles in an air line, the "Mountain House," the famous resort for hundreds of people who escape from the dust of cities during the heat of summer. The river is crossed on a steam ferry-boat, and good omnibuses convey travellers from it to the pleasant village of Katz-Kill, which lies upon a slope on the left bank of the stream bearing the same name, less than half a mile from its mouth. At the village, conveyances are ready at all times to take the tourist to the Mountain House, twelve miles distant by the road, which passes through a picturesque and highly cultivated country, to the foot of the mountain. Before making this

ENTRANCE TO THE KATZBERGS.

tour, however, the traveller should linger awhile on the banks of the Katz-Kill, from the Hudson a few miles into the country, for there may be seen, from different points of view, some of the most charming scenery in the world. Every turn in the road, every bend in the stream, presents new and attractive pictures, remarkable for beauty and diversity in outline, colour, and aërial perspective. The solemn Katzbergs, sublime in form, and mysterious in their dim, incomprehensible, and ever-changing aspect, almost always form a prominent feature in the landscape. In the midst of this scenery, Cole, the eminent painter, loved to linger when the shadows of the early morning were projected towards the mountain, then bathed in purple mists; or at evening, when these lofty hills, then dark and awful, cast their deep shadows over more than half the country below, between their bases and the river. Charmed with this region, Cole made it at first a summer retreat, and finally his permanent residence, and there, in a fine old family mansion, delightfully situated to command a full view of the Katzberg range and the intervening country, his spirit passed from earth, while a sacred poem, created by his wealthy imagination and deep religious sentiment, was finding expression upon his easel in a series of fine pictures, like those of " The Course of Empire," and " The Voyage of Life." He entitled the series, " The Cross and the World." Only one of the pictures was finished. One had found form in a " study " only, and two others were partly finished on the large canvas. Another, making the fifth (the number in the series), was about half completed, with some figures sketched in with white chalk. So they remain, just as the master left them, and so remains his studio. It is regarded by his devoted widow as a place too sacred for the common gaze. The stranger never enters it.

The range of the Katzbergs * rises abruptly from the plain on their eastern side, where the road that leads to the Mountain House enters them, and follows the margin of a deep, dark glen, through which flows a clear mountain stream seldom seen by the traveller, but heard continually for a mile and a half, as, in swift rapids or in little cascades, it hurries to the plain below. The road is sinuous, and in its ascent along the side of that glen, or more properly magnificent gorge, it is so enclosed by the towering hills on one side and the lofty trees that shoot up on the

---

* The Indians called this range of hills *On-ti-O-ra*, signifying, Mountains of the Sky, for in some conditions of the atmosphere they are said to appear like a heavy cumulous cloud above the horizon. The Dutch called them Katzbergs, or Cat Mountains, because of the prevalence of panthers and wild-cats upon them. The word Cats-Kill is partly English and partly Dutch: Katz-Kill, Dutch; Cats-Creek, English.

other, that little can be seen beyond a few rods, except the sky above, or glimpses of some distant summit, until the pleasant nook in the mountain is reached, wherein the Cabin of Rip Van Winkle is nestled. After that the course of the road is more nearly parallel with the river and the

RIP VAN WINKLE'S CABIN.

plain, and through frequent vistas glimpses may be caught of the country below, that charm the eye, excite the fancy and the imagination, and make the heart throb quicker and stronger with pleasurable emotions.

Rip's cabin was a decent frame-house, as the Americans call dwellings made of wood, with two rooms, standing by the side of the road half-way from the plain to the Mountain House, at the head of the gorge, along whose margin the traveller has ascended. It was so called because it stood within the "amphitheatre" reputed to be the place where the ghostly nine-pin players of Irving's charming story of Rip Van Winkle held their revel, and where thirsty Rip lay down to his long repose by "that wicked flagon," watched by his faithful dog Wolf, and undisturbed by the tongue of Dame Van Winkle. As one stands upon the rustic bridge, in front of the cabin, and looks down the dark glen, up to the impending cliffs, or around in that rugged amphitheatre, the scene comes up vividly in memory, and the "company of odd-looking personages playing at nine-pins" reappear. "Some wore short doublets, others jerkins, with long knives in their belts, and most of them had enormous breeches, of similar style with that of the guides. Their visages, too, were peculiar: one had a large head, broad face, and small piggish eyes; the face of another seemed to consist entirely of a nose, and was surmounted by a white sugar-loaf hat, set off with a little red cock's tail. They all had beards, of various shapes and colours. There was one who seemed to be the commander. He was a stout old gentleman, with a weather-beaten countenance; he wore a laced doublet, broad belt and hanger, and high-crowned hat and feather, red stockings, and high-heeled shoes with roses in them. What seemed particularly odd to Rip was, that though these folks were evidently amusing themselves, yet they maintained the gravest faces, the most mysterious silence, and were withal the most melancholy party of pleasure he had ever witnessed. Nothing interrupted the stillness of the scene but the noise of the balls, which, whenever they were rolled, echoed along the mountains like rumbling peals of thunder."

Such was the company to whom hen-pecked Rip Van Winkle, wandering upon the mountains on a squirrel hunt, was introduced by a mysterious stranger carrying a keg of liquor, at autumnal twilight. And there it was that thirsty Rip drank copiously, went to sleep, and only awoke when twenty years had rolled away. His dog was gone, and his rusty gun-barrel, bereft of its stock, lay by his side. He doubted his identity. He sought the village tavern and its old frequenters; his own house, and his faithful Wolf. Alas! everything was changed, except the river and the mountains. Only one thing gave him real joy—Dame Van Winkle's terrible tongue had been silenced for ever by death! He was a mystery to all, and more a mystery to himself than to others. Whom had he met in the mountains? those queer fellows that reminded him of "the figures in an old Flemish painting, in the parlour of Dominic Van Schaick, the village parson. Sage Peter Vonderdonck was called to explain the mystery; and Peter successfully responded. He asserted that it was a fact, handed down from his ancestor, the historian, that the Kaats-Kill Mountains had always been haunted by strange beings. That it was affirmed that the great Hendrick Hudson, the first discoverer of the river and country, kept a kind of vigil there every twenty years, with his crew of the *Half-Moon*, being permitted in this way to revisit the scenes of his enterprise, and kept a guardian eye upon the river and the great city called by his name. That his father had once seen them, in their old Dutch dresses, playing at nine-pins in a hollow of the mountain; and that himself had heard, one summer afternoon, the sound of their balls, like distant peals of thunder." Rip's veracity was vindicated; his daughter gave him a comfortable home; and the grave historian of the event assures us that the Dutch inhabitants, "even to this day, never hear a thunder-storm of a summer afternoon about the Kaats-Kill, but they say, Hendrick Hudson and his crew are at their game of nine-pins."

The Van Winkle of our day, who lived in the cottage by the mountain road-side as long as a guest lingered at the great mansion above him, was no kin to old Rip, and we strongly suspect that his name was borrowed; but he kept refreshments that strengthened many a weary toiler up the mountain—liquors equal, no doubt, to those in the "wicked flagons" that the ancient one served to the ghostly company—and from a rude spout poured cooling draughts into his cabin from a mountain spring, more delicious than ever came from the juice of the grape.

There are many delightful resting-places upon the road, soon after leaving Rip's cabin, as we toil wearily up the mountain, where the eye takes in a magnificent panorama of hill and valley, forest and river, hamlet and village, and thousands of broad acres where herds graze and the farmer gathers his crops,—much of it dimly refined because of distance —a beautifully coloured map rather than a picture. These delight the eye and quicken the pulse, as has been remarked; but there is one place upon that road where the ascending weary ones enjoy more exquisite pleasure for a moment than at any other point in all that mountain region. It is at a turn in the road where the Mountain House stands suddenly before and above the traveller, revealed in perfect distinctness—column, capital, window, rock, people—all apparently only a few rods distant. There, too, the road is level, and the traveller rejoices in the assurance that the toilsome journey is at an end; when, suddenly, he finds himself, like the young pilgrim in Cole's "Voyage of Life," disappointed in his

MOUNTAIN HOUSE, FROM THE ROAD.

course. The road that seemed to be leading directly to that beautiful mansion, upon the crag just above him, turns away, like the stream that appeared to be taking the ambitious young voyager directly to the shadowy temple of Fame in the clouds; and many a weary step must be taken, over a crooked, hilly road, before the traveller can reach the object of his journey.

The grand rock-platform, upon which the Mountain House stands, is reached at last; and then comes the full recompense for all weariness. Bathed—immersed—in pure mountain air, almost three thousand feet above tide-water, full, positive, enduring rest is given to every muscle after a half hour's respiration of that invigorating atmosphere; and soul and limb are ready for a longer, loftier, and more rugged ascent.

There is something indescribable in the pleasure experienced during the first hour passed upon the piazza of the Mountain House, gazing upon the scene toward the east. That view has been described a thousand times. I shall not attempt it. Much rhetoric, and rhyme, and sentimental platitudes have been employed in the service of description, but none have conveyed to my mind a picture so graphic, truthful, and satisfactory as Natty Bumpo's reply to Edward's question, in one of Cooper's "Leather-Stocking Tales," "What see you when you get there?"

"Creation!" said Natty, dropping the end of his rod into the water, and sweeping one hand around him in a circle, "all creation, lad. I was on that hill when Vaughan burnt 'Sopus, in the last war, and I saw the vessels come out of the Highlands as plainly as I can see that lime-scow rowing into the Susquehanna, though one was twenty times further from me than the other.* The river was in sight for seventy miles under my feet, looking like a curled shaving, though it was eight long miles to its banks. I saw the hills in the Hampshire Grants, the Highlands of the river, and all that God had done, or man could do, as far as the eye could reach—you know that the Indians named me for my sight, lad†—and from the flat on the top of that mountain, I have often found the place where Albany stands; and as for 'Sopus! the day the royal troops burnt the town, the smoke seemed so nigh that I thought I could hear the screeches of the women."

"It must have been worth the toil, to meet with such a glorious view."

"If being the best part of a mile in the air, and having men's farms at your feet, with rivers looking like ribands, and mountains bigger than the 'Vision,' seeming to be haystacks of green grass under you, give any satisfaction to a man, I can recommend the spot."

---

* Reference is here made to the burning of the village of Kingston (whose Indian name of *E-so-pus* was retained until a recent period), by a British force under General Vaughan, in the Autumn of 1777.
† "Hawk-Eye."

The aërial pictures seen from the Mountain House are sometimes marvellous, especially during a shower in the plain, when all is sunshine above, while the lightning plays and the thunder rolls far below the dwellers upon the summits ; or after a storm, when mists are driving over the mountains, struggling with the wind and sun, or dissolving into invisibility in the pure air. At rare intervals, an apparition, like the spectre of the Brocken, may be seen. A late writer, who was once there during a summer storm, was favoured with the sight. The guests were in the parlour, when it was announced that "the house was going past on the outside !" All rushed to the piazza, and there, sure enough, upon a moving cloud, more dense than the fog that enveloped the mountain, was a perfect picture of the great building, in colossal proportions. The mass of vapour was passing slowly from north to south, directly in front, at a distance, apparently, of two hundred feet from the building, and reflected the noble Corinthian columns which ornament the front of the building, every window, and all the spectators. The cloud moved on, and "ere long," says the writer, " we saw one pillar disappear, and then another. We, ourselves, who were expanded into Brobdignags in size, saw the gulf into which we were to enter and be lost. I almost shuddered when my turn came, but there was no eluding my fate ; one side of my face was veiled, and in a moment the whole had passed like a dream. An instant before, and we were the inhabitants of a 'gorgeous palace,' but it was the 'baseless fabric of a vision,' and now there was left 'not a wreck behind.'"

As a summer shower passes over the plain below, the effect at the Mountain House is sometimes truly grand, even when the lightning is not seen or the thunder heard. A young woman sitting at the side of the writer when this page was penned, and who had recently visited that eyrie, recorded her vision and impressions on the spot. "The whole scene before us," she says, " was a vast panorama, constantly varying and changing. The blue of the depths and distances—clouds, mountains, and shadows—was such that the perception entered into our very souls. How shall I describe the colour? It was not mazarine, because there was no blackness in it ; it was not sunlit atmosphere, because there was no white brightness in it ; and yet there was a sort of hidden, beaming brilliancy, that completely absorbed our eyes and hearts. It was not the blue of water, because it was not liquid or crystal-like; it was something as the calm, soft, lustre of a steady blue eye. . . . . And how various were the forms and motions of the vapour! Hills, mountains, domes, pyramids, wreaths and sprays of mist arose, mounted, hung, fell, curled, and almost leaped before us, white with their own spotlessness, but not bright with the sun's rays, for the luminary was still obscured. . . . . We looked down to behold what we might discover. A breath of heaven cleared the mist

VIEW FROM SOUTH MOUNTAIN.

from below,—softly at first, but gradually more decisive. Larger and darker became a spot in the magic depths, when, lo! as in a vision, fields, trees, fences, and the habitations of men were revealed before our eyes. For the first time something real and refined lay before us, far down in that wonderful gulf. Far beneath heaven and us slept a speck of creation, unlighted by the evening rays that touched us, and colourless in the twilight obscurity. Intently we watched the magic glass, but—did we breathe upon its surface?—a mist fell before us, and we looked up as if awakened from a dream."

that-a-way, striving to get out of the hollow, till it finally comes to the plain. . . . . The rock sweeps like mason-work in a half-round on both sides of the fall, and shelves over the bottom for fifty feet; so that when I've been sitting at the foot of the first pitch, and my hounds have run

KATERS-KILL FALLS.

into the caverns behind the sheet of water, they've looked no bigger than so many rabbits. To my judgment, lad, it's the best piece of work I've met with in the woods; and none know how often the hand of God is seen in the wilderness, but them that rove it for a man's life."

"Does the water run into the Delaware?" asked Edwards.

"No, no, it's a drop for the old Hudson : and a merry time it has until it gets down off the mountain."

And if the visitor would enjoy one of the wildest and most romantic rambles in the world, let him follow that little stream on its way "off the mountains," down the deep, dark, mysterious gorge, until it joins the Katers-Kill proper, that rushes through the "Clove" from the neighbourhood of Hunter, among the hills above, and thence onward to the plain.

It was just after a storm when we last visited these falls. The traces of "delicate-footed May" were upon every shrub and tree. Tiny leaves were just unfolding all over the mountains, and the snowy dogwood blossoms were bursting into beauty on every hand. Yet mementoes of winter were at the falls. In the cavern at the back of them, heaps of ice lay piled, and a chilling mist came sweeping up the gorge, at quick intervals, filling the whole amphitheatre with shadowy splendour when sunlight fell upon it from between the dissolving clouds. While sketching the cascades, memory recurred to other visits we had made there in midsummer, when the wealth of foliage lay upon tree and shrub; and also to a description given us by a lady, of her visit to the falls in winter, with Cole, the artist, when the frost had crystallised the spray into gorgeous fret-work all over the rocks, and made a spendid cylinder of milk-white ice from the base to the crown of the upper cascade. Of these phases Bryant has sung :—

> "Midst greens and shades the Katers-Kill leaps,
>   From cliffs where the wood-flower clings;
> All summer he moistens his verdant steeps;
>   With the sweet light spray of the mountain springs;
> And he shakes the woods on the mountain side,
> When they drip with the rains of autumn tide.
>
> "But when, in the forests bare and old,
>   The blast of December calls,
> He builds, in the star-light clear and cold,
>   A palace of ice, where his torrent falls,
> With turret, and arch, and fret-work fair,
> And pillars blue as the summer air."

The tourist, if he fails to traverse the rugged gorge, should not omit a ride from the Mountain House, down through the "Clove" to Palensville

and the plain, a distance of about eight miles. Unpleasant as was the day
when we last visited the mountains, we returned to Katz-Kill by that
circuitous route. After leaving the falls, we rode about three miles before
reaching the "Clove." Huge masses of vapour came rolling up from its
lower depths, sometimes obscuring everything around us, and then,

THE FAWN'S LEAP.

drifting away, laving the lofty summits of the mountains that stretch far
southward, gleaming in the fitful sunlight, and presenting unsurpassed
exhibitions of aërial perspective. Down, down, sometimes with only a
narrow space between the base of a high mountain on one side, and steep

precipices upon the other, whose feet are washed by the rushing Katers-Kill, our crooked road pursued its way, now passing a log-house, now a pleasant cottage, and at length the ruins of a leather manufacturing village, deserted because the bark upon the hills around, used for tanning, is exhausted. Near this picturesque scene, the Katers-Kill leaps into a

SCENE ON THE KATERS-KILL, NEAR PALENSVILLE.

seething gulf between cleft rocks, and flows gently on to make still greater plunges into darker depths a short distance below. This cleft in the rocks is called the Fawn's Leap, a young deer having there escaped a hunter and his dog, that pursued to the verge of the chasm. The fawn leaped it, but the dog, attempting to follow, fell into the gulf below and was drowned. The foiled hunter went home, without dog or game. By some, less poetical than others, the place is called the Dog Hole.

A few rods below the Fawn's Leap, the road crosses a rustic bridge, at the foot of a sheer precipice, and for half a mile traverses a shelf cut from the mountain side, two hundred feet above the stream that has found its way into depths so dark as to be hardly visible. Upon the opposite side of the creek a perpendicular wall rises many hundred feet, and then in slight inclination the mountain towers up at least a thousand feet higher, and forms a portion of the range known as the South Mountain. At the mouth of this cavernous gorge lies the pretty little village of Palensville, where we again cross the stream, and in a few moments find ourselves upon a beautiful and highly cultivated plain. From this point, along the base of the mountains to the road by which we enter them, or more directly to Katz-Kill, the drive is a delightful one.

From the lower borders of Columbia County, opposite Katz-Kill village, to Hyde Park, in Duchess County, a distance of thirty miles, the east bank of the Hudson is distinguished for old and elegant country seats, most of them owned and occupied by the descendants of wealthy proprietors who flourished in the last century, and were connected by blood and marriage with Robert Livingston, a Scotch gentleman, of the family of the Earls of Linlithgow, who came to America in 1672, and married a member of the Schuyler family, the widow of a Van Rensselaer. He lived at Albany, and was secretary to the Commissioners of Indian Affairs for a long time. From 1684 to 1715 he had, from time to time, purchased of the Indians, and secured by patents from the English crown, large tracts of land in the present Columbia County. This land was then mostly wild and unprofitable, but became the basis of great family wealth.

In the year 1710 Livingston's grants were consolidated, and Hunter, the royal governor, gave him a patent for a tract of a little more than one hundred and sixty-two thousand acres, for which he was to pay into the king's treasury "an annual rent of twenty-eight shillings, lawful money of New York," a trifle over fourteen shillings sterling! This magnificent estate was constituted a manor, with political privileges.

The freeholders upon it were allowed a representative in the colonial legislature, chosen by themselves, and in 1716 the lord of the manor, by virtue of that privilege, took his seat as a legislator. He had already built a manor-house, on a grassy point upon the banks of the Hudson, at

OLD CLERMONT.

the mouth of Roeleffe Jansen's Kill, or Ancram Creek, of which hardly a vestige now remains.*

The lord of the manor gave, by his will, the lower portion of his domain to his son Robert, who built a finer mansion than the old manor-house, and named his seat Clermont. This was sometimes called the

---

* In the year 1710 Governor Hunter, by order of Queen Anne, bought of Mr. Livingston 6,000 acres of his manor, for the sum of a little more than £200, for the use of Protestant Germans then in England, who had been driven from their homes in the Lower Palatinate of the Rhine, then the dominions of a cousin of the British Queen. About 1,800 of them settled upon the manor lands, and at a place on the opposite shore of the river, the respective localities being known as East and West Camp. These Germans were called Palatines, and are represented as the most enlightened people of their native land. Among them was the widow Hannah Zenger, whose son, John Peter, apprenticed to William Bradford, the printer, became, in after life, the impersonation of the struggling democratic idea. He published a democratic newspaper, and because he commented freely upon the conduct of the royal governor, he was imprisoned and prosecuted for a libel. A jury acquitted him, in the midst of great cheering by the people. His counsel was presented with the freedom of the city of New York in a gold box. By that verdict democratic ideas, and the freedom of the press, were nobly vindicated.

Hoboken, on the Jersey shore, where John Stevens (Mr. Livingston's brother-in-law) had been experimenting in the same direction for fifteen years. That first successful steamboat was named *Clermont*, in compli-

VIEW AT DE KOVEN'S BAY.

ment to Chancellor Livingston, and made her first voyage to Albany at the beginning of September, 1807.*

At Tivoli is the mansion of John Swift Livingston, Esq., built before

---

* The *Clermont* was 100 feet long, 12 feet wide, and 7 feet deep. The following advertisement appeared in the *Albany Gazette* on the 1st of September, 1807:—

THE CLERMONT.

"The *North River Steamboat* will leave Paulus's Hook [Jersey City] on Friday, the 4th of September, at 9 in the morning, and arrive at Albany on Saturday, at 9 in the afternoon. Provisions, good berths, and accommodation are provided. The charge to each passenger is as follows:—

To Newburgh,	Dollars,	3	Time,	14 hours.
,, Poughkeepsie	,,	4	,,	17 ,,
,, Esopus	,,	5	,,	20 ,,
,, Hudson	,,	5½	,,	30 ,,
,, Albany	,,	7	,,	36 ,,

"Mr. Fulton's new steamboat," said the same paper, on the 5th of October, "left New York on the 2nd, at 10 o'clock, A.M., against a strong tide, very rough water, and a violent gale from the north. She made a headway, against the most sanguine expectations, and without being rocked by the waves!"

the war for independence. It is surrounded by a pleasant park and gardens, and commands a view of the village of Saugerties, on the west shore of the Hudson, and that portion of the Katzbergs on which the Mountain House stands. That building may be seen, as a white spot on the distant hills, in our sketch. Mr. Livingston's house was occupied by one of that name when the British burnt Old Clermont and the residence of the chancellor. They landed in De Koven's Cove, or Bay, just below, and came up with destructive intent, supposing this to be the residence

LIVINGSTON'S MANSION AT TIVOLI.

of the arch offender. The proprietor was a good-humoured, hospitable man. He soon convinced the invaders of their error, supplied them bountifully with wine and other refreshments, and made them so kindly and cheery, that had he been the "rebel" himself, they must have spared his property. They passed on, performed their destructive errand, partook of the good things of Mr. Livingston's larder and wine-cellar on their return, and sailed down the river to apply the torch to Kingston, a few miles below.

Opposite Tivoli, in Ulster County, is the pleasant village of Saugerties,* near the mouth of the Esopus Creek, which comes flowing from the south through a beautiful valley, and enters the Hudson here. Iron, paper, and white-lead are manufactured there extensively, and between the river and the mountains are almost inexhaustible quarries of flagging stone. A once picturesque fall or rapid, around which a portion of the village is clustered, has been partially destroyed by a dam and unsightly

MOUTH OF ESOPUS CREEK, SAUGERTIES.

bridge above it, yet some features of grandeur and beauty remain. The chief business part of the village lies upon a plain with the Katzbergs for a background, and on the high right bank of the creek, where many of the first-class residences are situated, an interesting view of the mouth of Zaeger's Kill, or Esopus Creek, with the lighthouse, river, and the fertile lands on the eastern shore, may be obtained. Near this village was the West Camp of the Palatines, already mentioned.

About five miles below Tivoli is Annandale, the seat of John

---

* Incorporated *Ulster* in 1831. The name is derived from the Dutch word Zaeger, a sawyer. Peter Pietersen having built a saw-mill at the Falls, where the village stands, the stream was called Sawyer's Creek, or Zaeger's Kill, since, by corruption, Saugerties.

Bard, Esq. As we approached it from the north on a pleasant day in June, along the picturesque road that links almost a score of beautiful villas, the attention was suddenly arrested by the appearance of an elegant little church, built of stone in the early Anglo-Gothic style, standing on the verge of an open park. Near it was a long building, in similar style of architecture, in course of erection. On inquiry, we found the church to be that of the Holy Innocents, built by the proprietor of Annandale upon his estate, for the use of the inhabitants of that region as a free chapel. The new building was for St. Stephen's College, designed as a training school for those who are preparing to enter the General Theological Seminary of the Protestant Episcopal Church, in New York city. For this purpose Mr. Bard had appropriated, as a gratuity, the munificent sum of 60,000 dollars. He had deeded eigh-

ST. STEPHEN'S COLLEGE.

teen acres of land to the College, and pledged 1,000 dollars a year for the support of a professor in it. The institution had been formally recognised as the Diocesan Training College; the legislature of New York had granted the trustees an act of incorporation, and liberal subscriptions had been made to place it upon a stable foundation. In the midst of the grove of fine old trees seen in the direction of the river bank from the road near the College, stands the Villa of Annandale, like all its neighbours commanding extensive river and mountain scenery.

Adjoining Annandale on the south is Montgomery Place, the residence of the family of the late Edward Livingston, brother of the Chancellor, who is distinguished in the annals of his country as a leading United States senator, the author of the penal code of the State of Louisiana, and ambassador to France. The elegant mansion was built by the widow of General Richard Montgomery, a companion-in-arms of Wolfe when he fell at Quebec, and who perished under the walls of that city at the head of a storming party of Republicans on the 31st of December, 1775. Montgomery was one of the noblest and bravest men of his age. When he gave his young wife a parting kiss at the house of General Schuyler, at Saratoga, and hastened to join that officer at Ticonderoga, in the campaign that proved fatal to him, he said, "You shall never blush for your Montgomery." Gallantly did he vindicate that pledge. And when his virtues were extolled by Barré, Burke, and others in the British parliament, Lord North exclaimed, "Curse on his virtues; he has undone his country."

The wife of Montgomery was a sister of Chancellor Livingston. With ample pecuniary means and good taste at command, she built this mansion,

MONTGOMERY PLACE.

and there spent fifty years of widowhood, childless, but cheerful. The mansion and its 400 acres passed into the possession of her brother Edward, and there, as we have observed, members of his family now reside. Of all the fine estates along this portion of the Hudson, this is said to be the most perfect in its beauty and arrangements. Waterfalls, picturesque bridges, romantic glens, groves, a magnificent park, one of the most beautiful of the ornamental gardens in this country, and views of the river and mountains, unsurpassed, render Montgomery Place a retreat to be coveted, even by the most favoured of fortune.

Four miles by the railway below Tivoli is the Barrytown Station, or Lower Red Hook Landing. The villages of Upper and Lower Red Hook, like most of the early towns along the Hudson, lie. back from the river. Tivoli and Barrytown are their respective ports. A short distance below the latter, connected by a winding avenue with the public road already mentioned, is Rokeby, the seat of William B. Astor, Esq., who is distinguished as the wealthiest man in the United States. It was formerly the residence of his father-in-law, General John Armstrong, an officer in

THE KATZBERGS FROM MONTGOMERY PLACE.

the war for independence, and a member of General Gates's military family. Armstrong was the author of the celebrated addresses which were privately circulated among the officers of the Continental Army lying at Newburgh, on the Hudson, at the close of the war, and calculated to stir up a mutiny, and even a rebellion against the civil power. The feeble Congress had been unable for a long time to provide for the pay of the soldiers about to be disbanded and sent home in poverty and rags. There was apathy in Congress and among the people on the subject; and these addresses were intended to stir up the latter and their representatives to the performance of their duty in making some provision for their faithful servants, rather than to excite the army to take affairs into their own hand, as was charged. Through the wisdom and firmness of Washington, the event was so overruled as to give honour to the army and benefit the country. Washington afterwards acquitted Major Armstrong of all evil intentions, and considered his injudicious movement (instigated, it is supposed, by Gates) as a patriotic act.

Armstrong afterwards married a sister of Chancellor Livingston, and

ROKEBY.

was chosen successively to a seat in the United States senate, an ambassador to France, a brigadier-general in the army, and secretary-of-war. He held the latter office while England and the United States were at war, in 1812-14. He was the author of a "Life of General Montgomery," "Life of General Wayne," and "Historical Notices of the War of 1812." Rokeby, where this eminent man lived and died, is delightfully situated, in the midst of an undulating park, farther from the river than the other villas, but commanding some interesting glimpses of it, with more distant landscapes and mountain scenery. Among the latter may be seen the range of the Shawangunk (pronounced shon-gum), in the far south-west. Here Mr. Astor's family reside about eight months of the year.

A few miles below Rokeby, and lying upon an elevated plain two miles from the river, is the beautiful village of Rhinebeck, containing little more than 1,000 inhabitants. The first settler was William Beekman, or Beckman, who came from the Rhine, in Germany, in 1647, purchased all this region from the Indians, and gave homes to several poor families who came with him. The name of the river in his fatherland, and his own, are commemorated in the title of the town—Rhine-Beck. The house built by him is yet standing, upon a high point near the Rhinebeck station. It is a stone building. The bricks of which the chimney is constructed were imported from Holland. In this house the first public religious services in that region were held,

BEEKMAN'S HOUSE.

and it was used as a fortress in early times, against the Indians. It now belongs to the Heermance family, descendants of early settlers there. Beekman's son, Henry, afterwards procured a patent from the English government for a very extensive tract of land in Duchess County, including his Rhinebeck estate.

Just below the Rhinebeck Station is Ellerslie, the seat of the Hon. William Kelly. No point on the Hudson commands a more interesting view of the river and adjacent scenery, than the southern front of the mansion at Ellerslie. The house is at an elevation of two hundred feet above the river, overlooking an extensive park. The river is in full view for more than fourteen miles. At the distance of about thirty-five miles are seen the Fish-Kill Mountains, and the Hudson Highlands, while on the west, the horizon is bounded by the lofty Katzbergs.

Ellerslie is ninety miles from New York city, and contains about seven hundred acres of land, with a front on the river of a mile and a-half. Its character is different from that of an ordinary villa residence, being cultivated with much care as a farm, whilst great regard is had to improving its beauty, and developing landscape effects. The lawn and gardens occupy thirty acres; the greenhouse, graperies, &c., are among

the most complete in this country.   The park contains three hundred
acres; its surface is undulated, with masses of old trees scattered over it,
and upon it feeds a large herd of thorough-bred Durham cattle, which the
proprietor considers a more appropriate ornament than would be a herd
of deer.

A mile below Ellerslie is Wildercliff,* the seat of Miss Mary Garrettson,
daughter of the eminent Méthodist preacher, Freeborn Garrettson, who
married a sister of Chancellor Livingston.   The mansion is a very modest

ELLERSLIE.

one, compared with some in its neighbourhood.   It was built in accordance
with the simple tastes of the original proprietor.   Mr. Garrettson was a
leader among the plain Methodists in the latter part of the last century,
when that denomination was beginning to take fast hold upon the public
mind in America, and his devoted, blameless life did much to commend
his people to a public disposed to deride them.

* More properly *Wilder Klippe.* This is a Dutch word, signifying wild man's, or wild Indian's,
cliffe. The first settlers found upon a smooth rock, on the river shore, at this place, a rude delineation
of two Indians, one with a tomahawk, and the other a calumet, or pipe of peace. This gave them the
idea of the name.

The very beautiful view from this mansion, down the river, is exceedingly charming for its simple beauty, so much in harmony with the associations of the place. In the centre of the lawn stood a sun-dial. On the left was a magnificent wide-spreading elm. On the right, through the trees, might be seen the cultivated western shore of the Hudson, with the mountains beyond, and in front was the river, stretching away southward, at all times dotted with the white sails of water-craft. This mansion has many associations connected with the early struggles of

VIEW FROM WILDERCLIFF.

Methodism, very dear to the hearts of those who love that branch of the Christian church.

When Mr. Garrettson left the Church of England, in which he had been educated, the Methodists were despised in most places. He was a native of Maryland. Eminently conscientious, he gave his slaves their freedom, and entering upon his ministry, preached everywhere, on all occasions and at all times, offending the wicked and delighting the good, and fearless of all men, having full faith in a special Providence, and oftentimes experiencing proofs of the truth of the idea to which he clung. One example of his proofs may be cited. A mob had seized him on one

Many of the persecuted Huguenot families who fled from France settled at Kingston and in its vicinity, towards the close of the seventeenth century ; and when the war for independence broke out in 1775, their descendants were found on the side of the republicans. Kingston was called a "nest of rebels." There, in the spring of 1777, the representatives of the people of the State formed a state constitution, and organised civil government under it. The first session of the legislature was held there in July-following, but the members were obliged to flee in the autumn, on

KINGSTON.

the approach of Vaughan and his troops. These ascended the river from the Highlands, where Sir Henry Clinton had gained a victory, taken possession of Forts Clinton and Montgomery, and destroyed the obstructions in the river which prevented vessels passing northward. The object of Vaughan's expedition, as we have said, was to draw the attention of Gates and his army (then casting their meshes around Burgoyne) to the country below, where devastation and ruin were threatened. After passing the Highlands, they distressed the people along the shores of the river very much by burnings and plunderings. They landed at the port of Esopus, or Kingston, on the 13th of October, and proceeded to the village in two divisions. The town contained about 300 inhabitants, and the houses were mostly of stone. The people fled with what property they could carry away, and the soldiery burned every house but one.

It is related that when the British landed at Kingston Point, some Dutchmen were at work just below it, and were not aware of the fact until they saw the dreaded "red-coats" near them. It was low water, and across the flats on the river shore they fled toward the place of the present village of Rondout as fast as their legs could carry them, not presuming to look behind them, lest, like Lot's wife, they might be detained. The summer haymakers had left a rake on the marsh meadow, and upon this one of the fugitives trod. The handle flew up behind him, and gave him a severe blow on the back of his head. Not doubting that a "Britisher" was close upon his heels, he stopped short, and throwing up his hands imploringly, exclaimed, "O mein Got! mein Got! I kivs up. Hoorah for King Shorge!" The innocent rake was all the enemy that was near, and the fugitive's sudden conversion was known only to a companion in the race, who had outstripped him a few paces.

Hurley, a few miles from Kingston, became the place of refuge for the sufferers from the conflagration of the latter town. There, while Esopus was in flames, the republicans hanged a spy, who had been caught in the American camp near Newburgh, a few days before. He had been sent by Sir Henry Clinton with a message to Burgoyne. When apprehended on suspicion, he was seen to cast something into his mouth and swallow it. An emetic was administered, and a silver bullet, hollow and elliptical in shape, was produced. In it, written upon tissue paper, was the following note, dated Fort Montgomery, October 8, 1777:—

" *Nous y voici*, and nothing now between us and Gates. I sincerely hope this little succour of ours may facilitate your operation. In answer to your letter of the 28th, by C. C., I shall only say I cannot presume to order, or even advise, for reasons obvious. I heartily wish you success.

"Faithfully yours,   "H. CLINTON."

The prisoner was tried: out of his own mouth he was condemned. He was taken to Hurley, and there hanged upon an apple-tree. That silver bullet and the note are preserved in the family of Governor George Clinton.

Kingston village is a very pleasant one, and the country about it affords delightful drives. Its population in 1860 was about 4,000, and the space between it and Rondout, a mile and a half distant, was rapidly filling up with dwellings. The two villages were already connected by gas-pipes, and public conveyances ply between them continually.

Rondout (Redoubt), at the mouth of Rondout Creek, is one of the busiest places on the river between Albany and New York. It was formerly called the Strand, then Kingston Landing, and finally Bolton,

RONDOUT CREEK.

in honour of the then president of the Delaware and Hudson Canal Company. That canal, which penetrates the coal region of Pennsylvania, has its eastern terminus at Eddyville, two and a half miles up the Rondout Creek; and the mouth of that stream is continually crowded with vessels engaged in carrying coals and other commodities. Immense piers have been erected in the middle of the stream for the reception and forwarding of coal. Here, and in the vicinity, are manufactories of cement, and also extensive quarries of flagstone—all of which, with the agricultural products of the adjacent country, giving freights to twenty steamboats and many sailing vessels. Lines of steamers run regularly from Rondout to Albany and New York, and intermediate places, and a steam ferry-boat connects the place with the Rhinebeck Station.

The population of Rondout was about 6,000 in 1860. The greater proportion of the able-bodied men and boys were, in some way, connected with the coal business. Another village, the offspring of the same trade, and of very recent origin, stands just below the mouth of the Rondout Creek. It was built entirely by the Pennsylvania Coal Company. From that village, laid out in 1851, and containing a population of about 1,400 souls, a large portion of the coal brought to the Hudson on the canal was shipped in barges for the north and west. It is called Port Ewen, in honour of John Ewen, then president of the company.

Placentia is the name of the beautifully situated country seat of the late James Kirke Paulding, a mile above the village of Hyde Park, and seven north from Poughkeepsie. It stands upon a gentle eminence, over-looking a pleasant park of many acres, and commanding an extensive prospect of a fertile farming country on both sides of the river. Almost opposite Placentia is the model farm of Robert L. Pell, Esq., whose apples, gathered from thousands of trees, are familiar to those who make purchases in the American and English fruit markets. Placentia has no history of special interest. It is a simple, beautiful retreat, now conse-crated in memory as the residence of a venerable novelist and poet—the friend and associate of Washington Irving in his early literary career. They were associated in the conducting of an irregular periodical entitled "Salmagundi," the principal object of which was to satirise the follies and foibles of fashionable life. Contrary to their expectation, it obtained a wide circulation, and they found many imitators throughout the country. It was brought to an abrupt conclusion by the refusal of the publisher to allow them any compensation. Paulding and Irving were personal friends through a period of more than fifty years. Mr. Paulding lived in elegant retirement, at his country seat, for many years, enjoying his books, his pictures, and his friends. He passed away, at the beginning of 1860, at the age of more than fourscore years.

Our last visit to Placentia was at the close of a most delightful afternoon in early June.　A sweet repose rested upon land and water.　The golden sun was delicately veiled in purple exhalations, and over all the scene silence deepened the solemnity of the thought that we were treading paths where a child of genius had daily walked, but who had lately turned aside to be laid to rest in the cool shadows of the tomb.

The village of Hyde Park is upon a pleasant plain, high above the river, and half a mile from it.　It received its name from Peter Faulconier, the private secretary of Sir Edward Hyde (afterwards Lord Cornbury),

PLACENTIA.

the governor of the province of New York at the beginning of the last century.　Faulconier purchased a large tract of land at this place, and named it Hyde Park in honour of the governor.　Here the aspect of the western shores of the river changes from gently sloping banks and cultivated fields to rocky and precipitous bluffs; and this character they exhibit all the way to Hoboken, opposite New York,— with few interruptions.

At Hyde Park the river makes a sudden bend between rocky bluffs, and in a narrower channel.　On account of this the Dutch settlers called the place *Krom Elleboge,* or Crooked Elbow.　As is frequently the case along the Hudson, the present name is a compound of Dutch and English, and is called Crom Elbow.

Six miles below Hyde Park is the large rural city of Poughkeepsie, containing about 17,000 inhabitants. The name is a modification of the Mohegan word, *Apo-keep-sinck*,* signifying " safe and pleasant harbour." Between two rocky bluffs was a sheltered bay (now filled with wharves),

POUGHKEEPSIE, FROM LEWISBURG.

into the upper part of which leaped, in rapids and cascades, the Winnakee, called Fall Kill by the Dutch. The northerly bluff was called by the

---

* The name of this city, as found in records and on maps, exhibits a most curious specimen of orthographic caprice, it being spelt in forty-two different ways, as follows :—Pakeepsie, Pacapsey, Pakepsey, Paughkepsie, Pecapesy, Pecapsy, Pecapshe, Pochkeepsinck, Poeghkeepsing, Poeghkeeksingk, Poeghkeepsink, Pochkeepsey, Pochkeepsen, Pochkeepsy, Pochkepsen, Pochkyphsingh, Pockeepsy, Pockepseick, Pockepseng, Pokepsing, Poghkeepsie, Poghkeepsinck, Poghkeepsing, Poghkepse, Poghkepsen, Poghkeepsink, Poghkeepson, Poghkeepse, Pokeepsigh, Pokeepsingh, Pokeepsink, Pokeepsy, Pokepsinck, Pokkepsen, Poughkeepsey, Poukeepsie, Poukeepsy, Pikipsi, Picipsi, Pokepsie, Pokeepsie, Poughkeepsie.

and acacia trees, and their cleanliness is proverbial. It is celebrated for
its numerous seminaries of learning for both sexes, the salubrity of its
climate, the fertility of the surrounding country, and the wealth and
general independence of its inhabitants.   The eye and ear are rarely
offended by public exhibitions of squalor or vice, while evidences of thrift
are seen on every hand.

From a high rocky bluff on the river front of Poughkeepsie, named the
Call Rock, exquisite views of the Hudson, north and south, may be
obtained. The scene southward, which includes a distant view of the

THE HIGHLANDS, FROM POUGHKEEPSIE.

Highlands, is the most attractive. At all times the river is filled with
water-craft of almost every description. The most striking objects on its
surface are fleets of barges from the northern and western canals, loaded
with the products of the fields and forests, lashed or tethered together,
and towed by a steamboat. On these barges whole families sometimes
reside during the season of navigation; and upon lines stretched over
piles of lumber, newly-washed clothes may be frequently seen fluttering
in the breeze. One of these fleets appears in our sketch.

Two miles below Poughkeepsie is Locust Grove, the seat of Professor

Samuel F. B. Morse, an eminent artist and philosopher, the founder of the American Academy of Design, but better known to the world as the author of the system of telegraphing by electro-magnetism, now used in almost every civilised country on the globe. For this wonderful contribution to science and addition to the world's inventions for moral and material advancement, he has been honoured by several royal testimonials, honorary and substantial, and by the universal gratitude and admiration of his countrymen. Locust Grove is his summer retreat, and from his study he has electrographic communication with all parts of the United

LOCUST GROVE.

States and the British provinces. The mansion is so embowered that it is almost invisible to the traveller on the highway. But immediately around it are gardens, conservatories, and a pleasant lawn, basking in the sunshine, and through vistas between magnificent trees, glimpses may be caught of the Hudson, the northern and southern ranges of mountains, and villages that dot the western shore of the river. Here the master dispenses a generous hospitality to friends and strangers, and with the winning graces of a modest, unobtrusive nature, he delights all who enter the charmed circle of Locust Grove. For the man of taste and genius his

home is one of the most charming retreats to be found on the banks of
the Hudson from the wilderness to the sea.

About four miles below Poughkeepsie is an ancient stone farm-house
and a mill, at the mouth of Spring Brook, at the eastern terminus of the
Milton Ferry. Here, during the old war for independence, lived Theophilus
Anthony, a blacksmith, farmer, miller, and staunch Whig, who used his
forge for most rebellious purposes. He assisted in making a great chain
(of which I shall hereafter write), that was stretched across the Hudson
in the Highlands at Fort Montgomery, to prevent the British ships of war

MILTON FERRY AND HORSE-BOAT.

ascending the river and carrying invading troops into the heart of the
country. For this offence, when the chain and accompanying boom were
forced, and the vessels of Vaughan carried the firebrand to Esopus or
Kingston, the rebel blacksmith's mill was laid in ashes, and he was
confined in the loathsome *Jersey* prison-ship at New York, where he had
ample time for reflection and penitence for three weary years. Alas! the
latter never came. He was a sinner against ministers, too hardened for
repentance, and he remained a rebel until the close of his life. Another
mill soon arose from the ashes of the old one, and there his grandsons, the

Messrs. Gill were grinding wheat when we were there for the descendants of both Whigs and Tories, and never inquired into the politics of the passengers upon their boat at the Milton Ferry. That boat was keeping alive the memory of times before steam was used for navigation. It was one of only two vessels of the kind upon the Hudson in 1860, that were propelled by horse-power. The other was at Coxsakie. The Milton ferry-boat has since been withdrawn.

Opposite Spring Brook is the village of Milton, remarkable, like its

NEW HAMBURG TUNNEL.

sister, Marlborough, a few miles below, for the picturesque beauty of the surrounding country and the abundance of Antwerp raspberries produced in its vicinity every year. There and at some places on the eastern shore, are the chief sources of the supply of that delicious fruit for the city of New York; and the quantity raised is so great, that a small steamboat is employed for the sole purpose of carrying raspberries daily to the city. These villages are upon high banks, and are scarcely visible from the river. They have a background of rich farming lands, terminating beyond a sweet valley by a range of lofty hills that are covered with the primeval forest. They are the resort of New Yorkers during the heat of summer.

Eight miles below Poughkeepsie is the little village of New Hamburg, situated at the foot of a rocky promontory thickly covered with the Arbor Vitæ, or white cedar, and near the mouth of the Wappingi's Creek. Through this bluff the Hudson River Railway passes in a tunnel 800 feet in length, and then crosses the mouth of the Wappingi, upon a causeway

THE ARBOR VITÆ.

and drawbridge. All over this rocky bluff, including the roof of the tunnel, the Arbor Vitæ shrubs stand thickly; and present, according to Loudon, the eminent English writer on horticulture and kindred subjects, some of the finest specimens of that tree to be found in the world. Here they may be seen of all sizes and most perfect forms, from the tiny shrub to the tall tree that shows its stem for several feet from the ground. The most beautiful are those of six to ten feet in height, whose branches shoot out close to the ground, forming perfect cones, and exhibiting nothing to the eye but delicate sprays and bright green leaves. When quite small these shrubs may be successfully transplanted; but under cultivation they sometimes lose their perfect form, and become irregular, like the common cedar tree. They are beginning to be extensively used for hedges, and the ornamentation of pleasure grounds.*

A pleasant glimpse of Marlborough, through a broad ravine, may be obtained from the rough eminence above the New Hamburg tunnel, and also from the lime-kilns at the foot of the bluff, on the edge of the river, where a ferry connects the two villages. But one of the most interesting views on the Hudson, in this vicinity, is from the gravelly promontory

MARLBOROUGH, FROM THE LIME-KILNS.

near the town, at the mouth of the Wappingi's Creek—a large stream that comes down from the hills in the north-eastern part of Duchess County, dispensing fertility and extensive water-power along its whole course. It is navigable for a mile and a half from its mouth, when it falls seventy-five feet, and furnishes power used by quite a large manufacturing village. It is usually incorrectly spelled Wappingers. Its name is derived from

* The Arbor Vitæ is the *Thuya Occidentalis* of Linnæus. It is not the genuine white cedar, although it frequently bears that name. In New England it is often called Hackmatack. Its leaves lie in flattened masses along the stems, and each is filled with a vesicle containing a thin aromatic turpentine. It bears yellowish brown cones, about five lines in length.

CHAPTER XI.

HE house at Newburgh, which was occupied by Washington, was built by Jonathan Hasbrouck, in 1750, and is known by the respective names of "Hasbrouck House" and "Washington Headquarters." It has been the property of the State for several years, and a sufficient annual appropriation from the State treasury is made, to keep it, with the grounds around, in good order. Within it are collected many relics of the revolution, the war of 1812-15, and the war with Mexico.

In connection with this house, as the head-quarters of the army, occurred one of the most interesting events in the life of Washington, to which allusion has already been made. It was in the spring of 1783. Peace had been declared, a preliminary treaty had been signed by Great Britain and the United States, and the Continental Army was soon to be disbanded. The civil confederacy was weak. For a long time the Congress had been unable to pay the army, and officers and soldiers were likely to be sent home penniless, large pecuniary creditors of the country whose independence they had achieved. Secret consultations were held among a few of the officers. They had lost faith in the Congress, and began to doubt the feasibility of republican government, and some of them indirectly offered the power and title of King to Washington. He spurned the proposition with indignation. Then an appeal to the officers of the army was written, and secretly disseminated, in which grievances were set forth, and they were advised to take matters into their own hands, and, in effect, form a military despotism if the Congress should not speedily provide for their pay. Washington was informed of the movement. He resolved to control, without seeming to oppose it. He called a meeting of the officers, and the suspected ringleader of the movement was asked to preside. When all were assembled, Washington stepped forward and read to them a powerful appeal to their patriotism. His first words, before unfolding the paper, touched every heart. "You see, gentlemen," he said, as he placed his spectacles before his eyes, "that I have grown not only *grey*, but *blind*, in your service." His address, as usual, was short, pointed, convincing, and most persuasive. All eyes were filled with tears. The spirit of mutiny and revolt shrank abashed, and the assembly resolved unanimously, "That the officers of the American army view with abhorrence, and reject with disdain, the infamous propositions contained in a late anonymous address to the officers

WASHINGTON'S HEAD-QUARTERS AT NEWBURGH.

of the army." This scene did not occur at head-quarters, but in a large temporary building a few miles in the interior, near where the army lay at that time.

In the centre of the Hasbrouck House, or Head-quarters, is a large hall, having on one side an enormous fire-place, and containing seven doors, but only one window. Here Washington received his friends; here large companies dined; and here, from time to time, some of the most distinguished characters of the revolution, civil and military, were assembled. Colonel Nicholas Fish, of the Continental Army, used to

relate an interesting fact connected with this room. He was in Paris a
short time before the death of the Marquis de Lafayette, who had lodged
many nights beneath the roof of the "Hasbrouck House." Colonel Fish
was invited, with the American minister, on one occasion, to sup at the
house of the distinguished Marbois, who was the French Secretary of
Legation in the United States during the revolution. Lafayette was one
of the guests. At the supper hour the company was shown into a room
which contrasted quite oddly with the Parisian elegance of the other
apartments, where they had spent the evening. A low, boarded, painted

INTERIOR OF WASHINGTON'S HEAD-QUARTERS.

ceiling, with large beams, a single small, uncurtained window, with
numerous small doors, as well as the general style of the whole, gave, at
first, the idea of the kitchen, or largest room, of a Dutch or Belgian farm-
house. On a long rough table was a repast, just as little in keeping with
the refined *cuisines* of Paris, as the room was with its architecture. It
consisted of a large dish of meat, uncouth-looking pastry, and wine in
decanters and bottles, accompanied by glasses and silver mugs, such as
indicated other habits and tastes than those of modern Paris. "Do you
know where we now are?" said Marbois to Lafayette and his American

companions. They paused in surprise for a few minutes. They had seen something like it before, but when? and where? "Ah! the seven doors and one window," exclaimed Lafayette, "and the silver camp-goblets, such as the Marshals of France used in my youth! We are at Washington's Head-quarters, on the Hudson, fifty years ago!"

Upon the lawn, a little eastward of the Head-quarters, is a tall flag-staff, and near it a chaste monument, in the form of a mausoleum, made of brown sandstone, and erected early in the summer of 1860, over the grave of the latest survivor of Washington's life-guard. The monument

LIFE-GUARD MONUMENT.

was dedicated on the 18th of June, with appropriate services in connection with a large civic and military parade. It is about six feet in height, and is surmounted by a large recumbent wreath. On the river-front are the words:—"THE LAST OF THE LIFE GUARDS. UZAL KNAPP, BORN, 1759; DIED 1856. MONMOUTH, VALLEY FORGE, YORKTOWN." On the opposite side:—"ERECTED BY THE NEWBURGH GUARDS, COMPANY F., 19th REGIMENT, N. Y. S. M., JUNE, 1860." It is surrounded by a chain supported by granite posts, and is flanked by two pieces of heavy cannon. The monument was designed by H. K. Brown, the sculptor.

Mr. Knapp, the recipient of these honours, was, for a long time, the only surviving member of the body-guard of Washington, which was organised at Boston in the spring of 1776, and continued throughout the war. They were selected from all the regiments of the Continental Army, and chosen for their peculiar fitness of person and moral character. Mr. Knapp was a sergeant of the Guard, and was presented by Washington with a badge of Military Merit—the American Legion of Honour. In the autumn of 1855, the writer was at a public dinner where the old guardsman was a guest. He was then almost ninety-six years of age. When he was

NEWBURGH BAY.

about to leave the table, the company arose. The veteran addressed a few words to them, and concluded by inviting them all to his funeral! Just four months afterwards he died, and many who were at the feast were at the burial. By permission of his family, the citizens of Newburgh, after his body had lain in state for three days, buried him at the foot of the flag-staff, near the old head-quarters of his chief, where he had watched and sported three-quarters of a century before. It was over that grave the monument we have delineated was recently erected.

The natural scenery around Newburgh has an aspect of mingled grandeur and beauty, peculiar and unrivalled. Before the town is the lofty range of the Fishkill Mountains, on which signal fires were lighted during the revolution ; and the group of the Highlands, through which the Hudson flows. These are reflected in a broad and beautiful bay, at all times animated with a variety of water-craft and wild-fowl. Even in winter, when the frost has bridged the entire river, Newburgh Bay presents a lively scene almost every day, for ice-boats and skaters are there in great abundance. Its broad surface is broken by only a solitary rock island. One of the finest and most comprehensive views of Newburgh

FISHKILL LANDING AND NEWBURGH.

Bay may be obtained from the hill, just below the Fishkill and Newburgh railway-station, looking south-west. This view is given in our sketch. It includes the lower part of Newburgh, the mouth of the Quassaic Creek, the villages of New Windsor, and Cornwall, the beautiful low peninsula called Denning's Point on the left, and the higher one of Plum Point, on the western shore, seen in the centre. Just beyond the latter is the mouth of the Moodna, a fine clear stream that comes down from the hill-country of Orange County. The view is bounded on the left by the lofty hills extending westward from the Storm King, at whose base the Hudson enters the Highlands.

At Newburgh is the eastern terminus of a branch of the New York and Erie Railway, which passes through some of the most picturesque scenery in the world, between the Hudson and Delaware rivers.   In the vicinity of the village are charming drives, but no one is more attractive towards evening, than that along the river-bank, through New Windsor to

IDLEWILD FROM THE BROOK.

Idlewild, the residence of the well-known author, N. P. Willis, Esq.   I travelled that road on a hot afternoon in August.   The shadows were short; a soft breeze came up the river from the open northern door of the Highlands, whose rugged forms were bathed in golden light.   On the land not a leaf was stirred by a zephyr.   I crossed the Moodna, in whose shallow waters the cattle were seeking cool retreats, and I was glad to take shelter from the hot sun in the shadows of the old trees on the margin of the brook that rushes from the Glen at Idlewild. There all was cool, quiet, and delightful. The merry laugh of children came ringing like the tones of silver bells through the open grove. I sat down

IN THE GLEN AT IDLEWILD.

upon the bank of the brook, to enjoy the sweet repose of the scene, when, looking up, the cottage of Idlewild, half concealed by evergreens, stood in full view on the brow of the glen, two hundred feet above me. The whole acclivity is covered with the primeval wood, which presents an apparently impenetrable barrier to approach from below.

After sketching the attractive scene, I went leisurely up the deep, cool, dark glen, to its narrowest point, where the brook occupies the whole bottom of the gorge, and flows in picturesque rapids and cascades over and among rugged rocks and overhanging trees and shrubbery, with a rustic foot-bridge, the solitary testimony that man had ever penetrated that wild retreat.

A winding pathway lead from the slender bridge in the glen up to the cottage of Idlewild, which is at the north-eastern angle of the Highland Terrace, on which the village of Cornwall stands. The views from it are exceedingly beautiful. From the southern porch a lawn rises gently, beyond which nothing can be seen but the purple sides and summit of the Storm King, rising nearly 1,600 feet above the river. A little way from the cottage, a full view of Newburgh Bay and the river and country above may be obtained; and on the left, the placid estuary into which the Moodna* flows, reflects all the glories of sunset.

The Highland Terrace owes its name and fame to Mr. Willis, whose pen has been as potent as the wand of a magician in peopling that delightful spot with summer residents from New York. He has thoroughly "written it up." It is a fertile strip of land, quite elevated, lying at the foot of the north-western slopes of the mountains. The grape is cultivated there with success; and as its banks yield some of the finest brick-clay in the country, it has become a celebrated brick-making place. Cornwall Landing is at the base of the Terrace near the foot of the Storm King, and is reached from the plateau by a steep, winding road. During the summer months it exhibits gay scenes at the hours when the steamboats arrive. Many of the temporary residents of that vicinity have their own carriages, and these, filled with pleasure-seeking people, expecting

---

* This was called Murderer's Creek, because, in early times, a family of white people, who lived upon its banks, was murdered by the Indians. Mr. Willis, with a laudable desire to get rid of a name so unpleasant, sought reasons for establishing the belief that it is a corruption of the sweet Indian word *Moodna*. He has been successful, and the stream is now generally called Moodna's Creek. Such is also the name of the post-office there, established by the government. It is to be hoped that the old name will be speedily forgotten.

to meet friends, or only hoping to see new faces, quite cover the wharf at times, especially at evening.

From the Cornwall Landing an interesting view of the upper entrance to the Highlands, between the Storm King and Breakneck Hill, may be obtained. In our sketch, the former is seen on the right, the latter on the left. The river is here deep and narrow. The rocky shores, composed principally of granite and gneiss, embedding loose nodules and fixed veins

UPPER ENTRANCE TO THE HIGHLANDS.

of magnetic iron ore, rise from 1,000 to almost 1,600 feet above the river, and are scantily clothed with stunted trees. The range extends in a north-eastern and south-western direction across the Hudson, in the counties of Duchess and Putnam, Orange and Rockland, and connects with the Alleghanies. Geologists say that it is unequivocally a primitive chain, and in the early ages of the world must have opposed a barrier to the passage of the waters, and caused a vast lake which covered the

present Valley of the Hudson, extending to, if not over, Lake Champlain,
eastward to the Taghkanick Mountain, in Columbia County, and the
Highlands along the western borders of Massachusetts, and westward to
the Kayaderosseras Mountain, near Lake George, alluded to in our
description of the Upper Hudson. Such, they say, must have been in
former ages the "Ancient Lake of the Upper Valley of the Hudson,"
indicated by the levels and surveys of the present day, and by an
examination of the geological structure and alluvial formations of this
valley. The Indians called the range eastward of the Hudson, including
the Fishkill Mountains, *Matteawan*, or the Country of Good Fur. They
gave the same name to the stream that flows into the Hudson, on the
south side of Denning's Point, which the Dutch called *Vis Kill*, or Fish
Creek, and now known as the Fish Kill.

Toward the evening of the same hot day in August (1860), when I
rode from Newburgh to Idlewild and the Highland Terrace, I went in a
skiff around to the shaded nooks of the western shore below the Storm
King, and viewed the mountains in all their grandeur from their bases.
The Storm King, seen from the middle of the river abreast its eastern
centre, is almost semicircular in form, and gave to the minds of the
utilitarian Dutch skippers who navigated the Hudson early, the idea of a
huge lump of butter, and they named it *Boter Berg*, or Butter Hill. It
had borne that name until recently, when Mr. Willis successfully appealed
to the good taste of the public by giving it the more appropriate and
poetic title of Storm King. The appeal was met with a sensible response,
and the directors of the Hudson River Railway Company recognised its
fitness by naming a station at Breakneck Hill (when will a better name
for this be given?), opposite the Boter Berg, "Storm King Station." The
features of the mountain have been somewhat changed. For many years
past vast masses of stone have been quarried from its south-eastern face ;
until now the scene from its foot has the appearance given in the sketch.

Serrated Breakneck opposite has also been much quarried, and through
its narrow base, upon the brink of the river, a tunnel for the railway has
been pierced. Several years ago a powder blast, made by the quarriers
high up on the southern declivity of the mountain, destroyed an object
interesting to voyagers upon the river. From abreast the Storm King a

huge mass of rock was seen projected against the eastern sky in the perfect form of a human face, the branches of a tree forming an excellent representation of thick curly beard upon the chin. It was called the

AT THE FOOT OF THE STORM KING.

Turk's Head. By many it was mistaken for " Anthony's Nose," the huge promontory so called at the southern entrance to the Highlands a few miles below. Its demolition caused many expressions of regret, for it was regarded as a great curiosity, and an interesting feature in the Highland scenery on the river.

Just below the Storm King, at the foot of a magnificent valley composed of wooded slopes that come down from the high hills two or three miles westward, is the cottage of Mr. Lambertson, a resident of New York, who has chosen that isolated spot for a summer retreat. He has only one neighbour, who lives in another cottage beneath willow trees at the base of the Cro' Nest. This group of hills forms the southern boundary of their wild domain, and the Storm King the northern. In the slopes of

THE "POWELL" OFF THE STORM KING VALLEY.

the grand valley between these hills wild ravines are furrowed, and form channels for clear mountain streams, and every rood of that wilderness of several hundred acres is covered with timber. When in full foliage in summer it has the appearance, in every light, of green velvet. I have seen it in the morning and at evening, at meridian and in the light of the full moon, and on all occasions it had the same soft aspect in contrast with the rugged forms of Cro' Nest and the Storm King. That valley is always a delightful object to the eye, and should be sought for by the tourist. The last time I passed it was at sunset. I was on the swift steamer *Thomas Powell*, and at that hour the deep green of the foreground was fading higher up into a mingled colour of olive and pink, and softening into delicate purple, while the rocky summit of the Storm King cast over the whole the reflected effulgence of a brilliant evening sunlight. In this isolated spot among the mountains, Joseph Rodman Drake, whilst rambling alone many years ago, wrote *con amore* his beautiful poem,

SCENE OFF THE STORM KING VALLEY.

"The Culprit Fay," in which he thus summoned the fairies to a dance :—

"Ouphe and goblin! imp and sprite!
Elf of eve and starry fay!
Ye that love the moon's soft light,
Hither, hither, wend your way.
Twine ye in a jocund ring;
Sing and trip it merrily;
Hand to hand, and wing to wing,
Round the wild witch-hazel tree."

Whilst at the landing-place at Mr. Lambertson's, one of those black

electrical clouds, which frequently gather suddenly among the Highlands during the heats of July and August, came up from the west, obscured the sun, hovered upón the summit of the Storm King a few minutes, and then passed eastward, giving out only a few drops of rain where I stood, but casting down torrents in Newburgh Bay, accompanied by shafts of forked lightning and heavy peals of thunder. There was a perfect calm while the darkness brooded. Not a vessel was in sight, and no living thing was visible, except the white sea-gulls, which seem to be always on the

HIGHLAND ENTRANCE TO NEWBURGH BAY.

wing in the van or in the wake of a tempest. The shower passed eastward over the Matteawan Hills, when suddenly there appeared

"That beautiful one,
Whose arch is refraction, whose keystone the sun,
In the hues of its grandeur, sublimely it stood
O'er the river, the village, the field, and the wood,"

and cast a beautiful radiance over the great hills of the Shattemuc,*

---

* The Wappengi and Matteawan tribes called the Hudson *Shattemuc,* and the Highlands below the Matteawan, or Fishkill Mountains, the Hills of the Shattemuc.

among which I stood, gazing upon a sublime scene with wonder and delight.

After the shower had passed by, I rowed to the middle of the river, in the direction of Cold Spring village, on the eastern shore, and obtained a fine view of the Highland entrance to Newburgh Bay. The evening sun was pouring a flood of light upon the scene. On the left, in shadow, stood the Storm King, on the right was rugged Breakneck, with its neighbour, round Little Beacon Hill, and between was Pollopell's Island, a solitary rocky eminence, rising from the river, a mile north of them. Beyond these were seen the expanse of Newburgh Bay, the village, the cultivated country beyond, and the dim pale blue peaks of the Katzbergs, almost sixty miles distant. This view is always admired by travellers as one of the most agreeable in the whole village from New York to Albany.

On a cool, bright morning in August, I climbed to the bald summit of the Storm King, accompanied by a few friends. We procured a competent guide at Cornwall landing, and ascended the nearest and steepest part, where a path was to be found. It was a rough and difficult one, made originally by those who gathered hoop-poles upon the mountains. It was gullied in some places, and filled with stones in others, because it serves for the bed of a mountain torrent during showers and storms. Nearly half-way up to the first summit we found a spring of delicious water, where we rested. Occasionally we obtained glimpses of the country westward, where the horizon was bounded by the level summits of the Shawangunk Mountains.

We reached the first summit, after a fatiguing ascent of a mile and a half. It was not the highest, yet we had a very extensive prospect of the country around, except on the east, which was hidden by the higher points of the mountain. At last the greatest altitude was reached, after making our way another mile over rocky ledges, and through gorges filled with shrub-oaks, and other bushes. There a glorious picture filled us with exquisite pleasure. We felt amply rewarded for all our toil. The sky was cloudless, and the atmosphere perfectly clear. The scenery, in some features, was similar to, but in all others totally unlike, that of the Adirondack region. Looking northward, the river was seen in its slightly winding course to Crom Elbow, twenty-six miles distant, with the intermediate villages along its banks. On each side of the river, and sloping back to high ranges of hills (the shores of the ancient lake already alluded to), was spread out one of the most fertile and wealthy regions on the continent.

Our view included portions of seven counties in the State of New York, and of three in Connecticut, with numerous little inland villages. In the extreme north-west were the Katzbergs, and, in the north-east, the

NORTHERN VIEW FROM THE STORM KING.

Taghkanick range, with the hills of western Massachusetts and Connecticut. Almost at our feet lay Cornwall, and a little beyond were New Windsor and Canterbury, and the whole country back of Newburgh, made memorable by events of the war for independence. Before us lay the old camp-grounds of the Continental Army, the spot where the patriotism of the officers was tried to the utmost in the spring of 1783, as already explained; the quarters occupied by Washington at New Windsor and Newburgh; of Lafayette, at the Square; of Greene and Knox, at Morton's; and of Steuben, at Verplanck's. There was Plum Point and Pollopell's Island, between which a sort of *chevaux-de-frise* was constructed in 1776. Pollopell's Island lay beneath us. The solitary house of a fisherman upon it appeared like a wren's cage in size, and the kingdom of his insane wife, who imagines herself to be the Queen of England, and her husband the Prince Consort, seemed not much larger than one of her spouse's drag-nets. If he is not a Prince Consort, he is the sole ruler of the little domain which he inhabits, and he may say, as did Selkirk—

"I am monarch of all I survey,
My right there is none to dispute,
From the centre all round to the sea,
I am lord of the fowl and the brute."

The passing trains upon the Hudson River Railway, and large steamers, and more than forty sail of vessels of all sizes, seen upon the river at the same time, appeared almost like toys for children. Yet small as they seemed, and diminutive as we must have appeared from below, signals with white handkerchiefs, given by some of our party, brought responses in kind from the windows of the railway cars.

The view southward from the summit of the Storm King is not so extensive as northward and westward, but includes an exceedingly interesting region. In the distance, on the south-east, beyond the range of wooded hills that bound the view from less elevated eminences of the Highlands, the fine cultivated hill country of Putnam County was seen. Anthony's Nose, Bear Mountain, and the Dunderberg, at their southern entrance, were too high to permit glimpses of Westchester and Rockland counties below. These may be seen from the Great Beacon Hill of the Fishkill range, on the opposite side of the river. With a good telescope the city of New York may also be seen. But within the range of our unaided vision, lay fields of action, the events of which occupy large spaces in history. There was Philipsburg, where the Continental Army was encamped, and almost every soldier was inoculated with the kine-pox, to shield him from the ravages of the small-pox. The camp, for a while, became a vast lazar-house. There was Constitution Island, clustered with associations connected with the fall of Forts Clinton and Montgomery, and the Great Chain, which we shall presently consider; and beyond, among the shadows of old trees at the foot of the Sugar-Loaf Mountain, was seen the house occupied as head-quarters by Arnold, from which he escaped to the *Vulture* sloop-of-war, when his treason was discovered. Only a small portion of West Point could be seen, for the Cro' Nest group loomed up between; but over these, more westward, the landscape included the entire range of higher hills away toward Chester, the Clove,

SOUTHERN VIEW FROM THE STORM KING.

and the Ramapo Pass, with the solid-looking mass of the Shunnemunk beyond Canterbury.

It was after meridian when we had finished our observations from the lofty head of the Storm King, and sat down to lunch in the broken shadows of a stunted pine-tree. We descended the mountain by the path that we went up, and at Cornwall took a skiff and rowed to West Point, making some sketches and observations by the way. When a little below the Storm King Valley, we came to the high bluff known as Kidd's Plug Cliff, where the rocks rise almost perpendicularly several hundred feet from *débris* near the water's edge, which is covered with shrubbery.

KIDD'S PLUG CLIFF.

High up on the smooth face of the rock, is a mass slightly projecting, estimated to be twelve feet in diameter, and by form and position suggesting, even to the dullest imagination, the idea of an enormous plug stopping an orifice. The fancy of some one has given it the name of Captain Kidd's Plug, in deference to the common belief that that noted pirate buried immense sums of money and other treasures somewhere in the Highlands. Within a few years ignorant and credulous persons, misled by pretended seers in the clairvoyant condition, have dug in search of those treasures in several places near West Point; and some, it is said, have been ignorant and credulous enough to believe that the almost

CROW'S NEST.

mythical buccaneer had, by some supernatural power, mounted these rocks to the point where the projection is seen, discovered there an excavation, deposited vast treasures within it, and secured them by inserting the enormous stone plug seen from the waters below. It is plainly visible from vessels passing near the western shore.

Kidd's Plug Cliff is a part of the group of hills which form Cro' Nest (the abbreviation of Crow's Nest), a name given to a huge hollow among the summits of these hills. They are rocky heights, covered with trees and shrubbery, and, by their grouping, seen from particular points of view, suggest the idea of an enormous crow's nest. By some the signal high summit above the Plug Cliff is called Cro' Nest; and it is in allusion to that lofty hill that Morris, its "neighbour over the way," wrote—

> "Where Hudson's waves o'er silvery sands
> Winds through the hills afar,
> And Cro' Nest like a monarch stands,
> Crowned with a single star."

CHAPTER XII.

AS we passed the foot of Cro' Nest, we caught pleasant glimpses of West Point, where the government of the United States has a military school, and in a few moments the whole outline of the promontory and the grand ranges of hills around and beyond it, was in full view. We landed in a sheltered cove a little above Camp Town, the station of United States troops and other residents at the Point, and climbed a very steep hill to the Cemetery upon its broad and level summit, more than a hundred feet above the river. It is a shaded, quiet, beautiful retreat, consecrated to the repose of the dead, and having thoughtful visitors at all hours on pleasant days.

> "There, side by side, the dark green cedars cluster,
>   Like sentries watching by that camp of death;
> There, like an army's tents, with snow-white lustre,
>   The grave-stones gleam beneath.
>
> "Few are the graves, for here no populous city
>   Feeds, with its myriad lives, the hungry Fate;
> While hourly funerals, led by grief or pity,
>   Crowd through the open gate.
>
> "Here sleep brave men, who, in the deadly quarrel,
>   Fought for their country, and their life-blood poured;
> Above whose dust she carves the deathless laurel,
>   Wreathing the victor's sword.
>
> "And here the young cadet, in manly beauty,
>   Borne from the tents which skirt those rocky banks,
> Called from life's daily drill and perilous duty
>   To these unbroken ranks"

The most conspicuous object in the Cemetery is the Cadet's Monument, situated at the eastern angle. It is a short column, of castle form, composed of light brown hewn stone, surmounted by military emblems and a foliated memorial urn, wrought from the same material. It was erected in the autumn of 1818, to the memory of Vincent M. Lowe, of New York, by his brother cadets. He was accidentally killed by the discharge of a cannon, on the 1st of January, 1817. The names of several other officers and cadets are inscribed upon the monument, it having been adopted by the members of the institution as " sacred to the memory of the deceased " whose names are there recorded.

CADET'S MONUMENT.

From the brow of the hill, near the Cadet's Monument, is a comprehensive view of the picturesque village of Cold Spring, on the east side of the river, occupying a spacious alluvial slope, bounded by rugged heights on the north, and connected, behind a range of quite lofty mountains, with the fertile valleys of Duchess and Putnam Counties. We shall visit it

presently.   Meanwhile let us turn our eyes southward, and from another
point on the margin of the Cemetery, where a lovely shaded walk invites
the strollers on warm afternoons, survey Camp Town at our feet, with
West Point and the adjacent hills.   In this view we see the Old Landing-
place, the road up to the plateau, the Laboratory buildings, the Siege
Battery, the Hotel, near the remains of old Fort Clinton, upon the highest
ground on the plain, the blue dome of the Chapel, the turrets of the great

COLD SPRING, FROM THE CEMETERY.

Mess Hall, on the extreme right, the Cove, crossed by the Hudson River
Railway, and the range of hills on the eastern side of the river.

Following this walk to the entrance gate, we traverse a delightful
winding road along the river-bank, picturesque at every turn, to the
parting of the ways.   One of these leads to the Point, the other up Mount
Independence, on whose summit repose the grey old ruins of Fort Putnam.
We had ascended that winding mountain road many times before, and
listened to the echoes of the sweet bugle, or the deeper voices of the
morning and evening gun at the Point.   Now we were invited by a
shady path, and a desire for novelty, from the road between Forts Webb
and Putnam, into the deep rocky gorge between Mount Independence and

the more lofty Redoubt Hill, to the rear of the old fortress, where it wears the appearance of a ruined castle upon a mountain crag. The afternoon sun was falling full upon the mouldering ruin, and the chaotic mass of rocks beneath it; while the clear blue sky and white clouds presented the whole group, with accompanying evergreens, in the boldest relief. Making our way back, by another but more difficult path, along the foot of the steep acclivity, we soon stood upon the broken walls of Fort Putnam, 500 feet above the river, with a scene before us of unsurpassed interest and beauty, viewed in the soft light of the evening sun. At our

WEST POINT, FROM THE CEMETERY.

feet lay the promontory of West Point, with its Military Academy, the quarters of the officers and the cadets, and other buildings of the institution. To the left lay Constitution Island, from a point of which, where a ruined wall now stands, to the opposite shore of the main, a massive iron chain was laid upon floating timbers by the Americans, at the middle of the old war for independence. Beyond the island arose the smoke of the furnaces and forges, the spires, and the roofs of Cold Spring. Toward the left loomed up the lofty Mount Taurus, vulgarly called Bull Hill, at whose base, in the shadow of a towering wall of rock, and in the midst of grand old trees, nestles Under Cliff, then the home of Morris, whose songs have delighted thousands in both hemispheres.   On the extreme left arose old Cro' Nest; and over its right shoulder lay the rugged range of Break Neck, dipping to the river sufficiently to reveal the beautiful country beyond, on the borders of Newburgh Bay.   This is one of the most attractive points of view on the Hudson.

FORT PUTNAM, FROM THE WEST.

Fort Putnam was erected by the Americans in 1778, for the purpose of defending Fort Clinton, on West Point below, and to more thoroughly secure the river against the passage of hostile fleets.   It was built under the direction of Colonel Rufus Putnam, and chiefly by the men of his Massachusett's regiment.   It commanded the river above and below the Point, and was almost impregnable, owing to its position.   In front, the mountain is quite steep for many yards, and then slopes gently to the plain; while on its western side, a perpendicular wall of rock, fifty feet in height, would have been presented to the enemy. Redoubts were also built upon other eminences in the vicinity. These being chiefly earth works, have been almost obliterated by the action of storms; and Fort Putnam was speedily disappearing under the hands of industrious neighbours, who were carrying off the stone for building purposes, when

VIEW FROM FORT PUTNAM.

the work of demolition was arrested by the Government. Its remains, consisting of only broken walls and two or three arched casemates, all overgrown with vines and shrubbery, are now carefully preserved. Even the cool spring that bubbles from the rocks in its centre, is kept clear of choking leaves; and we may reasonably hope that the ruins of Fort Putnam will remain, an object of interest to the passing traveller, for more than a century to come.

The winding road from the fort to the plain is quite steep much of the way, but is so well wrought that carriages may safely traverse it; and the tourist is led by it to one of the loveliest of river and mountain views northward from the Point, in front of the residences of Mr. Weir, the eminent artist, and other professors employed in the Military Academy. Passing along the shaded walk in front of these mansions, on the margin of a high bank, a white marble obelisk is seen upon a grassy knoll on the left, shooting up from a cluster of dark evergreen trees. It was erected by Major-General Jacob Brown, of the United States army, in memory of

LIEUTENANT-COLONEL WOOD'S MONUMENT.

his youthful and well beloved companion-in-arms, Lieutenant-Colonel E. D. Wood, of the corps of Engineers, who fell while heading a charge, at the sortie of Fort Erie, in Upper Canada, on the 17th of September, 1814. He had been a pupil of the Military Academy at West Point. "He was," says one of the inscriptions, "exemplary as a Christian, and distinguished as a soldier."

Passing a little farther on, a gravelled walk diverges riverward, and leads down to the Siege Battery of six guns, erected by the cadets while in the performance of their practical exercises in engineering. The cannon were housed, and no gunners were near, yet the works appeared formidable. They were composed of gabions, covered with turf, soft and even as fine velvet. The battery commands one of the most pleasing views from the Point, comprising Constitution Island, Mount Taurus, and Break Neck on the right; Cro' Nest and the Storm King on the left; and ten miles of the river, with Pollopell's Island and the shores above Newburgh in the centre. A similar view is obtained from the piazza of Roe's Hotel, on the brow of the hill just above.

A little westward of the Siege Battery are the buildings of the

VIEW FROM THE SIEGE BATTERY.

Laboratory of the institution, in which are deposited some interesting relics of the old war for independence. One of the most attractive groups among these relics was composed of several links of the great iron chain, already mentioned, that spanned the river, enclosing a large brass mortar, taken from the British at Stoney Point, by Wayne, and two smaller ones, that were among the spoils of victory at Saratoga. There were a dozen links of the chain, and two huge clevises. The links were made of iron bars, $2\frac{1}{2}$ inches square. Their average length was a little over 2 feet, and their weight about 140 pounds each. The chain was stretched across the river at the narrowest place, just above Gee's Point (the extreme rocky end of West Point) and Constitution Island.   It was laid across a boom of heavy logs, that floated near together.   These were 16 feet long, and pointed at each end, so as to offer little resistance to the tidal currents. The chain was fastened to these logs by staples, and at each shore by huge blocks of wood and stone.   This chain and boom seemed to afford an efficient barrier to the passage of vessels ; but their strength was never tested, as the keel of an enemy's ship never ploughed the Hudson after

THE GREAT CHAIN.

the fleet of Vaughan passed up and down in the autumn of 1777, and performed its destructive mission.

The views from Roe's Hotel, on the extreme northern verge of the summit of the plain of West Point, are very pleasing in almost every direction.   The one northward, similar to that from the Siege Battery, is the finest.   Westward the eye takes in the Laboratory, Lieutenant-Colonel Wood's Monument, a part of the shaded walk along the northern margin of the plain, and Mount Independence, crowned with the ruins of Fort Putnam.   Southward the view comprehends the entire Parade, and glimpses, through the trees, of the Academy, the Chapel, the Mess Hall, and other buildings of the institution, with some of the officers' quarters and professors' residences on the extreme right. The earthworks of Fort Clinton have recently been restored, in their original form and general proportions, exactly upon their ancient site, and present, with the beautiful trees growing within their green banks, a very pleasant object from every point of view. The old fort was constructed in the spring of 1778, under the direction of the brave Polish soldier, Thaddeus Kosciuszko, who was then a colonel in the Continental Army, and chief

WESTERN VIEW, FROM ROE'S HOTEL.

of the Engineers' corps. The fort, when completed, was 600 yards around, within the walls. The embankments were 21 feet at the base, and 14 feet in height. Barracks and huts sufficient to accommodate six hundred persons were erected within the fort. It stood upon a cliff, on the margin of the plain, 180 feet above the river.

Kosciuszko was much beloved by the Revolutionary Army, and his memory is held in reverence by the American people. He was only twenty years of age when he joined that army. He had been educated at the Military School of Warsaw. He had not completed his studies, when he eloped with a beautiful girl of high rank. They were overtaken by the maiden's father, who made a violent attempt to seize his daughter. The young Pole was compelled either to slay the father or abandon the daughter. He chose the latter, and obtaining the permission of his sovereign, he went to France, and there became a student in drawing and military science. In Paris he was introduced to Dr. Franklin, and, fired with a desire to aid a people fighting for independence, he sailed for America, bearing letters from that minister. He applied to Washington

THE PARADE.

for employment. "What do you seek here?" asked the leader of the armies of the revolted colonies. "I come to fight as a volunteer for American independence," the young Pole replied. "What can you do?" Washington asked. "Try me," was Kosciuszko's prompt reply. Pleased with the young man, Washington took him into his military family. The Congress soon afterwards appointed him engineer, with the rank of colonel. He returned to Poland at the close of the Revolution, and was made a major-general under Poniatowski. He was at the head of the military movements of the Revolution in Poland, in 1794, and was made a prisoner, and carried to St. Petersburg. This event caused Campbell to write—

> "Hope for a season bade the earth farewell,
> And freedom shrieked when Kosciuszko fell."

After the Empress Catherine died, the Emperor Paul liberated him, offered him command in the Russian service, and presented him with his

KOSCIUSZKO'S MONUMENT.

own sword. He declined it, saying, "I no longer need a sword, since I have no longer a country to defend." He revisited the United States in 1797, when the Congress granted him land in consideration of his services. He afterwards lived in Switzerland, and there he died in 1817. A public funeral was made for him at Warsaw. Twelve years afterwards, the cadets of West Point, actuated by love for the man and reverence for his deeds, erected a beautiful marble monument to his memory, within the ruins of Old Fort Clinton, at a cost of about $5,000. It bears upon one side the name of—" KOSCIUSZKO," and on another, the simple inscription —" ERECTED BY THE CORPS OF CADETS, 1828." It is a conspicuous and pleasing object to voyagers upon the river.

Passing along the verge of the cliff, southward from Kosciuszko's monument, the visitor soon reaches another memorial stone. It is of white marble, the chief member being a fluted column, entwined by a laurel wreath, held in the beak of an eagle, perched upon its top. The

DADE'S COMMAND'S MONUMENT.

pedestal is of temple form, square, with a row of encircling stars upon its entablature, and a cannon, like a supporting column, at each corner. It was erected to commemorate a battle fought between a detachment of United States troops, under Major Francis L. Dade, and a party of Seminole Indians, in the Everglades of Florida, on the 28th of December, 1835. The detachment consisted of one hundred and eight men, all of whom, save three, were massacred by the savages on that occasion. The troops nobly defended themselves, and made no attempt to retreat. Their remains repose near St. Augustine, in Florida. This monument was erected by the three regiments and the medical staff, from which the detachment was selected.

A few feet from Dade's Command's Monument, a narrow path, through a rocky passage, overhung with boughs and shrubbery, leads down to a pleasant terrace in the steep bank of the river, which is called Kosciuszko's Garden. At the back of the terrace the rock rises perpendicularly, and

KOSCIUSZKO'S GARDEN.

from its outer edge descends as perpendicularly to the river. This is said to have been Kosciuszko's favourite place of resort for reading and meditation, while he was at West Point. He found a living spring bubbling from the rocks, in the middle of the terrace, and there he constructed a pretty little fountain. Its ruins were discovered in 1802, and repaired. The water now rises into a marble basin. Seats have been provided for visitors, ornamental shrubs have been planted, and the whole place wears an aspect of mingled romance and beauty. A deep circular indentation in the rock back of the fountain was made, tradition affirms, by a cannon-ball sent from a British ship, while the Polish soldier was occupying his accustomed loitering place, reading Vauban, and regaled by the perfume of roses. From this quiet, solitary retreat, a pathway, appropriately called Flirtation Walk, leads up to the plain.

A short distance from Kosciuszko's Garden, upon a higher terrace, is Battery Knox, constructed by the cadets. It commands a fine view of

VIEW FROM BATTERY KNOX.

the eastern shore of the Hudson, in the Highlands, and down the river to Anthony's Nose. Near by are seen the Cavalry Stables and the Cavalry Exercise Hall, belonging to the Military School; and below there is seen the modern West Point Landing. A little higher up, on the plain, are the groups of spacious edifices, used for the purposes of the institution.

West Point was indicated by Washington, as early as 1783, as an eligible place for a military academy. In his message to the Congress in

1793, he recommended the establishment of one at West Point. The subject rested until 1802, when Congress made provision by law for such an institution there. Very little progress was made in the matter until the year 1812, when, by another act of Congress, a corps of engineers and professors were organised, and the school was endowed with the most attractive features of a literary institution, mingled with that of a military character. From that time until the present, the academy has been increasing in importance, as the nursery of army officers and skilful practical engineers.

The buildings of the West Point Military Academy consisted, at the time we are considering, of cadets' barracks, cadets' guard-house, academy, mess hall, hospital of cadets, chapel, observatory, and library, artillery laboratory, hospital for troops, equipments shed, engineer troops' barracks, post guard-house, dragoons' barracks, artillery barracks, cavalry exercise hall, cavalry stables, powder magazine, the quarters of the officers and professors of the Academy, workshops, commissary of cadets and sutlers' store, shops and cottages for the accommodation of non-commissioned officers and their families, laundresses of the cadets, &c. The principal edifices are built of granite.

The post is under the general command of a superintendent, who bears the rank of brevet-colonel. The average number of cadets was about two hundred and fifty. Candidates for admission are selected by the War Department at Washington city, and they are required to report themselves for examination to the superintendent of the academy between the first and twentieth day of June. None are admitted who are less than sixteen or more than twenty-one years of age, who are less than five feet in height, or who are deformed or otherwise unfit for military duty. Each cadet, on admission, is obliged to subscribe his name to an agreement to serve in the army of the United States four years, in addition to his four years of instruction, unless sooner discharged by competent authority.

The course of instruction consists of infantry tactics and military policy, mathematics, the French language, natural philosophy, drawing, chemistry, mineralogy, artillery tactics, the science of gunnery and the duties of a military laboratory, engineering and the science of war, geography, history and ethics, the use of the sword, and cavalry exercise and tactics. The rules and regulations of the academy are very strict and salutary, and the instruction in all departments is thorough and complete.

The road from the plain to the landing at West Point was cut from the steep rocky bank of the river, at a heavy expense to the government. The wharf is spacious, and there a sentinel was continually posted, with a slate and pencil, to record the names of all persons who arrive and depart. This was for the use of the Superintendent, by which means he

THE BEVERLY HOUSE.

is informed daily of the arrival of any persons to whom he might wish to extend personal or professional courtesies.

A steam ferry-boat connects West Point with the Garrison Station of the Hudson River Railway, opposite. Near the latter is the old ferry-place of the Revolution, where troops crossed to and from West Point. Here Washington crossed on the morning when General Arnold's treason was discovered, and here he held a most anxious consultation with Colonel Hamilton when that event was suspected.

We crossed the ferry to Garrison's, and from the road near the station obtained a pleasant view of West Point, glimpses of the principal buildings there, and the range of lofty hills beyond, which form the group of the Cro' Nest and the Storm King. Following a winding road up the east bank of the river from this point, we came to a mill, almost hidden among the trees at the head of a dark ravine, through which flows a clear mountain stream, called Kedron Brook, wherefore, I could not learn, for there is no resemblance to Jerusalem or the Valley of Jehoshaphat near. It is a portion of the beautiful estate of Ardenia, the property of Richard Arden, Esq. His son, Lieutenant Thomas Arden, a graduate of the West Point Military Academy, owns and occupies Beverly, near by, the former residence of Colonel Beverly Robinson (an eminent American loyalist during the war for independence), and the head-quarters of General Benedict Arnold at the time of his treason. It is situated upon a broad and fertile terrace, at the foot of Sugar-Loaf Mountain, one of the eastern ranges of the Highlands, which rises eight hundred feet above the plain.

CHAPTER XIII.

T was mid-autumn when we visited Beverly House, and the Sugar-Loaf Mountain, at the foot of which it stands, exhibited those gorgeous hues which give such unequalled splendour to American forests at that season of the year. The beautiful hues of the foliage of the maple, hickory, chestnut, birch, sassafras, and several other kinds of deciduous trees in the Northern and Middle States, seen just before the falling of the leaf in autumn, are almost unknown in Europe. A picture by Cropsey, one of the most eminent of living American landscape painters, in which this peculiarity of foliage was represented, drew from one of the minor English poets the following sonnet:—

CROPSEY'S "AUTUMN ON THE HUDSON."

[ADDRESSED TO J. T. FIELD, OF BOSTON.]

Forgot are Summer and our English air;
Here is your Autumn with her wondrous dyes;
Silent and vast your forests round us rise:
God, glorified in Nature, fronts us there,
In His transcendent works as heavenly fair
As when they first seemed good unto His eyes.
See, what a brightness on the canvas lies!
Hues, seen not here, flash on us everywhere;
Radiance that Nature here from us conceals;
Glory with which she beautifies decay
In your far world, this master's hand reveals,
Wafting our blest sight from dimmed streets away,—
With what rare power!—to where our awed soul kneels
To Him who bade these splendours light the day.

W. C. BENNETT.

From the summit is a grand and extensive view of the surrounding scenery, which Dr. Dwight (afterwards President of Yale College) described, in 1778, as "majestic, solemn, wild, and melancholy." Dwight was then chaplain of a Connecticut regiment stationed at West Point, and ascended the Sugar Loaf with the soldier-poet, Colonel Humphreys.

Under the inspiration of feeling awakened by the grandeur of the sight, he conceived and partly composed his prophetic hymn, beginning with the words—

"Columbia! Columbia! to glory arise,
The queen of the world and the child of the skies."

General Arnold was at the mansion of Colonel Robinson (Beverly House) on the morning of the 24th of September, 1780, fully persuaded that his treasonable plans for surrendering West Point and its dependencies into the hands of Sir Henry Clinton, the British commander-in-chief,—then in possession of New York,—for the consideration of a brigadier's commission in the British army, and £10,000 in gold, were working prosperously. This subject we shall consider more in detail hereafter. We will only notice, in this connection, events that occurred at the Beverly House.

Major André, Arnold's immediate accomplice in treasonable designs, had, in a personal interview, arranged the details of the wicked bargain, and left for New York. Arnold believed he had arrived there in safety, with all requisite information for Sir Henry; and that before Washington's return from Connecticut, whither he had gone to hold a conference with Rochambeau and other French officers, Clinton would have sailed up the Hudson and taken possession of the Highland fortresses. But André did not reach New York. He was captured on his way, by militia-men, as a suspicious-looking traveller. Evidences of his character as a spy were found upon his person, and he was detained. Washington returned sooner than Arnold expected him. To the surprise of the traitor, Hamilton and Lafayette reached the Beverly House early on the morning of the 24th, and announced that Washington had turned down to the West Point Ferry, and would be with them soon. At breakfast Arnold received a letter from an officer below, saying, "*Major André, of the British Army, is a prisoner in my custody.*" The traitor had reason to expect that evidences of his own guilt might arrive at any moment. He concealed his emotions. With perfect coolness he ordered a horse to be made ready, alleging that his presence was needed "over the river" immediately. He then left the table, went into the great passage, and hurried up the broad staircase to his wife's chamber. In brief and hurried words he told her that they must instantly part, perhaps for ever, for his life depended on his reaching the enemy's lines without detection. Horror-stricken, the poor young creature, but one year a mother, and not two a wife, swooned and sank senseless upon the floor. Arnold dare not call for assistance, but kissing, with lips blasted by words of guilt and treason, his boy, then sleeping in angel innocence and purity, he rushed from the room, mounted a horse, hastened to the river, flung himself into his barge, and directing the six oarsmen to row swiftly down the Hudson, escaped to the *Vulture*, a British sloop-of-war, lying far below.

THE STAIRCASE OF THE ROBINSONS' HOUSE.

Washington arrived at the Beverly House soon after Arnold left it. As yet no suspicion of treason had entered his mind. After a hasty breakfast, he crossed to West Point, expecting to find Arnold there. " I have heard nothing from him for two days," said Colonel Lamb, the commanding officer. Washington's suspicions were awakened. He soon re-crossed the river, where he was met by Hamilton with papers just received revealing Arnold's guilt. He called in Knox and Lafayette for counsel. " Whom can we trust now ? " he inquired with calmness, while deep sorrow evidently stirred his bosom. At the same time the condition of Mrs. Arnold, who was frantic with grief and apprehension, awakened his liveliest sympathies. "The general went up to see her," wrote

THE INDIAN FALLS.

Hamilton in describing the scene. "She upbraided him with being in a plot to murder her child, for she was quite beside herself. One moment she raved; another she melted into tears. Sometimes she pressed her

infant to her bosom, and lamented its fate, occasioned by the imprudence
of its father, in a manner that would have moved insensibility itself."
Washington believed her innocent of all previous knowledge of her husband's guilt, and did all in his power to soothe her. "She is as good and
innocent as an angel, and as incapable of doing wrong," Arnold wrote to
Washington, from the *Vulture*, imploring protection for his wife and
child. Ample protection was afforded, and Mrs. Arnold and her infant

VIEW SOUTH FROM DU'ILH'F.

were conveyed in safety to her friends. She was the traitor's second wife,
and the daughter of Mr. Shippen, a loyalist of Philadelphia; and she was
only eighteen years of age at the time of her marriage to Arnold, while
he was military governor of that city, in 1778. The child above-
mentioned was named James Robertson Arnold. He entered the British
army, and rose to the rank of Colonel of Engineers. He was at one time
the aide-de-camp of her Majesty. In 1841 he was transferred from the

Engineers' corps, and in 1846 was a major-general and a Knight of the Royal Hanoverian Guelphic Order.

Mr. Arden kindly took us in his carriage from Beverly to Indian Brook, a clear mountain stream that makes its way in rapids and cascades, through a wild ravine, from the hills to the river. It falls into the deep marshy bay between Garrison's and Cold Spring. We stopped on the way to

INDIAN BROOK.

view the river and mountains below West Point, from the residence of Eugene Dutihl, Esq. His mansion is upon a point of the plain, shaded by a grove of pines, overlooking a deep dark dell, with a sparkling brook in its bosom, on one side, and the river and grand mountain scenery on the other. The view southward from his piazza is one of the most interesting and beautiful (though not the most extensive) among the

Highlands, comprehending the site of Forts Clinton and Montgomery— the theatre of stirring and most important events in the war for independence. From thence we passed along the brow of the declivity next the river, to the mansion of Ardenia, from which one of the finest views of West Point may be obtained; and then rode to Indian Brook, passing, on the way, the ancient Philipsburg Church—in which the officers of the Continental Army had worshipped during the Revolution—and the grounds and mansions of wealthy residents in that vicinity.

We crossed Indian Brook on a rustic bridge, just below the Indian Falls, whose murmur fell upon the ear before we came in sight of the stream. These falls have formed subjects for painting and poetry, and are the delight of the neighbourhood in summer. In the small space allotted for each of our illustrations and accompanying descriptions, we can convey only faint ideas of the wild beauty of the scenes we are called upon to depict in this mountain region of the Hudson. We were on the Indian Brook on a bright October day, when the foliage was in its greatest autumnal splendour, and the leaves were falling in gentle showers among the trees, the rocks, and in the sparkling water, appearing like fragments of rainbows cast, with lavish hand, into the lap of earth. At every turn of the brook, from its springs to its union with the Hudson, a pleasant subject for the painter's pencil is presented. Just below the bridge, where the highway crosses, is one of the most charming of these "bits." There, in the narrow ravine, over which the tree tops intertwine, huge rocks are piled, some of them covered with feathery fern, others with soft green mosses, and others as bare and angular as if just broken from some huge mass, and cast in there by Titan hands. In midsummer this stream is still more attractive, for there, as Street has sung of the Willewemoc,—

> "A fresh, damp sweetness fills the scene,
>   From dripping leaf and moistened earth,
> The odour of the winter green
>   Floats on the airs that now have birth;
> Plashes and air-bells all about
> Proclaim the gambols of the trout,
> And calling bush and answering tree
> Echo with woodland melody."

In the neighbourhood of this mountain stream are delightful summer honourable Gouverneur Kemble, an intimate and life-long friend of Irving and Paulding, and a former proprietor, withdrew from active participation in the business of the establishment several years ago, and is now enjoying life there in elegant retirement, and dispensing a generous hospitality. He has a gallery of rare and excellent pictures, and a choice library; and is surrounded by evidences of refined taste and thorough cultivation.

Leaving the residence of Mr. Kemble at twilight, we made our way

WEST POINT FOUNDRY.

through the grove, and the village of Cold Spring beyond, to "Undercliff," the summer dwelling of America's best lyric poet, George P. Morris, wh

cupolas and three air furnaces; two boring mills; three blacksmiths' shops; a trip-hammer weighing eight tons for heavy wrought iron-work; a turning shop; a boiler shop; and several other buildings use for various purposes. The quantity of iron then used varied with the nature and demand of work. Upward of fifty tons of pig metal had been melted for a single casting. The annual consumption varied from 5,000 to 10,000 tons, with about 1,000 tons of boiler-plate and wrought-iron. The number of hands the employed was about 500. Sometimes 700 men were at work there. The establishment is conducted b Robert P. Parrott, Esq., formerly a captain of Ordnance in the United States Army, and the inventor the celebrated "Parrott gun," so extensively used, as among the best of the heavy ordnance, during th late Civil War. These, with appropriate projectiles, were manufactured in great numbers at the We Point Foundry, during the war, from 1861 to 1865.

residences, fitted for occupation all the year round. Among the most pleasing of these, in their relation to the surrounding scenery, are those of Dr. Moore, late President of Columbia College, and Mr. De Rham, a retired merchant. We passed through their grounds on our way to Cold Spring village, and wished for space, among our sketches of the Highland scenery, for pen and pencil pictures of charming spots upon these and the neighbouring estates.

Our road to Cold Spring lay through the region occupied by portions of

VIEW FROM ROSSITER'S MANSION.

the American army at different times during the old war for independence. There, in the spring of 1781, the troops and others stationed there were inoculated with the small-pox. "All the soldiers, with the women and children," wrote Dr. Thacher, an army surgeon, "who have not had the small-pox, are now under inoculation." "Of five hundred who were inoculated here," he wrote subsequently, "only four have died." This was about fifteen years before Jenner made successful experiments in vaccination.

This portion of the Highlands is a charming region for the tourist on the Hudson; and the lover of nature, in her aspects of romantic beauty and quiet majesty, should never pass it by.

The first glimpse of Cold Spring village from the road is from the northern slope of an eminence thickly sprinkled with boulders, which commands a perfect view of the whole amphitheatre of hills, and the river winding among them. We turned into a rude gate on the left, and followed a newly-beaten track to the brow of this eminence, on the southern verge of which Rossiter, the eminent painter (a copy of whose picture of 'Washington at Mount Vernon' was presented to the Prince of Wales at the National Capitol in 1860), is erecting an elegant villa. The house was nearly completed, but the grounds around were in a state of transition from the ruggedness of the wilderness to the mingled aspects of Art and Nature, formed by the direction of good taste. It is a delightful place for an artist to reside, commanding one of the most extensive and picturesque views to be found in all that Highland region. The river is seen broken into lakes, in appearance; and on all sides rise in majesty the everlasting hills. Only at one point—a magnificent vista between Mount Taurus and the Storm King—can the world without be seen. Through it a glimpse may be had of the beautiful country around Newburgh.

Below us we could hear the deep breathing of furnaces, and the sullen monotonous pulsations of trip-hammers, busily at work at the West Point Foundry, the most extensive and complete of the iron-works of the United States. Following a steep, stony ravine that forms the bed of a water-course during rain-storms, we descended to these works, which lie at the head of a marshy cove, and at the mouth of a deep gorge, through which flows a clear mountain stream called Foundry Creek. We crossed the marsh upon a causeway, and from a rocky point of Constitution Island obtained a good panoramic view of the establishment. Returning to the foundry, we followed a pleasant pathway near the bay, into a large grove spared from the original forest, in which are situated the dwellings of former and the present proprietors of the works.* One of these, the

* The West Point Foundry was established in 1817, by an association organized for the chief purpose of manufacturing heavy iron ordnance, under a contract with the government. That yet formed a large portion of its business in 1860. The works then consisted of a moulding house; a gun foundry; three

has since been numbered with the dead. Broad Morris Avenue leads to a spacious iron gate, which opens into the grounds around "Undercliff." From this, through an avenue of stately trees, the house is approached. It is a substantial edifice of Doric simplicity in style, perfectly embowered when the trees are in full leaf, yet commanding, through vistas, some charming views of the river and the neighbouring mountains. Northward, and near it, rises Mount Taurus, with its impending cliff that suggested the name of the poet's country seat. It is the old "Bull Hill" which, in Irving's exquisite story of "Dolph Heyliger," "bellowed back the

UNDERCLIFF.

storm" whose thunders had "crashed on the Donder Berg, and rolled up the long defile of the Highlands, each headland making a new echo."

A late writer has justly said of "Undercliff"—"It is a lovely spot—beautiful in itself, beautiful in its surroundings, and inexpressibly beautiful in the home affections which hallow it, and the graceful and genial hospitality which, without pretence or ostentation, receives the guest, and with heart in the grasp of the hand, and truth in the sparkle of the eye, makes him feel that he is welcome." Over that household, a daughter, the " fair and gentle Ida," celebrated in the following beautiful poem, presided for several years:—

> " Where Hudson's wave o'er silvery sands
>   Winds through the hills afar,
> Old Cro' Nest like a monarch stands,
>   Crowned with a single star!
> And there, amid the billowy swells
>   Of rock-ribbed, cloud-capped earth,
> My fair and gentle Ida dwells,
>   A nymph of mountain birth.
>
> " The snow flake that the cliff receives,
>   The diamond of the showers,
> Spring's tender blossoms, buds, and leaves,
>   The sisterhood of flowers,
> Morn's early beam, eve's balmy breeze,
>   Her purity define;
> Yet Ida's dearer far than these
>   To this fond breast of mine.
>
> " My heart is on the hills. The shades
>   Of night are on my brow:
> Ye pleasant haunts and quiet glades,
>   My soul is with you now!
> I bless the star-crowned Highlands, where
>   My Ida's footsteps roam:
> Oh for a falcon's wing to bear
>   Me onward to my home! "

Between Cold Spring and West Point lies a huge rocky island, now connected to the main by a reedy marsh already referred to. It was called by the Dutch navigators Martelaer's Island, and the reach in the river between it and the Storm King, Martelaer's Rack, or Martyr's Reach. The word martyr was used in this connection to signify *contending* and *struggling*, as vessels coming up the river with a fair wind would frequently find themselves, immediately after passing the point of the island into this reach, struggling with the wind right ahead.

The Americans fortified this island very early in the old war for independence. The chief military work was called Fort Constitution, and the island has ever since been known as Constitution Island. It contains very little arable land, and is chiefly composed of rugged rocky heights, every one of which now bears the ruins of the old military works. To its shore nearest approaching West Point the Great Chain, which we have already considered, was fastened; and upon a high bluff near (delineated in the sketch) are yet seen the remains of a heavy battery—a part of Fort Constitution—placed there to protect the river obstructions.

At the time of my visit, Constitution Island belonged to Henry Warner, Esq., the father of the gifted and popular writers, Susan and Anna B. Warner.* They resided in a pleasant cottage, near the southern border of the island. Its kitchen was one of the barracks of Fort Constitution. It fronted upon a beautiful lawn that slopes to the river, and was sheltered by evergreen and deciduous trees, and beautified by flowers

RUINS OF BATTERY ON CONSTITUTION ISLAND.

and shrubbery. Although within the sound of every paddle upon the river, every beat of the drum or note of the bugle at West Point, every roll and its echo of trains upon the railway, "Wood Crag," as their secluded residence was called, was almost as retired from the bustling

---

* "Miss Susan Warner," says Duyckinck, in the "Cyclopædia of American Literature," "made a sudden step into eminence as a writer, by the publication, in 1849, of ' The Wide, Wide World,' a novel in two volumes." Her second novel was "Queechy." She is also the author of a theological work entitled "The Law and the Testimony." Her sister is the author of "Dollars and Cents," a novel; and several very pleasing volumes for young people. "The Hills of the Shatemuc," a tale of the Highlands, is the joint production of these gifted sisters.

world as if it was in the deep wilderness of the Upper Hudson. It is a charming home for a child of genius.

On a pleasant morning in October, while the trees were yet in full leaf and brilliant with the autumnal tints, we went from our home to Garrison's station on the Hudson River Railway, and crossed to Cozzens's, a summer hotel in the Highlands, about a mile below West Point. It was situated near the brow of a cliff on the western shore of the river, about 180 feet above tide water, and afforded a most delightful home, during the heat of

VIEW AT GARRISON'S.

summer, to numerous guests, varying in number from two hundred and fifty to five hundred. There, ever since the house was opened for guests in 1849, Lieutenant-General Scott, the General-in-Chief of the American army, had made his head-quarters during the four or five warmer months of the year. It was a place of fashionable resort from June until October, and at times was overflowing with guests, who filled the mansion and the several cottages attached to it. Among the latter was the studio of Leutze, the historical painter. Only a few days before our visit, it had been the scene of great festivity on the occasion of the reception of the

Prince of Wales and his suite, who spent a day and a night there, and at West Point, enjoying the unrivalled mountain and river scenery that surround them.

The pleasure-grounds around Cozzens's were extensive, and were becoming more beautiful every year. They had been redeemed from the wilderness state, by labour, within ten years. We remember passing through that region before the hand of man was put forth for its redemp-

COZZENS'S.

tion, and seeing the huge boulders—the "wandering rocks" of the geologist—strewn over the surface of the earth like apples beneath fruitful trees after an autumn storm. The change that had been wrought was marvellous. Another was about to take place. A few weeks after the visit here mentioned, that fine building delineated in the picture was destroyed by fire. The writer was passing by, in the evening, on the railway on the eastern side of the river, with a copy of the London *Art*

Journal in which these sketches were first published, containing this picture, while the building was in flames. Mr. Cozzens soon erected a more spacious one on the high rocky bluff overlooking Buttermilk Falls, a very short distance from the site of the other.

Between Cozzens's and the mountains is a small cruciform stone church, erected years before the hotel was contemplated, chiefly by the contribution of Professor Robert W. Weir, of West Point, the eminent historical painter, and one of the best of men in all the relations of life. It is really a *memorial* church, built in commemoration of his two sainted children,

CHURCH OF THE HOLY INNOCENTS.

and called "The Church of the Holy Innocents." For this pious purpose he devoted a portion of the money which he received from the United States Government for his picture of 'The Embarkation of the Pilgrims,' now in the Rotunda of the National Capitol. Divine service, according to the modified ritual of the Church of England, is held there regularly, and the seats are free to all who choose to occupy them. We trust our friend, whose modest nature shrinks from notoriety, will pardon us for this revelation of his sacred deed. The world, which needs good teachings, is entitled to the benefit of his noble example.

All about the cliffs, on the river front of Cozzens's, are winding paths, some leading through romantic dells and ravines, or along and across a clear mountain stream that goes laughing in pretty cascades down the

THE ROAD TO COZZENS'S DOCK.

steep shore to the river. The main road, partly cut like a sloping terrace in the rocks, is picturesque at every turn, but especially near the landing, where pleasant glimpses of the river and its water craft may be seen.

Altogether Cozzens's and its surroundings form one of the most attractive places on the Hudson to those who seek health and pleasure.

At Cozzens's Dock we procured a waterman, who took us to several places of interest in the vicinity. The first was Buttermilk Falls, half a mile below, on the same side of the river. Here a small stream comes rushing down the rocks in cascades and foaming rapids, falling more than a hundred feet in the course of as many yards. The chief fall, where the

BUTTERMILK FALLS.

stream plunges into the river, is over a sloping granite rock. It spreads out into a broad sheet of milk-white foam, which suggested its name to the Dutch skippers, and they called it *Boter Melck Val*—Buttermilk Fall. The stream affords water-power for flour-mills at the brink of the river. The fall is so great, that by a series of overshot water-wheels, arranged at different altitudes, a small quantity of water does marvellous execution.

Large vessels come alongside the elevator on the river front, and there discharge cargoes of wheat and take in cargoes of flour.

Rude paths and bridges are so constructed that visitors may view the great fall and the cascades above from many points. The latter have a grand and wild aspect when the stream is brimful, after heavy rains and the melting of snows.

UPPER CASCADES, BUTTERMILK FALL.

On the rough plain above is the village of Buttermilk Fall, containing over three hundred inhabitants. The country around is exceedingly rough and picturesque, especially in the direction of Fort Montgomery, three or four miles below; while on the brow of the high river bank near, there are some pleasant summer residences. Among these was the dwelling of Mr. Bigelow, then the associate of Mr. Bryant, the poet, in the ownership and conduct of the New York *Evening Post*, but since appointed, first the Secretary of the American Legation at the French Court, in 1861, and afterward Minister Plenipotentiary at the same Court.

Here on the smooth faces of the rocks might be seen a desecration which deserves the severest reprobation. All through the Highlands, on the line of the Hudson River Railway, the same offence met the eye. We refer to the occupation of smooth rocks by great staring letters, announcing the fact that one shopkeeper in New York has "Old London

BEVERLY DOCK.

Dock Gin" for sale, and that another sells "Paphian Lotion for beautifying the Hair." We protest, in the name of every person of taste who travels upon the river and the road, against any disfiguring of the picturesque scenery of the Hudson Highlands, by making the out-cropping rocks of the grand old hills play the part of those itinerants who walk the streets of New York with enormous placards on their backs, advertising wares for sale; and the Legislature of the State of New York, which, in 1865, made such disfiguration a penal offence, deserves high praise.

We crossed the river from Buttermilk Fall to the "Beverly Dock," which is interesting only as the place where Arnold, the traitor, entered his barge in which he escaped to the *Vulture* sloop-of-war, on the morning when he fled from the "Beverly House," the cause of which we have already considered. Here he kept his barge moored, and here he embarked on that flight which severed him for ever from the sympathies of his countrymen—ay, of the world—for those who "accepted the treason, despised the traitor." His six oarsmen on that occasion, unconscious of the nature of the general's errand in such hot haste down the river, had their muscles strengthened by a promised reward of two gallons of rum; and the barge glided with the speed of the wind. They were awakened to a sense of their position only when they were detained on board the *Vulture* as prisoners, and saw their chief greeted as a friend by the enemies of their country. They were speedily set at liberty, in New York, by Sir Henry Clinton, who scorned Arnold for his meanness and treachery.

CHAPTER XIV.

E rowed to Garrison's, where we dismissed the waterman, and took the cars for Peek's Kill, six miles below, a pleasant village lying at the river opening of a high and beautiful valley, and upon slopes that overlook a broad bay and extensive mountain ranges.* We passed the night at the house of a friend (Owen T. Coffin, Esq.), and from the lawn in front of his dwelling, which commands the finest view of the river and mountains in that vicinity, made the sketch of the Lower Entrance to the Highlands. On the left is seen the Donder Berg, over and behind which Sir Henry Clinton's army marched to attack Forts Clinton and Montgomery. On the right is Anthony's Nose, with the site of Fort Independence between it and Peek's Kill; and in the centre is Bear Mountain, at whose base is the beautiful Lake Sinnipink—the "Bloody Pond" in revolutionary times. This view includes a theatre of most important historical events. We may only glance at them.

Peek's Kill, named from the "Kill of Jan Peek," that flows into the Hudson just above the rocky promontory on the north-western side of the town, was an American depôt of military stores, during the earlier years of the war for independence. These were destroyed and the post burnt by the British in the spring of 1777. There, during most of the war, was the head-quarters of important divisions of the revolutionary army, and there the British spy was hanged, concerning whom General Putnam

---

* Peek's Kill Village was incorporated in 1817. It is the most northerly place on the Hudson (being forty-one miles from New York), where business men in the metropolis reside. It is so sheltered by the Highlands, that it is an agreeable place of residence in the winter. It contains ten churches, excellent schools, and had a population of about 4,000 in 1860.

wrote his famous laconic letter to Sir Henry Clinton. The latter claimed the offender as a British officer, when Putnam wrote in reply :—

"*Head-quarters, 7th August*, 1777.

"Sir,—Edmund Palmer, an officer in the enemy's service, was taken as a spy, lurking within our lines. He has been tried as a spy, condemned as a spy, and shall be executed as a spy; and the flag is ordered to depart immediately.

"Israel Putnam."

"P.S.—He has been accordingly executed."

LOWER ENTRANCE TO THE HIGHLANDS, FROM PEEK'S KILL.

At Peek's Kill we procured a waterman, whose father, then eighty-five years of age, conveyed the writer across the King's Ferry, four or five miles below, twelve years before. The morning was cool, and a stiff breeze was blowing from the north. We crossed the bay, and entered Fort Montgomery Creek (anciently Poplopen's Kill) between the two rocky promontories on which stood Forts Clinton and Montgomery, within rifle-shot of each other. The banks of the creek are high and precipitous, the southern one covered with trees; and less than half a mile from its broad and deep mouth, in which large vessels may anchor, it is a wild mountain stream, rushing into the placid tide-water through narrow valleys and dark ravines. Here, at the foot of a wild cascade, we moored

FALLS IN FORT MONTGOMERY CREEK.

our little boat, and sketched the scene. A short dam has been constructed there for sending water through a flume to a mill a few rods below. This stream, like Indian Brook, presents a thousand charming pictures, where nature woos her lovers in the pleasant summer-time.

From the mill may be obtained a view of the promontories on each side of the creek, and of the lofty Anthony's Nose on the eastern side of the river, which appears in our sketch, dark and imposing, as we look toward the east. Fort Montgomery was on the northern side of the creek, and Fort Clinton on the southern side. They were constructed at the beginning of the war for independence, and became the theatre of a desperate and bloody contest in the autumn of 1777. They were strong fortresses, though feebly manned. From Fort Montgomery to Anthony's Nose a heavy boom and massive iron chain were stretched over the river,

SCENE IN FORT MONTGOMERY CREEK.

to obstruct British ships that might attempt a passage toward West Point. The two forts were respectively commanded by two brothers, Generals George and James Clinton, the former at that time governor of the newly organised State of New York.

Burgoyne, then surrounded by the Americans at Saratoga, was, as we have observed in a former chapter, in daily expectation of a diversion in his favour, on the Lower Hudson, by Sir Henry Clinton—in command of the British troops at New York. Early in October, the latter fitted out an expedition for the Highlands, and accompanied it in person. He deceived General Putnam, then in command at Peck's Kill, by feints on that side of the river, at the same time he sent detachments over the Donder Berg, under cover of a fog. They were piloted by a resident Tory or loyalist, and in the afternoon of the 6th of October, and in two divisions, fell upon the forts. The commanders of the forts had no suspicions of the proximity of the enemy until their picket guards were

LAKE SINNIPINK.

assailed. These, and a detachment sent out in that direction, had a severe skirmish with the invaders on the borders of Lake Sinnipink, a beautiful sheet of water lying at the foot of the lofty Bear Mountain, on the same general level as the foundations of the fort. Many of the dead were cast into that lake, near its outlet, and their blood so incarnadined its waters, that it has ever since been vulgarly called "Bloody Pond."

The garrisons at the two forts, meanwhile, prepared to resist the attack with desperation. They were completely invested at four o'clock in the afternoon, when a general contest commenced, in which British vessels in the river participated. It continued until twilight. The Americans then gave way, and a general flight ensued. The two commanders were among those who escaped to the mountains. The Americans lost in killed, wounded, and prisoners, about three hundred. The British loss was about one hundred and forty.

The contest ended with a sublime spectacle. Above the boom and chain the Americans had two frigates, two galleys, and an armed sloop. On the fall of the forts, the crews of these vessels spread their sails, and, slipping their cables, attempted to escape up the river. But the wind was adverse, and they were compelled to abandon them. They set them on fire when they left, to prevent their falling into the hands of an enemy. "The flames suddenly broke forth," wrote Stedman, a British officer and author, " and, as every sail was set, the vessels soon became magnificent pyramids of fire. The reflection on the steep face of the opposite mountain (Anthony's Nose), and the long train of ruddy light which shone upon the water for a prodigious distance, had a wonderful effect; while the ear was awfully filled with the continued echoes from the rocky shores, as the flames gradually reached the loaded cannons. The whole was sublimely terminated by the explosions, which left all again in darkness."

Early on the following morning, the obstructions in the river, which had cost the Americans a quarter of a million of dollars, continental money, were destroyed by the British fleet. Fort Constitution, opposite West Point, was abandoned. A free passage of the Hudson being opened, Vaughan and Wallace sailed up the river on their destructive errand to Kingston and Clermont, already mentioned.

A short distance below Montgomery Creek, at the mouth of Lake Sinnipink Brook, is one of the depôts of the Knickerbocker Ice Company, of New York. The spacious storehouses for the ice are on the rocky bank, thirty or forty feet above the river. The ice, cut in blocks from the lake above in winter, is sent down upon wooden "ways," that wind through the forest with a gentle inclination, from the outlet of Sinnipink, for nearly half a mile. A portion of the "ways," from the storehouses to the forwarding depôt below, is seen in our sketch. From that depôt the ice is conveyed into vessels in warm weather, and carried to market. More than thirty thousand tons of ice are annually shipped from this single depôt. Ice is an important article of the commerce of the Hudson, from whose surface, also, immense quantities are gathered every winter.

From the high bank above the ice depôt, a very fine view of Anthony's Nose and the Sugar Loaf in the distance may be obtained. The latter name the reader will remember as that of the lofty eminence in the rear of the

ANTHONY'S NOSE AND THE SUGAR LOAF, FROM THE ICE DEPÔT.

Beverly House. At West Point and its vicinity it forms a long range of mountains, but looking up from the neighbourhood of the Nose, it is a perfect pyramid in form. It is one of the first objects that attract the eye of the voyager, when turning the point of the Nose on entering the Highlands from below. Its form suggested to the practical minds of the Dutch a *Suycker Broodt*—Sugar Loaf—and so they named it.

We crossed the river from Lake Sinnipink to Anthony's Nose, through the point of which the Hudson River Railway passes, in a tunnel over two hundred feet in length. This is a lofty rocky promontory, whose summit is almost thirteen hundred feet above the river, and with the jutting point of the Donder Berg, a mile and a half below, gives the Hudson there a double curve, and the appearance of an arm of the sea, terminating at the mountains. Such was the opinion of Hendrick Hudson, as he approached this point from below. The true origin of the

TUNNEL AT ANTHONY'S NOSE.

name of this promontory is unknown. Irving makes the veracious historian, Diedrich Knickerbocker, throw light upon the subject :—

"And now I am going to tell a fact, which I doubt much my readers will hesitate to believe, but if they do they are welcome not to believe a word in this whole history—for nothing which it contains is more true. It must be known then that the nose of Anthony the trumpeter was of a very lusty size, strutting boldly from his countenance like a mountain of Golconda, being sumptuously bedecked with rubies and other precious stones—the true regalia of a king of good fellows, which jolly Bacchus grants to all who bouse it heartily at the flagon. Now thus it happened, that bright and early in the morning, the good Anthony, having washed his burly visage, was leaning over the quarter railing of the galley, contemplating it in the glassy wave below. Just at this moment the illustrious sun, breaking in all his splendour from behind a high bluff of the Highlands, did dart one of his most potent beams full upon the refulgent nose of the sounder of brass—the reflection of which shot straightway down hissing hot into the water, and killed a mighty sturgeon that was sporting beside the vessel. This huge monster, being with infinite labour hoisted on board, furnished a luxurious repast to all the crew, being accounted of excellent flavour excepting about the wound, where it smacked a little of brimstone—and this, on my veracity, was the first time that ever sturgeon was eaten in these parts by Christian people. When this astonishing miracle became known to Peter Stuyvesant, and that he tasted of the unknown fish, he, as may well be supposed, marvelled exceedingly; and as a monument thereof, he gave the name of Anthony's Nose to a stout promontory in the neighbourhood, and it has continued to be called Anthony's Nose ever since that time."

Down the steep rocky valley between Anthony's Nose and a summit almost as lofty half a mile below, one of the wildest streams of this region flows in gentle cascades in dry weather, but as a rushing torrent during rain-storms or the time of the melting of the snows in spring. The Dutch called it *Brocken Kill*, or Broken Creek, it being seen in "bits" as it finds its way among the rocks and shrubbery to the river. The name is now corrupted to Brockey Kill. It is extremely picturesque from every point of view, especially when seen glittering in the evening sun. It comes from a wild wet region among the hills, where the Rattlesnake,* the most venomous serpent of the American continent,

---

* The *Crotalus durissus*, or common northern Rattlesnake of the United States, is of a yellowish or reddish brown, sometimes of a chestnut black, with irregular rhomboidal black blotches; head large, flattened, and triangular; length from three to seven or eight feet. On the tail is a *rattle*, consisting of several horny enlargements, loosely attached to each other, making a loud rattling sound when shaken and rubbed against each other. These are used by the serpent to give warning of its presence. When disturbed, it throws itself into a coil, vibrates its rattles, and then springing, sometimes four or five feet, fixes its deadly fangs in its victim. It feeds on birds, rabbits, squirrels, &c.

abounds. They are found in all parts of the Highlands, but in far less abundance than formerly. Indeed they are now so seldom seen, that the tourist need have no dread of them.

THE BROCKEN KILL.

A little below the Brocken Kill, at Flat Point, is one of those tunnels and deep rock cuttings so frequently passed along the entire line of the Hudson River Railway; and in the river opposite is a picturesque island called Iona, containing about 300 acres of land, including a marsh meadow of 200 acres. Only about forty acres of the island proper, besides, is capable of tillage. It lies within the triangle formed by the Donder Berg, Anthony's Nose, and Bear Mountain. There we spent an hour pleasantly and profitably with the proprietor, C. W. Grant, M.D., who resided there, and was extensively engaged in the propagation of grape-vines and choice fruit-trees. He had a vineyard of twenty acres, from 2,000 to 3,000 bearing pear-trees, and small fruit of every kind. He had

RATTLESNAKE.

eleven propagation houses, and produced more grape and other fruit-plants than all other establishments in the United States combined.

Iona is upon the dividing line of temperature. The sea breeze stops here, and its effects are visible upon vegetation. The season is two weeks earlier than at Newburgh, only fourteen miles northward, above the Highlands. It is at the lower entrance to this mountain range. The width of the river between it and Anthony's Nose is only three-eighths of a mile—less than at any other point below Albany. The water is deep, and the tidal currents are so swift, that this part of the river is called " The Race."

herself, and sailed on as quietly as if in a mill-pond. Nothing saved her from utter wreck but the fortunate circumstance of having a horse-shoe nailed against the mast—a wise precaution against evil spirits, since adopted by all the Dutch captains that navigate this haunted river.

"There is another story told of this foul-weather urchin, by Skipper Daniel Ouslesticker, of Fish Kill, who was never known to tell a lie. He declared that, in a severe squall, he saw him seated astride of his bowsprit, riding the sloop ashore, full butt against Anthony's Nose, and that he was exorcised by Dominic Van Geisen, of Esopus, who happened to be on board, and who sang the hymn of St. Nicholas, whereupon the goblin threw himself up in the air like a ball, and went off in a whirlwind, carrying away with him the nightcap of the Dominic's wife, which was discovered the next Sunday morning hanging on the weather-cock of Esopus church steeple, at least forty miles off. Several events of this kind having taken place, the regular skippers of the river for a long time did not venture to pass the Donder Berg without lowering their peaks, out of homage to the Heer of the Mountains; and it was observed that all such as paid this tribute of respect were suffered to pass unmolested."

We have observed that the tempest is often seen brooding upon the Donder Berg in summer. We give a sketch of one of those scenes, drawn by the writer several years ago, when the steam-engine of an immense pumping apparatus was in operation at Donder Berg Point. Concerning that engine and its co-workers, there is a curious tale of mingled fraud, superstition, credulity, and "gullibility," that vies with many a plot born in the romancer's brain. It cannot be told here. The simple outlines are, that some years ago an iron cannon was, by accident, brought up from the river depths at this point. Some speculator, as the story goes, at once conceived a scheme of fraud, for the success of which he relied on the average ignorance and credulity of mankind. It was boldly proclaimed, in the face of recorded history, that Captain Kidd's piratical vessel was sunken in a storm at this spot with untold treasures on board, and that one of his cannons had been raised. Further, that the deck of his vessel had been penetrated by a very long augur, hard substances encountered by it, and pieces of silver brought up in its thread—the evidence of coffers of specie below. This augur with its bits of silver was exhibited, and the story believed. A stock company was formed. Shares were readily taken. The speculator was chief manager. A coffer dam was made over the supposed resting-place of the treasure-ship. A steam-engine and huge pumps, driven by it, were set in motion. Day after day, and month after month, the work went on. One credulous New York merchant invested 20,000 dollars in the scheme. The speculator took large commissions. Hope failed, the work stopped, and nothing now

DONDER BERG POINT.

remains to tell the tale but the ruins of the coffer dam and the remains of the pumps, which may   seen almost on a level with the surface of the river, at high water.

The true history of the cannon found there is, probably, that it is one of several captured by the Americans at Stony Point, just below, in 1779. They attempted to carry the cannon on galleys (flat boats) to West Point. According to the narrative of a British officer present, a shot from the

Vulture sloop-of-war sunk one of the boats off Donder Berg Point. This cannon, probably, went to the bottom of the river at that time. And so vanishes the right of any of Kidd's descendants to that old cannon.

A few weeks after my visit to the Donder Berg and its vicinity, I was again at Peek's Kill, and upon its broad and beautiful bay. But a great change had taken place in the aspect of the scene. The sober foliage of late autumn had fallen, and where lately the most gorgeous colours clothed the lofty hills in indescribable beauty, nothing but bare stems and branches, and grey rugged rocks, were seen, shrouded in the snow that covered hill and valley, mountain and plain. The river presented a smooth surface of strong ice, and winter, with all its rigours, was holding supreme rule in the realm of nature without.

It was evening when I arrived at Peek's Kill—a cold, serene, moon-light evening. Muffled in a thick cloak, and with hands covered by stout woollen gloves, I sallied out to transfer to paper and fix in memory the scene upon Peek's Kill (or Peek's Kill Creek, as it is erroneously written), of which I had obtained a glimpse from the window of the railway-car. The frost bit sharply, and cold keen gusts of wind came sweeping from the Highlands, while I stood upon the causeway at the drawbridge at the mouth of Peek's Kill, and made my evening sketch.* All was cold, silent, glittering, and solitary, except a group of young skaters, gliding spectre-like in the crisp night air, their merry laughter ringing out clear and loud when one of the party was made to "see stars"—not in the black arch above—as his head took the place of his heels upon the ice. The form of an iron furnace, in deep shadow, on the southern side of the creek, was the only token of human labour to be seen in the view, except the cabin of the drawbridge keeper at my side.

A little north of Peek's Kill Hollow, as the valley is called by the inhabitants, is another, lying at the bases of the rugged Highlands, called the Canopus Hollow. It is a deep, rich, and interesting valley, through which flows the Canopus Creek. In its bosom is pleasant little Continental

---

* This railway-bridge and causeway is called Cortlandt Bridge. It is 1,496 feet in length. At its north-western end is a gravelly hill, on which stood a battery, called Fort Independence, during the Revolution. The Indians called the Peek's Kill *Mag-ri-ga-ries*, and its vicinity *Sack-hoes*.

Village, so named in the time of the Revolution because the hamlet there was made a depôt for Continental or Government cattle and stores. These were destroyed, three days after the capture of Forts Clinton and Montgomery, by Governor Tyron, at the head of a band of German mercenaries known as Hessians, because a larger portion of the German troops, hired by the British Government to assist in crushing the rebellion in America, were furnished by the Prince of Hesse Cassel. Tryon, who

THE PEEK'S KILL.

had been governor of the colony of New York, and was now a brigadier in the royal army, hated the Americans intensely. He really seemed to delight in expeditions of this kind, having almost destroyed Danbury, in Connecticut, and East Haven, Fairfield, and Norwalk, on the borders of Long Island Sound, in the same State. Now, after destroying the public stores and slaughtering many cattle, he set fire to almost every house in the village. In allusion to this, and the devastations on the Hudson, above the Highlands, by General Vaughan, Trumbull, an American contemporary poet, wrote indignantly :—

> "Behold, like whelps of Britain's lion,
> Our warriors, Clinton, Vaughan, and Tryon,
> March forth with patriotic joy
> To ravish, plunder, and destroy.
> Great gen'rals! foremost in their nation,
> The journeymen of desolation,
> Like Samson's foxes, each assails,
> Let loose with fire-brands in their tails,
> And spreads destruction more forlorn
> Than they among Philistine corn."

It is proper to observe that Tryon's marauding expeditions were con-

SKATERS ON PEEK'S KILL BAY.

demned by the British public, and the ministry were censured by the opposition in parliament for permitting such conduct to pass unrebuked.

On the following morning, when the sun had climbed high towards meridian, I left Peek's Kill for a day's sketching and observation in the winter air. The bay was alive with people of all ages, sexes, and conditions. It was the first day since a late snow-storm that the river had offered good sport for skaters, and the navigators of ice-boats.* It was a gay scene. Wrapped in furs and shawls, over-coats and cloaks, men and women, boys and girls, were enjoying the rare exercise with the greatest pleasure. Fun, pure fun, ruled the hour. The air was vocal with shouts and laughter; and when the swift ice-boat, with sails set, gay pennon streaming, and freighted with a dozen boys and girls, came sweeping gracefully towards the crowd,—after making a comet-like orbit of four or five miles to the feet of the Donder Berg, Bear Mountain, and Anthony's Nose,—there was a sudden shout, and scattering, and merry laughter, that would have made old Scrooge, even before his conversion, tremulous with delight, and glowing with desires to be a boy again and singing Christmas Carols with a hearty good-will. I played the boy with the rest for awhile, and then, with long strides upon skates, my satchel with portfolio slung over my shoulder, I bore away towards the great lime-kilns on the shores of Tomkins's Cove, on the western side of the river, four or five miles below.

---

* The ice-boats are of various forms of construction. Usually a strong wooden triangular platform is placed upon three sled-runners, having skate-irons on their bottoms. The rear runner is worked on a pivot or hinge, by a tiller attached to a post that passes up through the platform, and thereby the boat is steered. The sails and rigging are similar to the common large sail-boat. The passengers sit flat upon the platform, and with a good wind are moved rapidly over the ice, oftentimes at the rate of a mile in a minute.

CHAPTER XV.

N my way to Tomkins's Cove I encountered other groups of people, who appeared in positive contrast with the merry skaters on Peek's Kill Bay. They were sober, thoughtful, winter fishermen, thickly scattered over the surface, and drawing their long nets from narrow fissures which they had cut in the ice. The tide was "serving," and many a striped bass, and white perch, and infant sturgeon at times, were drawn out of their warmer element to be instantly congealed in the keen wintry air.

These fishermen often find their calling almost as profitable in winter as in April and May, when they draw "schools" of shad from the deep. They generally have a "catch" twice a day when the tide is "slack," their nets being filled when it is ebbing or flowing. They cut fissures in the ice, at right angles with the direction of the tidal currents, eight or ten yards in length, and about two feet in width, into which they drop their nets, sink them with weights, and stretching them to their utmost length, suspend them by sticks that lie across the fissure. Baskets, boxes on hand-sledges, and sometimes sledges drawn by a horse, are used in carrying the "catch" to land. Lower down the river, in the vicinity of the Palisades, when the strength of the ice will allow this kind of fishing, bass weighing from thirty to forty pounds each are frequently caught. These winter fisheries extend from the Donder Berg to Piermont, a distance of about twenty-five miles.

I went on shore at the ruins of an old lime-kiln at the upper edge of Tomkins's Cove, and sketched the fishermen in the distance toward Peek's Kill. It was a tedious task, and, with benumbed fingers, I hastened to the office and store of the Tomkins Lime Company to seek warmth and information. With Mr. Searing, one of the proprietors, I visited the kilns. They are the most extensive works of the kind on the Hudson.

They are at the foot of an immense cliff of limestone, nearly 200 feet in height, immediately behind the kilns, and extend more than half a mile along the river.* The kilns were numerous, and in their management, and the quarrying of the limestone, about 100 men were continually employed. I saw them on the brow of the wooded cliff, loosening huge masses and sending them below, while others were engaged in blasting, and others again in wheeling the lime from the vents of the kilns to heaps in front,

WINTER FISHING.

where it is slaked before being placed in vessels for transportation to market. This is a necessary precaution against spontaneous combustion.

---

* This deposit of limestone occupies a superficial area of nearly 600 acres, extending in the rear of Stony and Grassy Points, where it disappears beneath the red sandstone formation. It is traversed by white veins of carbonate of lime. In 1837 Mr. Tomkins purchased 20 acres of land covering this limestone bed for 100 dollars an acre, then considered a very extravagant price. The stratum where they are now quarrying is at least 500 feet in thickness. It is estimated that an acre of this limestone, worked down to the water level, will yield 600,000 barrels of lime, upon which a mean profit of 25 cents a barrel is the minimum. Some of this limestone is black and variegated, and makes pleasing ornamental marbles. Most of it is blue.

Many vessels are employed in carrying away lime, limestone, and "gravel" (pulverized limestone, not fit for the kiln) from Tomkins's Cove, for whose accommodation several small wharves have been constructed.

One million bushels of lime were produced at the kilns each year. From the quarries, thousands of tons of the stone were sent annually to kilns in New Jersey. From 20,000 to 25,000 tons of the "gravel" were used each year in the construction of macadamised roads. The quarry had

FISHERMEN, FROM THE OLD LIME-KILNS.

been worked almost twenty-five years. From small beginnings the establishment had grown to a very extensive one. The dwelling of the chief proprietor was upon the hill above the kiln at the upper side of the cove; and near the water the houses of the workmen form a pleasant little village. The country behind, for many miles, is very wild, and almost uncultivated.

I followed a narrow road along the bank of the river, to the extreme southern verge of the limestone cliff, near Stony Point, and there sketched that famous, bold, rocky peninsula from the best spot where a view of its entire length may be obtained. The whole Point is a mass of granite rock, with patches of evergreen trees and shrubs, excepting on its northern side (at which we are looking in the sketch), where may be seen a black cliff of magnetic iron ore. It is too limited in quantity to tempt labour or capital to quarry it, and the granite is too much broken to be

TOMKINS'S LIME-KILNS AND QUARRY.

very desirable for building purposes. So that peninsula, clustered with historic associations, will ever remain almost unchanged in form and feature. A lighthouse, a keeper's lodge, and a fog-bell, occupy its summit. These stand upon and within the mounds that mark the site of the old fort which was built there at the beginning of the war for independence.

Stony Point was the theatre of stirring events in the summer of 1779. The fort there, and Fort Fayette on Verplanck's Point, on the opposite side of the river, were captured from the Americans by Sir Henry Clinton, on the 1st of June of that year. Clinton commanded the troops in person. These were conveyed by a small squadron under the command of Admiral Collier. The garrison at Stony Point was very small, and retired towards West Point on the approach of the British. The fort changed masters without bloodshed. The victors pointed the guns of the captured fortress, and cannon and bombs brought by themselves, upon Fort Fayette the next

STONY POINT.

morning. General Vaughan assailed it in the rear, and the little garrison soon surrendered themselves prisoners of war.

These fortresses, commanding the lower entrance to the Highlands, were very important. General Anthony Wayne, known as "Mad Anthony," on account of his impetuosity and daring in the service, was then in command of the Americans in the neighbourhood. Burning with a desire to retake the forts, he applied to Washington for permission to make the attempt. It would be perilous in the extreme. The position of the fort was almost impregnable. Situated upon a high rocky peninsula, an island at high water, and always inaccessible dry-shod, except across a narrow causeway, it was strongly defended by outworks and a double row of *abattis*. Upon three sides of the rock were the waters of the Hudson, and on the fourth was a morass, deep and dangerous. The cautious Washington considered; when the impetuous Wayne, scorning all obstacles, said, "General, I'll storm hell if you will only plan it!"

STONY POINT LIGHTHOUSE AND FOG-BELL.

Permission to attack Stony Point was given, preparations were secretly made, and at near midnight, on the 15th of July, Wayne led a strong force of determined men towards the fórtress. They were divided into two columns, each led by a forlorn hope of twenty picked men. They advanced undiscovered until within pistol-shot of the picket guard on the heights. The garrison were suddenly aroused from sleep, and the deep silence of the night was broken by the roll of the drum, the loud cry "To arms! to arms!" the rattle of musketry from the ramparts and behind the *abattis*, and the roar of cannon charged with deadly grape-shot. In the face of this terrible storm the Americans made their way, by force of bayonet, to the centre of the works. Wayne was struck upon the head by a musket ball that brought him upon his knees. "March on!" he cried. "Carry me into the fort, for I will die at the head of my column!" The wound was not very severe, and in an hour he had sufficiently recovered to write the following note to Washington :—

"*Stony Point, 16th July,* 1779, 2 *o'clock,* A.M.

"DEAR GENERAL,—The fort and garrison, with Colonel Johnston, are ours. Our officers and men behaved like men who are determined to be free.

"Yours most respectfully,

"ANTHONY WAYNE."

At dawn the next morning the cannon of the captured fort were again turned upon Fort Fayette on Verplanck's Point, then occupied by the British under Colonel Webster. A desultory cannonading was kept up during the day. Sir Henry Clinton sent relief to Webster, and the Americans ceased further attempts to recapture the fortress. They could not even retain Stony Point, their numbers were so few. Washington ordered them to remove the ordnance and stores, and destroy and abandon the works. A large portion of the heavy ordnance was placed upon a galley to be conveyed to West Point. It was sunk by a shot from the *Vulture,* off Donder Berg Point, and one of the cannon, as we have observed, raised a few years ago by accident, was supposed to have been brought up from the wreck of the ship of the famous Captain Kidd. Congress testified its gratitude to Wayne for his services by a vote of thanks for his "brave, prudent, and soldierly conduct," and also ordered a gold medal, emblematic of the event, to be struck and presented to him. Copies of this medal, in silver, were given to two of the subordinate officers engaged in the enterprise.

I climbed to the summit of Stony Point along a steep, narrow, winding road from a deserted wharf, the snow almost knee-deep in some places. The view was a most interesting one. As connected with the history and traditions of the country, every spot upon which the eye rested was classic ground, and the waters awakened memories of many legends. Truthful chronicles and weird stories in abundance are associated with the scenes around. Arnold's treason and André's capture and death, the "storm ship" and the "bulbous-bottomed Dutch goblin that keeps the Donder Berg," already mentioned, and a score of histories and tales pressed upon the attention and claimed a passing thought. But the keen wintry wind sweeping over the Point kept the mind prosaic. There was

VERPLANCK'S POINT, FROM STONY POINT LIGHTHOUSE.

no *poetry* in the attempts to sketch two or three of the most prominent scenes; and I resolved, when that task was accomplished, to abandon the amusement until the warm sun of spring should release the waters from their Boreal chains, clothe the earth in verdure, and invite the birds from the balmy south to build their nests in the branches where the snow-heaps then lay.

From the lighthouse is a comprehensive view of Verplanck's Point opposite, whereon no vestige of Fort Fayette now remains. A little village, pleasant pastures and tilled fields in summer, and brick manufactories the year round, now occupy the places of former structures of war, around ,which the soil still yields an occasional ball, and bomb, and musket shot. The Indians called this place *Me-a-nagh*. They sold it to Stephen Van Cortlandt, in the year 1683, with land east of it called *Ap-pa-magh-pogh*. The purchase was confirmed by patent from the English government. On this point Colonel Livingston held command at

GRASSY POINT AND TORN MOUNTAIN.

the time of Arnold's treason, in 1780 ; and here were the head-quarters of Washington for some time in 1782. It was off this point that Henry Hudson first anchored the *Half-Moon* after leaving Yonkers. The Highland Indians flocked to the vessel in great numbers. One of them was killed in an affray, and this circumstance planted the seed of hatred of the white man in the bosom of the Indians in that region.

From the southern slope of Stony Point, where the rocks lay in wild confusion, a fine view of Grassy Point, Brewster's Cove, Haverstraw Bay, the Torn Mountain, and the surrounding country may be obtained. The little village of Grassy Point, where brick-making is the staple industrial pursuit, appeared like a dark tongue thrust out from the surrounding whiteness. Haverstraw Bay, which swarms in summer with water-craft of every kind, lay on the left, in glittering solitude beneath the wintry clouds that gathered while I was there, and cast down a thick, fierce, blinding snow-shower, quite unlike that described by Bryant, when he sung—

> " Here delicate snow-stars out of the cloud,
>   Come floating downward in airy play,
> Like spangles dropped from the glistening crowd
>   That whiten by night the milky way;
> There broader and burlier masses fall;
> The sullen water buries them all:
>   Flake after flake,
> All drowned in the dark and silent lake.'"

The snow-shower soon passed by. The spires of Haverstraw appeared in the distance, at the foot of the mountain, and on the right was Treason Hill, with the famous mansion of Joshua Hett Smith, who was involved in the odium of Arnold's attempt to betray his country.

Here I will recall the memories of a visit there at the close of a pleasant summer day, several years ago. I had lingered upon Stony Point, until near sunset, listening to the stories of an old waterman, then eighty-five years of age, who assisted in building the fort, and then I started on foot for Haverstraw. I stopped frequently to view the beautiful prospect of river and country on the east, while the outlines of the distant shores were imperceptibly fading as the twilight came on. At dusk I passed an acre of ground, lying by the road-side, which was given some years before as a burial-place for the neighbourhood. It was already populous. The lines of Longfellow were suggested and pondered. He says,—

> " I like that ancient Saxon phrase which calls
>   The burial-ground *God's Acre!* It is just;
> It consecrates each grave within its walls,
>   And breathes a benison o'er the sleeping dust.
>
> " *God's Acre!* Yes, that blessed name imparts
>   Comfort to those who in the grave have sown
> The seed that they had garner'd in their hearts,
>   Their bread of life, alas! no more their own."

Night had fallen when I reached Treason Hill, so I passed on to the village near. Early on the following morning, before the dew had left the grass, I sketched Smith's House, where Arnold and André completed those negotiations concerning the delivery, by the former, of West Point and its defenders into the hands of the British, for a mercenary consideration, which led to the death of one, and the eternal infamy of the other.

The story of Arnold's treason may be briefly told. We have had occasion to allude to it several times already.

SMITH'S HOUSE, ON TREASON HILL.

Arnold was a brave soldier, but a bad man. He was wicked in boyhood, and in early manhood his conduct was marked by traits that promised ultimate disgrace. Impulsive, vindictive, and unscrupulous, he was personally unpopular, and was seldom without a quarrel with some of his companions in arms. This led to continual irritations, and his ambitious aims were often thwarted. He fought nobly for freedom during the earlier years of the war, but at last his passions gained the mastery over his judgment and conscience.

Arnold twice received honourable wounds during the war—one at Quebec, the other almost two years later at Saratoga; * both were in the leg. The one last received, while gallantly fighting the troops of Burgoyne, was not yet healed when, in the spring of 1778, the British army, under Sir Henry Clinton, evacuated Philadelphia, and the Americans, under Washington, came from their huts at Valley Forge to take their places. Arnold, not being able to do active duty in the field, was appointed military governor of Philadelphia. Fond of display, he there entered upon a course of extravagant living that was instrumental in his ruin. He made his head-quarters at the fine old mansion built by William Penn, kept a coach and four, gave splendid dinner parties, and charmed the gayer portions of Philadelphia society with his princely display. His station and the splendour of his equipage captivated the daughter of Edward Shippen, a leading loyalist, and afterwards chief justice of Pennsylvania; she was then only eighteen years of age. Her beauty and accomplishments won the heart of the widower of forty. They were married. Staunch Whigs shook their heads in doubt concerning the alliance of an American general with a leading Tory family.

Arnold's extravagance soon brought numerous creditors to his door. Rather than retrench his expenses he procured money by a system of fraud and prostitution of his official power : the city being under martial law, his will was supreme. The people became incensed, and official inquiries into his conduct were instituted, first by the local state council, and then by the Continental Congress. The latter body referred the whole matter to Washington. The accused was tried by court-martial, and he was found guilty of two of four charges. The court passed the mildest sentence possible—a mere reprimand by the commander-in-chief. This duty Washington performed in the most delicate manner. " Our

---

* Soon after Arnold joined the British Army, he was sent with a considerable force upon a marauding expedition up the James River, in Virginia. In an action not far from Richmond, the capital, some Americans were made prisoners. He asked one of them what his countrymen would do with him (Arnold) if they should catch him. The prisoner instantly replied, " Bury the leg that was wounded at Quebec and Saratoga with military honours, and hang the remainder of you."

profession," he said, "is the chastest of all; even the shadow of a fault tarnishes the lustre of our finest achievements. The least inadvertence may rob us of the public favour, so hard to be acquired. I reprimand you for having forgotten that, in proportion as you had rendered yourself formidable to our enemies, you should have been guarded and temperate in your deportment towards your fellow citizens. Exhibit anew those noble qualities which have placed you on the list of our most valued commanders. I will myself furnish you, as far as it may be in my power, with opportunities of regaining the esteem of your country."

What punishment could have been lighter? yet Arnold was greatly irritated. A year had elapsed since his accusation, and he expected a full acquittal. But for nine months the rank weeds of treason had been growing luxuriantly in his heart. He saw no way to extricate himself from debt, and retain his position in the army. For nine months he had been in secret correspondence with British officers in New York. His pride was now wounded, his vindictive spirit was aroused, and he resolved to sell his country for gold and military rank. He opened a correspondence in a disguised hand, and in commercial phrase, with Major John André, the young and highly accomplished adjutant-general of the British army.

How far Mrs. Arnold (who had been quite intimate with Major André in Philadelphia, and had kept up an epistolary correspondence with him after the British army had left that city) was implicated in these treasonable communications we shall never know. Justice compels us to say that there is no evidence of her having had any knowledge of the transaction until the explosion of the plot at Beverly already mentioned.

Arnold's deportment now suddenly changed. For a long time he had been sullen and indifferent; now his patriotism glowed with all the apparent ardour of his earlier career. Hitherto he had pleaded the bad state of his wounds as an excuse for inaction; now they healed rapidly. He appeared anxious to join his old companions in arms; and to General Schuyler, and other influential men, then in Congress, he expressed an ardent desire to be in the camp or in the field. They believed him to be sincere, and rejoiced. They wrote cheering letters to Washington on the subject; and, pursuant to Arnold's intimation, they suggested the propriety of appointing him to the command of West Point, the most important post in the country. Arnold visited Washington's camp at the same time, and, in a modest way, expressed a desire to have a command like that of West Point, as his wounds would not permit him to perform very active service on horseback.

The change surprised Washington, yet he was unsuspicious of wrong. He gave Arnold the command of "West Point and its dependencies," and furnished him with written instructions on the 3rd of August, 1780. Then it was that Arnold made his head-quarters at Beverly, and worked vigorously for the consummation of his treasonable designs. There he was joined by his wife and infant son. He at once communicated, in his disguised writing and commercial phraseology, under the signature of *Gustavus*, his plan to Sir Henry Clinton, through Major André, whom he addressed as "John Anderson." That plan we have already alluded to. Sir Henry was delighted with it, and eagerly sought to carry it out. He was not yet fully aware of the real character behind "Gustavus," although for several months he had suspected it to be General Arnold. Unwilling to proceed further upon uncertainties, he proposed sending an officer to some point near the American lines, who should have a personal interview with his correspondent. "Gustavus" consented, stipulating, however, that the messenger from Clinton should be Major André, his adjutant-general.

Arnold and André agreed to meet at Dobbs's Ferry, twenty-two miles above New York, upon what was then known as neutral ground. The British water-guard prevented the approach of Arnold. Sir Henry, anxious to complete the arrangement, and to execute the plan, sent the *Vulture* sloop of war up the river as far as Tarry Town, with Colonel Robinson, the owner of Beverly, who managed to communicate with Arnold. A meeting of Arnold and André was arranged. On the morning of the 20th of August, the latter officer left New York, proceeded by land to Dobbs's Ferry, and from thence to the *Vulture*, where it was expected the traitor would meet him that night. The wily general avoided the great danger. He repaired to the house of Joshua Hett Smith, a brother to the Tory chief justice of New York, and employed him to go to the *Vulture* at night, and bring a gentleman to the western shore of the Hudson.

There was delay, and Smith did not make the voyage until the night of
the 21st, after the moon had gone behind the high hills in the west.
With muffled oars he paddled noiselessly out of Haverstraw Creek, and,
at little past midnight, reached the *Vulture*.   It was a serene night, not
a ripple was upon the bosom of the river.   Not a word was spoken.   The

MEETING-PLACE OF ANDRE AND ARNOLD.

boat came alongside, with a concerted signal, and received Sir Henry's
representative.   André was dressed in his scarlet uniform, but all was
concealed by a long blue surtout, buttoned to the chin.   He was conveyed
to an estuary at the foot of Long Clove Mountain, a little below the

Village of Haverstraw. Smith led the officer to a thicket near the shore, and then, in a low whisper, introduced "John Anderson" to "Gustavus," who acknowledged himself to be Major-General Arnold, of the Continental Army. There, in the deep shadows of night, concealed from human cognizance, with no witnesses but the stars above them, they discussed the dark plans of treason, and plotted the utter ruin of the Republican cause. The faint harbingers of day began to appear in the east, and yet the conference was earnest and unfinished. Smith came and urged the necessity of haste to prevent discovery. Much was yet to be done. Arnold had expected a protracted interview, and had brought two horses with him. While the morning twilight was yet dim, they mounted and started for Smith's house. They had not proceeded far when the voice of a sentinel challenged them, and André found himself entering the American lines. He paused, for within them he would be a spy. Arnold assured him by promises of safety; and before sunrise they were at Smith's house, on what has since been known as Treason Hill. At that moment the sound of a cannon came booming over Haverstraw Bay from the eastern shore; and within twenty minutes the *Vulture* was seen dropping down the river, to avoid the shots of an American gun on Teller's Point. To the amazement of André, she disappeared. Deep inquietude stirred his spirit. He was within the American lines, without flag or pass. If detected, he would be called a *spy*—a name which he despised as much as that of *traitor*.

At noon the whole plan was arranged. Arnold placed in André's possession several papers—fatal papers!—explanatory of the condition of West Point and its dependencies. Zealous for the interests of his king and country, André, contrary to the explicit orders of Sir Henry Clinton, received them. He placed them in his stockings, under his feet, at the suggestion of Arnold, received a pass from the traitor in the event of his being compelled to return to New York by land, and waited with great impatience for the approaching night, when he should be taken in a boat to the *Vulture*. The remainder of the sad narrative will be repeated presently at a more appropriate point in our journey towards the sea.

Returning from this historical digression, I will recur to the narrative of the events of a winter's day on the Hudson, only to say, that after sketching the Lighthouse and Fog-bell structure upon Stony Point, I hastened to the river, resumed my skates, and at twilight arrived at Peek's Kill, in time to take the railway-car for home. I had experienced a tedious but interesting day. The remembrance of it is far more delightful than was its endurance.

CHAPTER XVI.

THE winter was mild and constant. No special severity marked its dealings, yet it made no deviations in that respect from the usual course of the season sufficient to mark it as an innovator. Its breath chilled the waters early, and for several weeks the Hudson was bridged with strong ice, from the wilderness almost to the sea. Meanwhile the whole country was covered with a thick mantle of snow. Skaters, ice-boats, and sleighs traversed the smooth surface of the river with perfect safety, as far down as Peek's Kill Bay, and the counties upon its borders, separated by its flood in summer, were joined by the solid ice, that offered a medium for pleasant intercourse during the short and dreary days of winter.

Valentine's Day came—the day in England traditionally associated with the wooing of birds and lovers, and when the crocus and the daffodil proclaim the approach of spring. But here the birds and the early flowers were unseen; the sceptre of the frost king was yet all-potent. The blue bird, the robin, and the swallow, our earliest feathered visitors from the south, yet lingered in their southern homes. Soon the clouds gathered and came down in warm and gentle rain; the deep snows of northern New York melted rapidly, and the Upper Hudson and the Mohawk poured out a mighty flood that spread over the valleys, submerged town wharves, and burst the ribs of ice yet thick and compact. Down came the turbid waters whose attrition below, working with the warm sun above, loosened the icy chains that for seventy days had held the Hudson in bondage, and towards the close of February great masses of the shivered fetters were moving with the ebb and flow of the tide. The snow disappeared, the buds swelled, and, to the delight of all, one beautiful morning, when even the dew was not congealed, the blue birds, first harbingers of approaching summer, were heard gaily singing in the

trees and hedges. It was a welcome and delightful invitation to the
fields and waters, and I hastened to the lower borders of the Highland
region to resume my pen and pencil sketches of the Hudson from the
wilderness to the sea.

The air was as balmy as May on the evening of my arrival at Sing
Sing, on the eastern bank of the Hudson, where the State of New York
has a large penitentiary for men and women. I strolled up the steep
and winding street to the heart of the village, and took lodgings for the

SLEIGH RIDING ON THE HUDSON.

night. The sun was yet two hours above the horizon. I went out
immediately upon a short tour of observation, and found ample compensation for the toil occasioned by the hilly pathways traversed.

Sing Sing is a very pleasant village, of almost four thousand inhabitants.
It lies upon a rudely broken slope of hills, that rise about one hundred
and eighty feet above the river, and overlook Tappan Bay,* or Tappaanse
Zee, as the early Dutch settlers called an expansion of the Hudson,

* *Tap-pan* was the name of a Mohegan tribe that inhabited the eastern shores of the bay.

extending from Teller's or Croton Point on the north, to the northern bluff of the Palisades near Piermont. The origin of the name is to be found in the word Sint-sinck, the title of a powerful clan of the Mohegan

CROTON AQUEDUCT AT SING SING.

or river Indians, who called this spot *Os-sin-ing*, from *ossin*, a stone, and *ing*, a place—stony place. A very appropriate name. The land in this vicinity, first parted with by the Indians, was granted to Frederick

Philipse (who owned a large manorial estate along the Hudson), in 1685.

Passing through the upper portion of the village of Sing Sing is a wild, picturesque ravine, lined with evergreen trees, with sides so rugged that the works of man have only here and there found lodgment. Through it flows the *Kill*, as the Dutch called it, or Sint-sinck brook, which rises among the hills east of the village, and 'falls into the Hudson after a succession of pretty rapids and cascades. Over it the waters of the Croton river pass on their way to supply the city of New York with a healthful beverage. Their channel is of heavy masonry, here lying upon an elliptical arch of hewn granite, of eighty-eight feet span, its keystone more than seventy feet from the waters of the brook under it. This great aqueduct will be more fully considered presently.

On the southern borders of the village of Sing Sing is a rough group of small hills, called collectively Mount Pleasant. They are formed of dolomitic, or white coarse-grained marble, of excellent quality, and almost inexhaustible quantity, cropping out from a thin soil in many places. At the foot of Mount Pleasant, on the shore of the river, is a large prison for men, with a number of workshops and other buildings, belonging to the State of New York. A little way up the slope is the prison for women, a very neat and substantial building, with a fine colonnade on the river front. These prisons were built by convicts about thirty years ago, when there were two establishments of the kind in the State, one in the city of New York, the other at Auburn, in the interior. A new system of prison discipline had been adopted. Instead of the old system of indolent, solitary confinement, the workhouse feature was combined with incarceration in separate cells at night. They were made to work diligently all day, but in perfect silence, no recognition by word, look, or gesture, being allowed among them. The adoption of this system, in 1823, rendered the prison accommodation insufficient, and a new establishment was authorised in 1824. Mount Pleasant, near Sing Sing, was purchased, and in May, 1826, Captain Lynds, a farm agent of the Auburn prison, proceeded with one hundred felons from that establishment to erect the new penitentiary. They quarried and wrought diligently among the marble rocks at Mount Pleasant, and the prison for men was completed in 1829, when the convicts in the old State prison in the city of New York were removed to it.· It had eight hundred cells, but these were found to be too few, and in 1831 another story was added to the building, and with it two hundred more cells, making one thousand in all, the present number. More are needed, for the number of convicts in the men's prison, at the beginning of 1861, was a little more than thirteen hundred. In the prison for women there were only

STATE PRISON AT SING SING.

one hundred cells, while the number of convicts was one hundred and fifty at that time.

The ground occupied by the prisons is about ten feet above high-water mark. The main building, in which are the cells, is four hundred and eighty feet in length, forty-four feet in width, and five stories in height. Between the outside walls and the cells there is a space of about twelve feet, open from floor to roof. A part of it is occupied by a series of galleries, there being a row of one hundred cells to each story on both fronts, and backing each other. Between the prison and the river are the several workshops, in which various trades are carried on. In front of the prison for women is the guard-house, where arms and instructions are given out to thirty-one guardsmen every morning. Between the guard-house and the prison the Hudson River Railway passes, partly through two tunnels and a deep trench. Upon the highest points of Mount Pleasant are guard-houses, which overlook the quarries and other places of industrial operations.

STATE PRISONERS.

It was just at sunset when I finished my sketch of the prisons and workshops. A large portion of Tappan Bay, and the range of high hills upon its western shore, were then immersed in a thin purple mist, so frequently seen in this region on balmy afternoons in the spring and autumn. The prison bell rang as I was turning to leave the scene, and soon a troop of convicts, dressed in the felon's garb, and accompanied by overseers, was marched towards the prison and taken to their cells, there to be fed and locked up for the night. Their costume consists of a short co.it, vest, pantaloons, and cap, made of white kerseymere cloth, broadly striped with black. The stripes pass around the arms and legs, but are perpendicular upon the body of the coat.

I visited the prisons early the following morning, in company with one of the officers. We first went through that in which the women are kept, and I was surprised at the absence of aspects of crime in the appearance of most of the convicts. The cells were all open, and many of them displayed evidences of taste and sentiment, hardly to be suspected in criminals. Fancy needlework, cheap pictures, and other ornaments, gave some of the cells an appearance of comfort; but the wretchedly narrow spaces into which, in several instances, two of the convicts are placed together at night, because of a want of more cells, dispelled the temporary illusion that prison life was not so very uncomfortable after all. The household drudgery and cookery were performed by the convicts, chiefly by the coloured ones, and a large number were employed in binding hats that are manufactured in the men's prison. They sat in a series of rows, under the eyes of female overseers, silent, yet not very sad. Most of them were young, many of them interesting and innocent in their appearance, and two or three really beautiful. The crime of a majority of them was grand larceny.

There was one woman there, six-and-thirty years of age, whose case was a sad one. She seemed to have been, through life, the victim of others' crimes, and doomed to suffer more for the sins of others than for her own. Years ago, a friend of the writer arrived at New York at an early hour one morning, and was led by curiosity to the police office, where persons arrested by watchmen during the night were disposed of at dawn. Whilst there, a beautiful young girl, shrinking from public gaze, and weeping as if her heart was breaking, was brought in. When her turn for examination came, the justice, too accustomed to the sight of vicious persons to exercise much compassion, accosted her rudely, she having been picked up as a street wanderer, and accused of vagrancy. She told a simple, touching story of her wrongs and misery. Only a month before, she had been the innocent daughter of loving parents in Connecticut. She came to the metropolis to visit an aunt, whose vicious son invited her to attend him to the theatre. She went without suspicion, took some refreshments which he offered her at the play, became oblivious within half an hour after partaking of the spiced wine which the young villain had drugged, and before morning found herself covered with shame in a strange house in a strange part of the city. Utterly cast down, she avoided both aunt and parents. She was soon cast away by her wicked cousin, and on the night of her arrest was wandering alone, without shelter or hope. She was compelled to bow to her fate, whilst the law, at that time, could not touch the author of her degradation, who further wronged her by foulest slander, to palliate his own wickedness. Justice was not then so kindly disposed towards the erring and unfortunate as now. There was no Magdalen refuge for her, and the magistrate, with almost brutal roughness, reproached her, and sent her to "the Island"* for six months as a vagrant. The gentleman who witnessed this scene became possessed of her subsequent history.

Associated with the vile, her degradation was complete, while her innate virtue struggled for existence. She was an outcast at the age of seventeen. Parental affection, yielding to the stern demands of social ethics, sought not to rescue or reform the child. She had "disgraced her family," and that offence was sufficient to win for her an eternal exile. When the law was satisfied, she went forth with virtuous resolves, and sought a livelihood through menial service. Twice she was pointed at as a Magdalen and convict, and sought refuge from recognition in other places. At length a gleam of hope beamed upon her. She was wooed by a man who seemed honest and true, who had been charmed by her beauty. They were married. She was again allied with human sympathy, and was happy. Years passed by. A cloud appeared. She suspected her husband to be in league with burglars and counterfeiters. She accused him inquiringly, and he confessed his guilt. She pleaded with him most tenderly, for the sake of herself and their three babes, to abandon his course of life. Her words were ineffectual. His vile associates became bold. His house became the receptacle of burglars' plunder, and the head-quarters of counterfeiting. To her the world was shut. She had sympathy only with her husband and children. She had

---

* Blackwell's Island, in the East River, which will be noticed hereafter.

not courage to leave the loathed atmosphere of crime that filled her dwelling, and encounter again the blasts of a selfish world. She became a passive participator in guilt. Detection soon followed transgression. She was arraigned as an accomplice of her husband and his associates in counterfeiting. The proof was clear, and conviction followed. Three years before my visit she had been sent to the state prison for five years, and her husband for ten years. They have never met since hearing their sentence. Their babes were taken to the almshouse, and that crushed woman sat desolate within the prison walls. Meekly she performed her daily duties. There was a sweet sadness in her pale face. She was not a *criminal* in the eye of Divine justice; she was a *victim* to be pitied—the wreck of an innocent and beautiful girl. Surely there must be something radically wrong in the constitution of our society, that permits tender flowers to be thus blasted and thus neglected, and become like worthless weeds, to be trampled upon and forgotten.

In the prison for men, and in the workshops, everything is carried on with the most perfect order; every kind of labour, the meals, the religious exercises in the chapel, are all conducted according to the most rigid rules. The discipline is consequently quite perfect. *Reformation*, not merely *punishment*, is the great aim, and the history of the prison attests the success of the effort. Severe punishments are becoming more and more rare, and the terrible Shower Bath, which has been so justly condemned by the humane, is now seldom used, and then in the presence of the prison physician. Only when all other means for forcing obedience have failed, is this horrid punishment inflicted. It is admitted, I believe, that the Mount Pleasant or Sing Sing prison is one of the best conducted penitentiaries in the world.

On returning to the village across the fields northward of Mount Pleasant, I obtained a full view of Teller's or Croton Point, which divides Tappan from Haverstraw Bay. It is almost two miles in length, and was called *Se-nas-qua* by the Indians, and by the English, Sarah's Point, in honour of Sarah, wife of William Teller, who purchased it of the Indians for a barrel of rum and twelve blankets. It was called Teller's Point until within a few years, when the name of Croton was given to it. Near its extremity, within a pleasant, embowered lawn, stood the Italian villa of R. T. Underhill, M.D., who was sixth in descent from the famous Captain Underhill, a leader in the Indian wars of New England. The Point was owned by himself and brother, both of whom had extensive vineyards and luxuriant orchards. They had about eighty acres covered with the Isabella and Catawba grape vine, sixty of which belonged to the doctor. They also raised fine apples and melons in great abundance. From our point of view, near Sing Sing landing, the village of Haverstraw is seen in the vista between Croton Point and the High Torn Mountain on the left.

CROTON POINT, FROM SING SING.

It was now the first day of March, and very warm; the surface of the river was unruffled by a breeze. Knowing how boisterous and blustering this first spring month generally is, I took advantage of the fine weather, and crossed Tappan Bay to Rockland Lake village (formerly Slaughter's Landing), opposite Sing Sing, the most extensive ice-station on the river. After considerable delay, I procured a boat and oarsman—the former very leaky, and the latter very accommodating. The bay is here between two and three miles wide. We passed a few masses of floating ice and some sailing vessels, and at little past noon landed at Rockland, where the Knickerbocker Ice Company had a wharf and barges, and a large inclined-plane railway, down which ice, brought from the adjacent lake, was sent to the vessels in the river.

ROCKLAND, OR SLAUGHTERER'S LANDING.

It was a weary way up the steep shore to the village and the lake, on the borders of a high and well-cultivated valley, half a mile from the river. This is the famous Rockland Lake, whose congealed waters have been so

long familiar to the thirsty dwellers in the metropolis.   It is a lovely
sheet of water, one hundred and fifty feet above the river.   On its south-
eastern borders, excepting where the village and ice-houses skirt it, are
steep, rugged shores.   Westward, a fertile country stretches away many
a mile to rough hills and blue mountains.   The lake is an irregular ellipse
in form, half a mile in length, and three-fourths of a mile at its greatest
width, and covers about five hundred acres.   It is supplied by springs in
its own bosom, and clear mountain brooks, and forms the head waters of
the Hackensack river, which flows through New Jersey, and reaches the

ROCKLAND LAKE.

salt water in Newark Bay.   Near its outlet, upon a grassy peninsula, is
the residence of Moses G. Leonard, Esq., seen in the picture; and in the
distance, from our point of view, is seen the peak of the great Torn
Mountain, back of Haverstraw.   Along the eastern margin of the lake
were extensive buildings for the storeage of ice in winter, at which time
a thousand men were sometimes employed.   The crop averaged nearly
two hundred thousand tons a-year; and during the warm season, one
hundred men were employed in conveying it to the river, and fifteen

barges were used in transporting it to New York, for distribution there, and exportation.

We crossed the bay to Croton Point, visited the villa and vineyards of

MOUTH OF THE CROTON.

Doctor Underhill, and then rowed up Croton Bay to the mouth of the river, passing, on our way, under the drawbridge of the Hudson River Railway. It was late in the afternoon. There was a remarkable stillness and dreamy repose in the atmosphere, and we glided almost noiselessly up the bay, in company with two or three duck-hunters, in their little cockles. The tide was ebbing, and as we approached the mouth of the Croton, the current became more and more rapid, until we found ourselves in a shallow rift abreast the Van Cortlandt Manor House, unable to proceed. After vain efforts of our united strength to stem the current, the boatman landed me on the southern shore of the stream. After satisfying his extortionate demand of about the price of three fares for his services, I dismissed him, with a strong desire never again to fall into his hands; and then clambered up the rough bank by the margin of a brook, and made my way to the "post road," a most picturesque highway along the lofty banks of the Croton. When near the "High Bridge," at the old head of boat navigation, I obtained a most interesting view of the Mouth of the Croton, including Dover Kill Island near, the railway-bridge in the distance, and the high hills on the western shore of the Hudson in the extreme distance. The scenery thereabout is both picturesque and beautiful, and such is its character to the very sources of this famous stream eastward of the Pawling Mountains, whose clear waters supply the city of New York with wholesome beverage.

The ancient name of the Croton was *Kitch-a-wan*, signifying a large and swift current. The Dutch called it Croton in memory of an Indian Sachem of that name, whose habitation was on the northern border of the bay, near the neck, a little below the mouth of the river. Its sources are among the hills of Putnam and Duchess, and it has five considerable tributaries, all of mountain birth. When the authorities of the city of New York were seeking sources of ample supply of pure water, their attention was early called to this stream. Commissioners reported in favour of its use, though far away; and in May, 1837, the construction of an aqueduct from a point six miles from its mouth to the metropolis was begun. At the head of the aqueduct a dam was constructed, for the purpose of forming a fountain reservoir. At the beginning of 1841 a flood, produced by a protracted rain-storm and melting snows, swept away the dam, and carried with it, riverward, a quantity of earth and gravel, sufficient to half fill the beautiful Croton Bay. The dam was immediately rebuilt, at greater altitude, and a lake was produced, almost

six miles in length, containing about 500,000,000 gallons. It is 166 feet
above mean tide-water at New York, and pours into the aqueduct from
40,000,000 to 50,000,000 gallons every twenty-four hours. Not having
time to visit the fountain reservoir, I have availed myself of the pencil
services of a friend, in giving a sketch of the dam from a point just
below it.

The Croton aqueduct runs parallel with the Hudson, at the mean
distance of half a mile from it throughout its entire length. Its course is

CROTON DAM.

marked by culverts and arches of solid masonry, and its line may be
observed at a distance by white stone towers, about fifteen feet in height,
placed at intervals of a mile. These are ventilators of the aqueduct;
some of them are quite ornamental, as in the case of the one at Sing Sing,
others are simple round towers, and every third one has a square base,
with a door by which a person may enter the aqueduct. At the top of
each is an iron screen, to prevent substances from being cast into the

ventilators. Our little group shows the different forms of these towers,
which present a feature in the landscape on the eastern shore of the river,
to voyagers on the Hudson. This great work was completed, and the
water opened to the use of the inhabitants of New York, in the autumn
of 1842. Its cost was about $12,000,000. We shall meet with it
frequently in our future tour towards the city.

The "High Bridge" over the Croton, at the old head of the navigation,
was a wooden, rickety structure, destined soon to fall in disuse and
absolute decay, because of a substantial new bridge, then being

VENTILATORS.

constructed across the head of the bay, almost a mile below, by which the
route from Croton to Sing Sing would be much shortened. Here was the
"Croton Bridge" of revolutionary times, frequently mentioned in
connection with military movements between New York and the Highlands ; and here is now the scene of most important experiments in the
production of malleable iron from the ore, by a simple process, which, if
successful, would produce a marked change in the iron manufacture. It
is a process of deoxidizing iron ore in a heated hollow screw, out of which,
when the process is completed, it drops into the furnace, avoids all fluxes,
and comes out "blooms" of the finest iron. Mr. Rogers, the inventor,

claimed that by this process there would be a saving of from eight to twelve dollars a ton in the production of iron—a matter of great importance to such isolated districts as that of the Adirondack works at the sources of the Hudson already mentioned. It was from Bayley's rolling mill, at the foot of the rapids in the Croton, just above the old High Bridge, where these experiments were going on, that I made the sketch of that dilapidated affair, just at sunset.

Crossing the bridge, I strolled down the right bank of the Croton, along

HIGH BRIDGE OVER THE CROTON.

the high margin of the stream, to the Van Cortlandt Manor House, passing the old Ferry House on the way, where a party of New York levies, under Captain Daniel Williams, were surprised by some British horsemen in the winter of 1782. At the entrance gate to the mansion grounds, at twilight, I met Colonel Pierre Van Cortlandt, the present proprietor, and accepted his cordial invitation to partake of the hospitalities of his house for the night.

The Van Cortlandt Manor House stands near the shore of Croton Bay. It was erected at the beginning of the last century, by John Van

Cortlandt, eldest son of the first lord of the manor, and is now more than one hundred and fifty years old. Orloff Stevenson Van Cortlandt, father of the first proprietor of this estate, was a lineal descendant of the Dukes of Courland, in Russia. His ancestors emigrated to Holland, when deprived of the Duchy of Courland. The family name was Stevens, or Stevensen, van (or from) Courland. They adopted the latter as a surname, the true orthography of which, in Dutch, is *Korte* (short), and

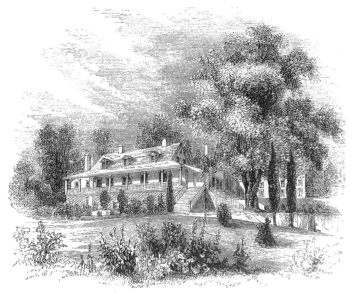

VAN CORTLANDT MANOR HOUSE.

landt (land), a term expressing the form of the ancient Duchy of Courland. Orloff emigrated to America, and settled in New Amsterdam (New York), and in 1697 his son Stephen purchased the large estate on the Hudson, afterwards known as the Van Cortlandt Manor. By intermarriages, the Van Cortlandts are connected with nearly all of the leading families of New York—the Schuylers, Beekmans, Van Renselaers, De Peysters, De Lancys, Bayards, &c. The Manor House was built of heavy stone; and the thick walls were pierced with loopholes for musketry to be used in defence against the Indians. It has been somewhat changed in aspect, by covering the round stone with stucco. Its front, graced by a pleasant lawn, commands an extensive view of the bay, and of the Hudson beyond. In that bay, under the shelter of Croton Point, Hendrick Hudson anchored the *Half-Moon*, on the evening of the first of October, 1609; and such a resort were these waters for canvas-back ducks, and other water-fowl, that, as early as 1683, Governor Dongan came there to enjoy the sport of fowling. There, too, great quantities of shad were caught. But its glory is departed. The flood of 1841, that swept away the Croton Dam, almost filled the bay with earth; it is accumulating there every hour; and, in the course of a few years, the Van Cortlandt estate will have many acres of fine meadow land added to it, where once large vessels might ride at anchor.

CHAPTER XVII.

HE Van Cortlandt mansion, of which a sketch appears in the last Chapter, is clustered with historic associations. It was the summer home of the master, whose town residence was a stately one for the colonial times. There, at early, as well as at later, periods, the wealthy and the high-born of the land frequently assembled as guests. From its broad piazza the famous Whitefield preached to a large audience upon the lawn. There, in 1774, Governor Tryon, and Edmund Fanning, his secretary, came on a mission of bribery to General Van Cortlandt, who had espoused the cause of the colonists. They offered him lands and titles for his allegiance to the crown, but they were refused. Under that roof the illustrious Washington was a frequent guest when the army was in that vicinity; and the parlour was once honoured by the presence of the immortal Franklin. There may be seen many mementoes of the past: the horns of a stag killed on the manor, when deer ran wild there; the buttons from the yager coat worn by one of the captors of André; a box made of the wood of the *Endeavour*, the ship in which Cook navigated the globe, et cetera.

On the morning after my arrival, accompanied by Mrs. Van Cortlandt, I rode to the village of Croton, a mile distant, to visit one of twin sisters, who were ninety years old in August, 1860.* On our way we turned into the cemetery of the Van Cortlandt family, upon a beautiful point of land, commanding an extensive view of the Hudson southward. A little west of the cemetery, at the neck of land which connects Croton Point with the main, stood the old fort or castle of *Kitch-a-wan*, said to have been one of the most ancient Indian fortresses south of the Highlands. It was built by the Sachem Croton, when he assembled his parties for

---

* These sisters were living at the beginning of 1866.

hunting or war. In a beautiful nook, a little east of the site of the fort, on the borders of Haunted Hollow, is the *Kitch-a-wan* burying-ground. Around this locality hovers the memory of many a weird story of the early times, when the superstitious people believed that they often saw, in the groves and glens there, the forms of the departed red men. They called them the Walking Sachems of Teller's Point.

We visited one of the twin sisters at Croton, Mrs. Miriam Williams. Her memory of long-past events seemed very faithful, but the mind of her sister had almost perished with age. They had both lived in that vicinity since their birth, having married and settled there in early life. Mrs. Williams had a perfect recollection of Washington, when he was quartered with the army near Verplanck's Point. On one occasion, she said, he dismounted in front of her father's house, and asked for some food. As he entered, the twins were standing near the door. Placing his hands upon their heads, he said, "You are as alike as two eggs. May you have long life." He entered with her father, and the children peeped curiously in at the door. A morsel of food and a cup of cold water was placed upon the table, when Washington stepped forward, laid his hand upon the board, closed his eyes, and reverently asked a blessing, their father having, meanwhile, raised his hat from his head. "And here," said Mrs. Williams, pointing to a small oval table near her, "is the very table at which that good man asked a blessing."

From the little village of Croton, or Collaberg Landing, I rode to the dwelling of a friend (James Cockroft, Esq.), about two miles northward, passing on the way the old house of Tellar (now Moodie), where the incident just related occurred. Accompanied by Mr. Cockroft and his neighbour, J. W. Frost, Esq., I climbed to the summit of Prickly Pear Hill (so called from the fact that a species of cactus, called Prickly Pear, grows there abundantly), almost five hundred feet above the river, from which may be obtained the most extensive and interesting views in all that region. From no point on the Hudson can be seen, at a glance, such a cluster of historic localities, as from this eminence. Here Washington was encamped in 1782, and made this pinnacle his chief observatory. At one sweep of the vision may be seen the lofty ranges of the Highlands, and the Fish Kill Mountains, with all the intervening country adjacent to Peek's Kill, Verplanck's and Stony Points, the theatres of important military events during the war for independence; Haverstraw, where Arnold and André had their conference; Teller's Point, off which the *Vulture* lay, and from which she received a cannonading that drove her down the river; King's Ferry, where André crossed the Hudson; the place of Pine's Bridge on the Croton, where he was suspected; Tarrytown, where he was captured, and the long wharf of Piermont, near Tappan, where he was executed. All of these, with the villages on the eastern

VIEW FROM PRICKLY PEAR HILL.

shore of the Hudson, from Cruger's to York Island, may be seen from this hill. Before it lies Haverstraw Bay, the widest expanse of the Hudson, with all its historic and legendary associations, which limited space forbids us to portray. Here the fresh and salt water usually contend most equally for the mastery; and here the porpoise,* a sea-water

---

* *Porpoise communis;* genus *Phocæna*, supposed to be the Tursio of Pliny. It is from four to eight feet in length, nearly of a black colour above, and whitish beneath. They are found in all our northern seas and bays. They swim in shoals, and pursue other fishes up bays and rivers, with the avidity of hounds after game. In fine weather they leap, roll, and tumble, in great glee, especially in late spring time. They yield a very fine oil.

fish, is often seen in large numbers, sporting in the summer sun. Here, in the spring, vast numbers of shad are caught while on their way to spawning places in fresh-water coves; and here, at all seasons, most delicious fish may be taken in great abundance. All things considered, this is one of the most interesting points for a summer residence to be found on the Hudson.

The highways, on land and water, from the Croton to the Spuyten Duyvil Creek, at the head of York Island, pass through exceedingly beautiful and picturesque scenery, made classical to the American mind

THE PORPOISE.

because of most interesting historical associations. On the west side of the Hudson, seen by the traveller on road, railway, or river, is a bold mountain shore, having a few cultivated slopes and pleasant villages as far down as the lower extremity of Tappan Bay. From that point there are presented, for about twenty miles southward, perpendicular walls of rock, with bases in buttress form, called the Palisades, fronting immediately on, and rising several hundred feet above, the river. On the east the voyager sees a beautiful, high, undulating country, well cultivated, and sprinkled with villages and hamlets.

The drive from Sing Sing to King's Bridge at Spuyten Duyvil Creek, along the old post-road, is attractive at all seasons of the year, but more especially in spring and early summer, when the trees are in leaf, because of the ever-varying aspects of the landscape. Fine mansions and villa residences are seen on every side, where, only a few years ago, good taste was continually offended by uncouth farmhouses, built for utility only,

GENERAL WARD'S MANSION.

without a single thought of harmony or beauty. Now all is changed, and the eye is as continually pleased.

One of the finest of the older country seats in this region was the mansion of General Aaron Ward, overlooking the village of Sing Sing, and commanding a very extensive view of the Hudson and its distant shores. General Ward is one of the most distinguished men in Westchester

County, and is descended from an early settler in that region. He was an officer in the American army during the war with Great Britain in 1812—15, and at its close conducted the first detachment of the British prisoners from the States to Canada. Law was his chosen profession, and in 1825 he became a law-maker, by election to the Lower House of the National Congress. He was an active and efficient worker, and the satisfaction of his constituency was certified by their retaining him as their representative, by re-election, twelve out of eighteen consecutive years. He assisted in framing the present constitution of the State of New York, in 1846, and since then has declined invitations to public service. During the years 1859 and 1860, he visited Egypt and the Holy Land. His narrative of his journey, published under the title of "Around the Pyramids," is considered one of the most truthful productions of its kind from the pen of an American. Sing Sing owes much to General Ward's enterprise and public spirit, and he is sincerely honoured and beloved in the community where he resides.

Pleasant residences—some embowered, others standing out in the bright sunlight near groves and woods—delight the eye more and more as we approach the large village of Tarrytown, twenty-seven miles from New York. Of these the most conspicuous between the little hamlet of Scarborough, below Sing Sing and Tarrytown, is that of Mr. Aspinwall, a wealthy New York merchant. Near it was the residence of General James Watson Webb, then the veteran editor and proprietor of the New York *Courier and Inquirer*, and well known, personally, and by reputation, in both hemispheres as a gentleman of rare abilities as a journalist. At the beginning of the Civil War, General Webb was appointed resident minister at the court of Pedro II., emperor of Brazil, in which position he continued during the entire struggle.

Approaching Tarrytown, we observe upon the left of the highway an already populous cemetery, covering the crown and slopes of a gentle hill. Near its base is an ancient church, and a little beyond it flows a clear stream of water, which the Indians called *Po-can-te-co*, signifying a "run between two hills." It makes its way in a swift current from the back country, between a hundred hills, presenting a thousand scenes of singular beauty in its course. The Dutch named it *Slaeperigh Haven*

Kill, or Sleepy Haven Creek, and the valley in the vicinity of the old church, through which it flowed, *Slaeperigh Hol*, or Sleepy Hollow, the scene of Washington Irving's famous legend of that name.

The little old church is a curiosity. It was built, says an inscription upon a small marble tablet on its front, by "Frederic Philips and Catharine Van Cortland, his wife, in 1699," and is the oldest church edifice existing in the State of New York. It was built of brick and stone, the former imported from Holland for the purpose. Over its little

ANCIENT DUTCH CHURCH.

spire still turns the flag-shaped vane of iron, in which is cut the monogram of its founder (VF in combination, his name being spelt in Dutch, Vedryck Flypsen); and in the little tower hangs the ancient bell, bearing the inscription in Latin, "*If God be for us, who can be against us?* 1685." The pulpit and communion table were also imported from Holland. The former was long since destroyed by the iconoclastic hand of "improvement."

At this quiet old church is the opening of Sleepy Hollow, upon the shores of the Hudson, and near it is a rustic bridge that crosses the

Po-can-te-co, a little below the one made famous in Irving's legend by an amusing incident.*   In this vicinity, according to the legend, Ichabod

SLEEPY HOLLOW BRIDGE.

Crane, a Connecticut schoolmaster, instructed " tough, wrong-headed,

---

* " Over a deep, black part of the stream, not far from the church," says Mr. Irving, in his " Legend of Sleepy Hollow," " was formerly thrown a wooden bridge ; the road that led to it, and the bridge itself, were thickly shaded by overhanging trees, which cast a gloom about it even in the daytime, but occasioned a fearful darkness at night."

broad-skirted, Dutch urchins" in the rudiments of learning. He was also the singing-master of the neighbourhood. Not far off lived old Baltus Van Tassel, a well-to-do farmer, whose house was called *Wolfert's Roost*. He had a blooming and only daughter named Katrina, and Ichabod was her tutor in psalmody, training her voice to mingle sweetly with those of the choir which he led at Sabbath-day worship in the Sleepy Hollow Church. Ichabod "had a soft and foolish heart toward the sex." He fell in love with Katrina. He found a rival in his suit in stalwart, bony Brom Van Brunt, commonly known as Brom Bones. Jealousies arose, and the Dutchman resolved to drive the Yankee school-master from the country.

Strange stories of ghosts in Sleepy Hollow were believed by all, and by none more implicitly than Ichabod. The chief goblin seen there was that of a Hessian trooper, whose head had been carried away by a cannon ball. This spectre was known all over the country as " The Headless Horseman of Sleepy Hollow."

Ichabod was invited to a social evening party at the house of Van Tassel. He went with alacrity, and borrowed a lean horse called Gun-powder for the journey. Brom Bones was also there. When the company broke up, Ichabod lingered to have a few words with Katrina. He then bestrode Gunpowder, and started for home. When within half a mile of the old church, a horse and rider, huge, black, and mysterious, suddenly appeared by his side. The rider was headless, and to the horror of the pedagogue it was discovered that he carried his head in his hand, on the pommel of his saddle. Ichabod was half dead with fear. He urged Gunpowder forward to escape the demon, but in vain. The headless horseman followed. The walls of the old church appeared in the dim starlight of the midnight hour. The log bridge, in the deep shadows of the trees, was near. "If I can but reach that bridge," thought Ichabod, "I shall be safe." Just then he heard the black steed panting and blowing close behind him; he even fancied that he felt his hot breath. Another convulsive kick in the ribs and old Gunpowder sprang upon the bridge: he thundered over the resounding planks; he gained the opposite side; and now Ichabod cast a look behind to see if his pursuer would vanish, according to rule, in a flash of fire and brimstone. Just then he saw the goblin rising in his stirrups, and in the very act of hurling his head at him. Ichabod endeavoured to dodge the horrible missile, but too late ; it encountered his cranium with a terrible crash ; he was tumbled headlong into the dust, and Gunpowder, the black steed, and the goblin rider, passed like a whirlwind. A shattered pumpkin was found in the road the next day, and Brom Jones not long afterwards led Katrina Van Tassel to the altar as his bride. Ichabod was never heard of afterwards. The people always believed he had been spirited away by the Headless Horseman of Sleepy Hollow, who, on that occasion, some knowing ones supposed to have been a being no more ghostly than Brom Bones himself.

Let us climb over this stile by the corner of the old church, into the yard where so many of the pilgrims of earth are sleeping. Here are mossy stones with half obliterated epitaphs, marking the graves of many early settlers, among whom is one, upon whose monumental slab it is recorded, that he lived until he was " one hundred and three years old," and had one hundred and twenty-four children and grandchildren at the time of his death! Let us pass on up this narrow winding path, and cross the almost invisible boundary between the old "graveyard" and the new "cemetery." Here, well up towards the summit of the hill near the "receiving vault," upon a beautiful sunny slope, is an enclosure made of iron bars and privet hedge, with open gate, inviting entrance. There in line stand several slabs of white marble, only two feet in height, at the head of as many oblong hillocks, covered with turf and budding spring flowers. Upon one of these, near the centre, we read :—

WASHINGTON,
SON OF
WILLIAM AND
SARAH S. IRVING,
DIED
NOV. 28, 1859,
AGED 76 YEARS 7 MO.
AND 25 DAYS.

This is the grave of the immortal Geoffrey Crayon!* Upon it lie

* In the Episcopal Church at Tarrytown, in which Mr. Irving was a communicant for many years, a small marble tablet has been placed by the vestry, with an appropriate inscription to his memory.

wreaths of withered flowers, which have been killed by frosts, and buried
by drifts of lately departed snow.   These will not long remain, for all
summer long fresh and fragrant ones are laid upon that honoured grave

IRVING'S GRAVE.

by fair hands that pluck them from many a neighbouring garden.   Here,
at all times, these sweet tributes of affection may be seen, when the trees
are in leaf.

This lovely burial spot, from which may be seen Sleepy Hollow, the ancient church, the sparkling waters of the *Po-can-te-co*, spreading out into a little lake above the picturesque old dam at the mill of Castle Philipse, Sleepy Hollow Haven, Tappan Bay and all its beautiful surroundings, was chosen long ago by the illustrious author of the "Sketch-Book," as his final resting-place. Forty years ago, in Birmingham, three thousand miles away from the spot where his remains now repose, and long before he even dreamed of converting Wolfert's Roost into Sunnyside, he wrote thus concerning Sleepy Hollow, in his introduction to the legend :—

"Not far from this village [Tarrytown], perhaps about two miles, there is a little valley, or rather a lap of land, among high hills, which is one of the quietest places in the whole world. A small brook glides through it, with just murmur enough to lull one to repose ; and the occasional whistle of a quail, or tapping of a woodpecker, is almost the only sound that ever breaks in upon the uniform tranquillity. . . . . If ever I should wish for a retreat, whither I might steal from the world and its distractions, and dream quietly away the remnant of a troubled life, I know of none more promising than this little valley."

When, more than a dozen years ago, the Tarrytown Cemetery was laid out, Mr. Irving chose the plot of ground where his remains now lie, for his family burial-place. A few years later, when the contents of the grave and vaults in the burial-ground of the "Brick Church" in New York, were removed, the remains of his family were taken to this spot and interred. A gentleman who accompanied me to the grave, superintended the removal. Mr. Irving had directed the remains to be so disposed as to allow himself to lie by the side of his mother. And when the burial was performed, the good old man stood thoughtfully for awhile, leaning against a tree, and looking into his mother's grave, as it was slowly filled with the earth. Then covering his face with his hands he wept as tenderly as a young child. According to his desire he now rests by the side of that mother, whom he loved dearly ; and at his own left hand is reserved a space for his only surviving brother, General Ebenezer Irving, ten years his senior, who yet (1866) resides at Sunnyside at the age of about ninety-four years.

The remains of Mr. Irving's old Scotch nurse were, at his request, buried in the same grave with his mother. Of this faithful woman Mr. Irving once said,—"I remember General Washington perfectly. There was some occasion when he appeared in a public procession ; my nurse, a good old Scotch woman, was very anxious for me to see him, and held me up in her arms as he rode past. This, however, did not satisfy her ; so the next day, when walking with me in Broadway, she espied him in a shop ; she seized my hand, and darting in, exclaimed in her bland Scotch,—' Please your excellency, here's a bairn that's called after ye !' General Washington then turned his benevolent face full upon me, smiled, laid his hand upon my head, and gave me his blessing, which," added Mr. Irving, "I have reason to believe has attended me through life. I was but five years old, yet I can feel that hand upon my head even now." Mr. Irving's last and greatest literary work was an elaborate life of Washington, in five octavo volumes.

We have observed that the *Po-can-te-co*, flowing through Sleepy Hollow, spreads out into a pretty little lake above an ancient and picturesque dam, near the almost as ancient church. This little lake extends back almost to the bridge in the dark weird glen, and furnishes motive power to a very ancient mill that stands close by Philipse Castle, as the more ancient manor-house of the family was called. The first lord of an extensive domain in this vicinity, purchased from the Sachem Goharius, in 1680, and which was confirmed by royal patent the same year, was a descendant of the ancient Viscounts Felyps, of Bohemia, who took an active part in favour of John Huss and Jerome of Prague. Here, at the mouth of the *Po-can-te-co*, he erected a strong stone house, with port and loop holes for cannon and musketry, and also a mill, about the year 1683. Because of its heavy ordnance, it was called Castle Philipse. At that time the extensive marsh and meadow land between it and the present railway was a fine bay, and quite large vessels bore freight to and from the mill. Here, and at the lower manor-house at Yonkers, the lords of Philipse's Manor lived in a sort of feudal state for almost a century, enjoying exclusive social and political privileges. The proprietor in possession when the war for independence broke out, espoused the cause of the crown. His estates were confiscated, and a relative of the family,

Gerardus Beekman, became the purchaser of the castle and many broad acres adjoining it. In that family it remained until the spring of 1860 (about three quarters of a century), when Mr. Storm, the present proprietor, purchased it. Beekman made a large addition to the Castle. In our little picture it is seen as it appeared in the time of the Philipses. In the basement wall, near the rear of the building, may be seen a porthole in which the muzzle of a cannon was seen for full half a century, as

PHILIPSE'S MILL-DAM.

a menace to any hostile intruders who might come up *Po-can-te-co* Bay, which is now filled with earth, and is a fine marsh meadow.

Upon an eminence eastward of Philipse Castle and the ancient church, whose base is washed by the *Po-can-te-co*, is Irving Park, a domain of about one hundred acres, which was laid out by Charles H. Lyon, Esq., for the purpose of villa sites, that should have all the advantages of highly ornamented grounds, pleasant neighbourhood, retirement, and extensive and varied views of a beautiful country, at a moderate expense. From this hill, and its river slopes, comprehensive views may be had of some of the most charming scenery of the lower Hudson. From its summit, overlooking Sleepy Hollow, the eye commands a sweep of the Hudson from New York to the Highlands, a distance of fifty miles, and views in five or six counties in the States of New York and New Jersey. From the veranda of one of the cottages in the park, most charming glimpses may

PHILIPSE CASTLE.

be obtained of portions of the village of Tarrytown,* near, with its wharf and railway station; and of the Palisades below Piermont, the village of Piermont and its pier jutting into the Hudson a mile from the shore, the village of Rockland (formerly Sneden's Landing), and the intervening

* The natives called this place *A-lip-conck*, or Place of Elms, that tree having been abundant there in early times, and still flourishes. The Dutch called it *Terwen Dorp*, or Wheat Town, because that cereal grew luxuriantly upon the Greenburgh Hills and valleys around. As usual, the English retained a part of the Dutch name, and called it Terwe Town, from which is derived the modern pronunciation, Tarrytown. In the legend of "Sleepy Hollow," Mr. Irving says,—"The name was given, we are told, in former days by the good housewives of the adjacent country, from the inveterate propensity of their husbands to linger about the village taverns on market days." So they called it Tarrytown.

river with its numerous water-craft. Our little picture of that scene gives some idea of the delights of a residence within Irving Park, afforded by broad views of nature in its lovely aspects, and the teeming commerce of a great river. Besides these attractions there are pleasant views of the *Po-can-te-co*, as it dashes through Sleepy Hollow in swift rapids and sparkling cascades, from various portions of the park. And all of these,

DISTANT VIEW AT TARRYTOWN.

with the pleasant roads and paths, belong to the owners of dwellings within the park. The proprietor of an acre of ground and his family may take their morning walk or evening drive through miles of varied scenery, without going into the public road, and with the agreeable consciousness of being on their own premises.

Soon after leaving the *Po-can-te-co*, on the way towards Tarrytown, a fine monument of white Westchester marble, about twenty-five feet in height, is seen at the side of the highway, and on the margin of a little stream called André's Brook. It is surrounded by an iron railing, and upon a tablet next to the road is the following inscription, which explains the object of the monument :—

"On this spot, the 22nd day of September, 1780, the spy, Major John

VIEW ON THE PO-CAN-TE-CO FROM IRVING PARK.

André, Adjutant-general of the British army, was captured by John Paulding, David Williams, and Isaac Van Wart, all natives of this county. History has told the rest.

"The people of Westchester County have erected this Monument, as well to commemorate a great event as to testify their high estimation of that integrity and patriotism which, rejecting every temptation, rescued the United States from most imminent peril, by baffling the arts of a Spy and the plots of a Traitor. Dedicated October 7, 1853."

The land on which this monument stands was given for the purpose, by William Taylor, a coloured man, who lives in a neat cottage close by, surrounded by ornamented grounds, through which flows André's Brook. Hon. Henry J. Raymond, editor of the *New York Daily Times*, addressed

MONUMENT AT TARRYTOWN.

the multitude on the occasion of the dedication. Monuments of white marble have been erected to the memory of two of the captors of André, over their respective remains. That to Paulding is in the burial-ground of St. Peter's Church, near Peek's Kill. It was erected by the corporation of the city of New York, as "a memorial sacred to PUBLIC GRATITUDE." William Paulding, then mayor of New York, addressed the assembled citizens on the occasion of its dedication, November 22, 1827. The monument to the memory of Van Wart is over his remains in the Greenburgh Presbyterian Church, near the lovely Neperan river, a few miles from Tarrytown. It was dedicated on the 11th of June, 1829, when the assembled citizens were addressed by General Aaron Ward, of Sing Sing. The monument was erected by the citizens of Westchester County. The remains of Williams are at Livingstonville, Schoharie County; no monument has yet been erected over them.

"History has told the rest," says the inscription upon the monument. In the next Chapter we will observe what history says.

CHAPTER XVIII.

E have already observed the progress of Arnold's treason, from its inception to his conference with André at the house of Joshua Hett Smith. There we left them, André being in possession of sundry valuable papers, revealing the condition of the post to be surrendered, and a pass. He remained alone with his troubled thoughts all day. The *Vulture*, as we have seen, had dropped down the river, out of sight, in consequence of a cannonade from a small piece of ordnance upon the extremity of Teller's Point, sent there for the purpose by Colonel Henry Livingston, who was in command at Verplanck's Point, a few miles above.

In the afternoon André solicited Smith to take him back to the *Vulture*. Smith refused, with the false plea of illness—but he offered to travel half the night with the adjutant-general if he would take the land route. There was no alternative, and André was compelled to yield to the force of circumstances. He consented to cross the King's Ferry (from Stony to Verplanck's Point), and make his way back to New York by land. He exchanged his military coat for a citizen's dress, placed the papers received from Arnold in his stockings under his feet, and at a little before sunset on the evening of the 22nd of September, accompanied by Smith and a negro servant, all mounted, made his way towards King's Ferry, bearing the following pass, in the event of his being challenged within the American lines:—

"*Head-quarters, Robinson's House, Sept.* 22, 1780.

"Permit Mr. John Anderson to pass the Guards to the White Plains, or below, if he chooses, he being on public business by my direction.

"B. ARNOLD, *Major-General.*"

At twilight they passed through the works at Verplanck's Point, unsuspected, and then turned their faces towards the White Plains, the interior route to New York. André was moody and silent. He had disobeyed the orders of his commander by receiving papers, and was involuntarily a spy, in every sense of the word, within the enemy's lines. Eight miles from Verplanck's they were hailed by a sentinel. Arnold's pass was presented, and the travellers were about to pass on, when the officer on duty advised them to remain until morning, because of dangers on the road. After much persuasion, André consented to remain, but passed a sleepless night. At an early hour the party were in the saddle, and at Pine's Bridge over the Croton, André, with a lighter heart, parted company with Smith and his servant, having been assured that he was then upon the neutral ground, beyond the reach of the American patrolling parties.

André had been warned to avoid the Cow Boys. These were bands of Tory marauders who infested the neutral ground. He was told that they were more numerous upon the Tarrytown road than that which led to the White Plains. As these were friends of the British, he resolved to travel the Tarrytown or river road. He felt assured that if he should fall into the hands of the Cow Boys, he would be taken by them to New York, his destination. This change of route was his fatal mistake.

On the morning when André crossed Pine's Bridge, a little band of seven volunteers went out near Tarrytown to prevent the Cow Boys driving the cattle to New York, and to arrest any suspicious travellers upon the highway. Three of these—Paulding, Van Wart, and Williams—were under the shade of a clump of trees, near a spring on the borders of the stream just mentioned, and now known by the name of André's Brook, playing cards, when a stranger appeared on horseback, a short distance up the road. His dress and manner were different from ordinary travellers seen in that vicinity, and they determined to step out and question him. Paulding had lately escaped from captivity in New York, in the dress of a German Yager, the mercenaries in the employment of the British; and on seeing him, André, thereby deceived, exclaimed, "Thank God! I am once more among friends." But Paulding presented his musket, and ordered him to stop. "Gentlemen," said André, "I hope you belong to our party?" "What party?" asked Paulding. "The Lower Party" (meaning the British), André replied. "I do," said Paulding; when André said, "I am a British officer, out in the country on particular business, and I hope you will not detain me a minute." Paulding told him to dismount, when André, conscious of his mistake, exclaimed, "My God! I must do anything to get along;" and with a forced good-humour, pulled out General Arnold's pass. Still they insisted upon his dismounting, when he warned them not to detain him, as he was on public business for the General. They were inflexible. They said there were many bad people on the road, and they did not know but he might be one of them. He dismounted, when they took him into a thicket, and searched him. They found nothing to confirm their suspicions that he was not what he represented himself to be. They then ordered him to pull off his boots, which he did without hesitation, and they were about to allow him to dress himself, when they observed something in his stockings under his feet. When these were removed they discovered the papers which Arnold had put in his possession. Finding himself detected, he offered them bribes to let him go. They refused; and he was conducted to the nearest American post, and delivered to a commanding officer. That officer, with strange obtuseness of perception, was about to send the prisoner to General Arnold with a letter detailing the circumstances of his arrest, when Major Tallmadge, a bright and vigilant officer, protested against the measure, and expressed his suspicions of Arnold's fidelity. But Jamieson, the commander, only half yielded. He detained the *prisoner*, but sent the *letter* to Arnold. That was the one which the traitor received while at breakfast at Beverly (Robinson's House), and which caused his precipitate flight to the *Vulture*. The circumstances of that flight have already been narrated.

André wrote a letter to Washington, briefly but frankly detailing the events of his mission, and concluded, after relating how he was conducted to Smith's House, and changed his clothes, by saying, "Thus, as I have had the honour to relate, was I betrayed (being adjutant-general of the British army) into the vile condition of an enemy in disguise within your posts."

Washington ordered André to be sent first to West Point, and then to

Tappan, an inland hamlet on the west side of the Hudson opposite Tarry-town, then the head-quarters of the American army. There, at his own quarters, he summoned a board of general officers on the 29th of September, and ordered them to examine into the case of Major André, and report the result. He also directed them to give their opinion as to the light in which the prisoner ought to be regarded, and the punishment that should be inflicted. André was arraigned before them, on the same day, in the church not far from Washington's quarters. He made to

WASHINGTON'S HEAD-QUARTERS AT TAPPAN.

them the same truthful statement of facts which he gave in his letter to Washington, and remarked; "I leave them to operate with the board, persuaded that you will do me justice." He was remanded to prison; and after long and careful deliberation, the board reported "That Major André, adjutant-general of the British army, ought to be considered as a spy from the enemy, and that agreeably to the law and usage of nations, it is their opinion he ought to suffer death."

Washington approved the sentence on the 30th, and ordered his execution the next day at five o'clock in the afternoon. The youth, candour, gentleness, and honourable bearing of the prisoner made a deep impression on the court and the commander-in-chief. Had their decision been in consonance with their feelings instead of their judgments and the stern necessities of war, he would never have suffered death. There was a general desire on the part of the Americans to save him. The only mode was to exchange him for Arnold, and hold the traitor responsible for all the acts of his victim. Sir Henry Clinton was a man of nice honour, and would not be likely to exhibit such bad faith towards Arnold, even to save his beloved adjutant-general. Nor would Washington make such a proposition. He, however, respited the prisoner for a day, and gave others an opportunity to lay an informal proposition of that kind before Clinton. A subaltern went to the nearest British outpost with a letter from Washington to Clinton, containing the official proceedings of the court-martial, and André's letter to the American commander. That subaltern, as instructed, informed the messenger who was to bear the packet to Sir Henry, that he believed André might be exchanged for Arnold. This was communicated to Sir Henry. He refused compliance, but sent a general officer up to the borders of the neutral ground, to confer with one from the American camp on the subject of the innocence of Major André. General Greene, the president of the court, met General Robertson, the commissioner from Clinton, at Dobbs' Ferry. The conference was fruitless of results favourable to André.

The unfortunate young man was not disturbed by the fear of death, but the *manner* was a subject of great solicitude to him. He wrote a touching letter to Washington, asking to die the death of a *soldier*, and not that of a *spy*. Again the stern rules of war interposed. The manner of death must be according to the character given him by the sentence. All hearts were powerfully stirred by sympathy for him. The *equity* of that sentence was not questioned by military men; and yet, only inexorable expediency at that hour when the Republican cause seemed in the greatest peril, caused the execution of the sentence in his case. The sacrifice had to be made for the public good, and the prisoner was hung as a spy at Tappan at noon on the 2nd of October, 1780.

It is said that Washington never saw Major André, having avoided a personal interview with him from the beginning. Unwilling to give him unnecessary pain, Washington did not reply to his letter asking for the death of a soldier, and the unhappy prisoner was not certain what was to be the manner of his execution, until he was led to the gallows. The lines of Miss Anne Seward, André's friend, commencing,

" O Washington ! I thought thee great and good,
Nor knew thy Nero-thirst for guiltless blood,
Severe to use the power that fortune gave,
Thou cool, determined murderer of the brave!"

were unjust, for he sincerely commiserated the fate of the prisoner, and would have made every proper sacrifice to save him.

ANDRE'S PEN AND INK SKETCH.

Major André was an accomplished young man, and a clever amateur artist. He was perfectly composed from the time that his fate was made known to him. On the day fixed for his execution, he sketched with pen and ink a likeness of himself sitting at a table, and gave it to the officer of his guard, who had been kind to him. It is preserved in the Trumbull Gallery of pictures, at Yale College, in Connecticut.

Major André was buried at the place of his execution. In 1832, his remains were removed, under instructions of his Royal Highness the Duke of York, by James Buchanan, the British consul at New York, and deposited in a grave near a monument in Westminster Abbey, erected by his king not long after his death. It is a mural monument, in the form of a sarcophagus, standing on a pedestal. It is surmounted by Britannia and her lion. On the front of the sarcophagus is a basso-relievo, in which is represented General Washington and his officers in a tent at the moment

ANDRE'S MONUMENT.

when he received the report of the court of inquiry. At the same time a messenger is seen with a flag, bearing a letter from André to Washington. On the opposite side is a guard of Continental soldiers, and the tree on which André was hung. Two men are preparing the prisoner for execution, in the centre of this design. At the foot of the tree sit Mercy and

Innocence bewailing his fate. Upon a panel of the pedestal is the following inscription:—"Sacred to the memory of Major JOHN ANDRÉ, who, raised by his merit at an early period of his life to the rank of Adjutant-General of the British forces in America, and employed in an important but hazardous enterprise, fell a sacrifice to his zeal for his king and country, on the 2nd of October, A.D. 1780, universally beloved and esteemed by the army in which he served, and lamented even by his foes. His gracious sovereign, KING GEORGE THE THIRD, has caused this monument to be erected." On the base is a record of the removal of his remains from the banks of the Hudson to their final resting-place near the banks of the Thames. Such is the sad story, in brief outline, of the closing days of the accomplished André's life. Arnold, the traitor, was despised even by those who accepted his treason for purposes of state; and his hand never afterwards touched the palm of an honourable Englishman. In his own country, he had ever occupied the "bad eminence" of arch traitor, until the beginning of the year 1861; others now bear the palm.

Upon a high and fertile promontory below Tarrytown, may be seen one of the finest and purest specimens of the Pointed Tudor style of domestic architecture in the United States, the residence of Philip R. Paulding, Esq., and called Paulding Manor. It was built in 1840. Its walls are of the Mount Pleasant or Sing Sing marble. The whole outline, ground and sky, is exceedingly picturesque, there being gables, towers, turrets, and pinnacles. There is also a great variety of windows decorated with mullions and tracery; and at one wing is a *Port Cochere*, or covered entrance for carriages. It has a broad arcaded piazza, affording shade and shelter for promenading. The interior is admirably arranged for convenience and artistic effect. The drawing-room is a spacious apartment, occupying the whole of the south wing. It has a high ceiling, richly groin-arched, with fan tracery or diverging ribs, springing from and supported by columnar shafts. The ceilings of all the apartments of the first story are highly elegant in decoration. "That of the dining-room," says Mr. Downing, "is concavo-convex in shape, with diverging ribs and ramified tracery springing from corbels in the angles, the centre being occupied by a pendant. In the saloon the ribbed ceiling forms two inclined planes. The floor of the second story has a much larger area than that of the first, as the rooms in the former project over the open portals of the latter. The spacious library, over the western portal, lighted by a lofty window, is the finest apartment of this story, with its carved foliated timber roof rising in the centre to twenty-five feet." The dimensions of this room are thirty-seven by eighteen feet, including an organ gallery. Ever since its erection, Paulding Manor has been the most conspicuous dwelling to be seen by the eye of the voyager on the Lower Hudson.

PAULDING MANOR.

About three miles below Tarrytown is Sunnyside, the residence of the late Washington Irving. It is reached from the public road by a winding carriage-way that passes here through rich pastures and pleasant woodlands, and then along the margin of a dell through which runs a pleasant brook, reminding one of the merry laughter of children as it dances away riverward, and leaps, in beautiful cascades and rapids, into a little bay a few yards from the cottage of Sunnyside. There, more than fifteen years ago, I visited the dear old man whom the world loved so well, and who so lately was laid beneath the greensward on the margin of Sleepy Hollow, made classic by his genius. Then I made the sketch of Sunnyside here presented to the reader. It was a soft, delicious day in June, when the trees were in full leaf and the birds in full song. I had left the railway-cars a fourth of a mile below where the germ of a village had just appeared, and strolled along the iron road to a stile, over which I climbed,

SUNNYSIDE.

and ascended the bank by a pleasant path to the shadow of a fine old cedar, not far from the entrance gate. There I rested, and sketched the quaint cottage half shrouded in English ivy. Its master soon appeared in the porch, with a little fair-haired boy whom he led to the river bank in search of daisies and buttercups. It was a pleasant picture, and yet there was a cloud-shadow resting upon it. His best earthly affections had been buried, long years before, in the grave with a sweet young lady who had promised to become his bride. Death interposed between the betrothal and the appointed nuptials. He remained faithful to that first love. Throughout all the vicissitudes of a long life, in society and in solitude, in his native land and in foreign countries, on the stormy ocean and in the repose of quiet homes, he had borne her miniature in his bosom in a plain golden case, and upon his table, for daily use, always lay a small Bible, with the name of his lost one, in the delicate handwriting of a female, upon the title-page. As I looked upon that good man of gentle, loving nature, a bachelor of sixty-five, I thought of his exquisite picture of a true woman, in his charming little story of "The Wife," and wondered whether his own experience had not been in accordance with the following beautiful passage in his "Newstead Abbey," in which he says:—"An early, innocent, and unfortunate passion, however fruitful of pain it may be to the man, is a lasting advantage to the poet. It is a well of sweet and bitter fancies, of refined and gentle sentiments, of elevated and ennobling thoughts, shut up in the deep recesses of the heart, keeping it green amidst the withering blights of the world, and by its casual gushings and overflowings, recalling at times all the freshness, and innocence, and enthusiasm of youthful days."

I visited Sunnyside again only a fortnight before the death of Mr. Irving. I found him in his study, a small, quiet room, lighted by two delicately curtained windows, one of which is seen nearest the porch, in our little sketch of the mansion. From that window he could see far down the river; from the other, overhung with ivy, he looked out upon the lawn and the carriage-way from the lane. In a curtained recess was a lounge with cushions, and books on every side. A large easy-chair, and two or three others, a writing-table with many drawers, shelves filled with books, three small pictures, and two neat bronze candelabra, completed the furniture of the room. It was warmed by an open grate of coals in a black variegated marble chimney-piece. Over this were the three small pictures. The larger represents "A literary party at Sir Joshua Reynolds's." The other two were spirited little pen-and-ink sketches, with a little colour—illustrative of scenes in one of the earlier of Mr. Irving's works—"Knickerbocker's History of New York"—which he picked up in London many years ago. One represented Stuyvesant confronting Risingh, the Swedish governor; the other, Stuyvesant's wrath in council.

Mr. Irving was in feeble health, but hopeful of speedy convalescence. He expressed his gratitude because his strength and life had been spared

IRVING'S STUDY.

until he completed the greatest of all his works, his "Life of Washington." "I have laid aside my pen for ever," he said; "my work is finished, and now I intend to rest." He was then seven years past the allotted age of man, yet his mental energy seemed unimpaired, and his genial good-humour was continually apparent. I took the first course of dinner with him, when I was compelled to leave to be in time for the next train of cars that would convey me home. He arose from the table, and passed into the little drawing-room with me. At the door he took my hand in both of his, and with a pleasant smile said, " I wish you success in all your undertakings. God bless you."

It was the last day of the " Indian summer," in 1859, a soft, balmy, glorious day in the middle of November. The setting sun was sending a blaze of red light across the bosom of Tappan Bay, when I left the porch and followed the winding path down the bank to the railway. There was peacefulness in the aspect of all nature at that hour, and I left Sunnyside, feeling sensibly the influence of a good man's blessing. Only a fortnight afterwards, on a dark, stormy evening, I took up a newspaper at an inn in a small village of the Valley of the Upper Hudson, and read the startling announcement, " *Death of Washington Irving.*" I felt as if a near and dear friend had been snatched away for ever. I was too far from home to be at the funeral, but one of my family, very dear to me, was in the crowd of sincere mourners at his grave, on the borders of Sleepy Hollow. The day was a lovely one on the verge of winter, and thousands stood reverently around, on that sunny slope, while the earth was cast upon the coffin and the preacher uttered the solemn words, " Earth to earth, ashes to ashes, dust to dust." Few men ever went to the tomb lamented by more sincere friends. From many a pulpit his name was spoken with reverence. Literary and other societies throughout the land expressed their sorrow and respect. A thousand pens wrote eulogies for the press, and Bryant, the poet, his life-long friend, pronounced an impressive funeral oration not long afterwards, at the request of the New York Historical Society, of which Mr. Irving was a member.

I visited Sunnyside again in May, 1860, and after drinking at the mysterious spring,* strolled along the brook at the mouth of the glen, where it comes down in cascades before entering the once beautiful little bay, now cut off from free union with the river by the railway. The

---

* This spring is at the foot of the bank on the very brink of the river. "Tradition declares," says Mr. Irving in his admirable story of " Wolfert's Roost," "that it was smuggled over from Holland in a churn by Femmetie Van Blarcom, wife of Goosen Garrett Van Blarcom, one of the first settlers, and that she took it up by night, unknown to her husband, from beside their farm-house near Rotterdam ; being sure she should find no water equal to it in the new country—and she was right."

channel was full of crystal water.   The tender foliage was casting delicate shadows where, at this time, there is half twilight under the umbrageous branches, and the trees are full of warblers.   It is a charming spot, and is

THE BROOK AT SUNNYSIDE.

consecrated by many memories of Irving and his friends who frequented this romantic little dell when the summer sun was at meridian.

After sketching the brook at the cascades, I climbed its banks, crossed the lane, and wandered along a shaded path by a gardener's cottage to a hollow in the hills, filled with water, in which a bevy of ducks were sporting. This pond, which Mr. Irving playfully called his "Mediter-

THE POND, OR "MEDITERRANEAN SEA."

ranean Sea," was made by damming the stream, and thus a pretty cascade at its outlet was formed. It is in the shape of the "palm leaf" that comes from the loom. On one side a wooded hill stretches down to it abruptly, leaving only space enough for a path, and on others it washes the feet of gentle grassy slopes. This is one of the many charming pictures to be found in the landscape of Sunnyside. After strolling along the pathways in various directions, sometimes finding myself upon the domains of the neighbours of Sunnyside (for no fence or hedge barriers exist between them), I made my way back to the cottage, where the eldest and only surviving brother of Mr. Irving, and his daughters, reside. These daughters were always as children to the late occupant, and by their affection and domestic skill they made his home a delightful one to himself and friends. But the chief light of that dwelling is removed, and there are shadows at Sunnyside that fall darkly upon the visitor who remembers the sunshine of its former days, for, as his friend Tuckerman wrote on the day after the funeral,—

" He whose fancy wove a spell
    As lasting as the scene is fair,
And made the mountain, stream, and dell,
    His own dream-life for ever share ;

" He who with England's household's grace,
    And with the brave romance of Spain,
Tradition's lore and Nature's face,
    Imbued his visionary brain :

" Mused in Granada's old arcade
    As gush'd the Moorish fount at noon,
With the last minstrel thoughtful stray'd,
    To ruin'd shrines beneath the moon ;

" And breathed the tenderness and wit
    Thus garner'd, in expression pure,
As now his thoughts with humour flit,
    And now to pathos-wisely lure ;

" Who traced with sympathetic hand
    Our peerless chieftain's high career,
His life that gladden'd all the land,
    And blest a home—is ended here !"

There was a fascination about Mr. Irving that drew every living creature towards him. His personal character, like his writings, was distinguished by extreme modesty, sweetness, and simplicity. "He was never willing to set forth his own pretensions," wrote a friend, after his death ; "he was willing to leave to the public the care of his literary reputation. He had no taste for controversy of any sort; his manners were mild, and his conversation, in the society of those with whom he was intimate, was most genial and playful." James Russell Lowell has given the following admirable outline of his character :—

" But allow me to speak what I humbly feel,—
To a true poet-heart add the fun of Dick Steele
Throw in all of Addison, *minus* the chill;
With the whole of that partnership's stock and good-will,.
Mix well, and while stirring, hum o'er as a spell,
The fine *old* English Gentleman; simmer it well.
Sweeten just to your own private liking, then strain,
That only the finest and purest remain;
Let it stand out of doors till a soul it receives
From the warm, lazy sun loitering down through green leaves,
And you'll find a choice nature, not wholly deserving
A name either English or Yankee—just IRVING."

I must remember that I am not writing an eulogy of Mr. Irving, but only giving a few outlines with pen and pencil of his late home on the banks of the Hudson. Around that home sweetest memories will ever cluster, and the pilgrim to Sunnyside will rejoice to honour those who made that home so delightful to their idol, and who justly find a place in the sunny recollections of the departed.

Around that cottage, and the adjacent lands and waters, Irving's genius has cast an atmosphere of romance. The old Dutch house—one of the oldest in all that region—out of which grew that quaint cottage, was a part of the veritable Wolfert's Roost—the very dwelling wherein occurred Katrina Van Tassel's memorable quilting frolic, that terminated so disastrously to Ichabod Crane, in his midnight race with the Headless Horseman of Sleepy Hollow. There, too, the veracious Dutch historian, Diedrich Knickerbocker, domiciled while he was deciphering the precious documents found there, " which, like the lost books of Livy, had baffled the research of former historians." But its appearance had sadly changed when it was purchased by Mr. Irving, about thirty years ago, and was by him restored to the original form of the Roost, which he describes as " a little, old-fashioned stone mansion, all made up of gable ends, and as full of angles and corners as an old cocked hat. It is said, in fact," continues Mr. Irving, "to have been modelled after the cocked hat of Peter the Headstrong, as the Escurial was modelled after the gridiron of

the blessed St. Lawrence." It was built, the chronicler tells us, by
Wolfert Acker, a privy councillor of Peter Stuyvesant, "a worthy, but
ill-starred man, whose aim through life had been to live in peace and
quiet." He sadly failed. "It was his doom, in fact, to meet a head
wind at every turn, and be kept in a constant fume and fret by the
perverseness of mankind. Had he served on a modern jury, he would
have been sure to have eleven unreasonable men opposed to him." He
retired in disgust to this then wilderness, built the gabled house, and

WOLFERT'S ROOST WHEN IRVING PURCHASED IT.

"inscribed over the door (his teeth clenched at the time) his favourite
Dutch motto, 'Lust in Rust' (pleasure in quiet). . The mansion was
thence called Wolfert's Rust (Wolfert's Rest), but by the uneducated,
who did not understand Dutch, Wolfert's Roost." It passed into the
hands of Jacob Van Tassel, a valiant Dutchman, who espoused the cause
of the Republicans. The hostile ships of the British were often seen in
Tappan Bay, in front of the Roost, and Cow Boys infested the land
thereabout. Van Tassel had much trouble: his house was finally
plundered and burnt, and he was carried a prisoner to New York. When

the war was over, he rebuilt the Roost, but in more modest style, as seen in our sketch. "The Indian spring"—the one brought from Rotterdam —"still welled up at the bottom of the green bank; and the wild brook, wild as ever, came babbling down the ravine, and threw itself into the little cove where of yore the water-guard harboured their whale-boats."

The "water-guard" was an aquatic corps, in the pay of the revolutionary government, organised to range the waters of the Hudson, and keep watch upon the movements of the British. The Roost, according to the chronicler, was one of the lurking-places of this band, and Van Tassel was one of their best friends. He was, moreover, fond of warring upon his "own hook." He possessed a famous "goose-gun," that would send its shot half-way across Tappan Bay. "When the belligerent feeling was strong upon Jacob," says the chronicler of the Roost, "he would take down his gun, sally forth alone, and prowl along shore, dodging behind rocks and trees, watching for hours together any ship or galley at anchor or becalmed. So sure as a boat approached the shore, bang! went the great goose-gun, sending on board a shower of slugs and buck shot."

On one occasion, Jacob and some fellow bush-fighters peppered a British transport that had run aground. "This," says the chronicler, " was the last of Jacob's triumphs; he fared like some heroic spider that has unwittingly ensnared a hornet, to the utter ruin of its web. It was not long after the above exploit that he fell into the hands of the enemy, in the course of one of his forays, and was carried away prisoner to New York. The Roost itself, as a pestilent rebel nest, was marked out for signal punishment. The cock of the Roost being captive, there was none to garrison it but his stout-hearted spouse, his redoubtable sister, Notchie Van Wurmer, and Dinah, a strapping negro wench. An armed vessel came to anchor in front; a boat full of men pulled to shore. The garrison flew to arms, that is to say, to mops, broomsticks, shovels, tongs, and all kinds of domestic weapons, for, unluckily, the great piece of ordnance, the goose-gun, was absent with its owner. Above all, a vigorous defence was made with that most potent of female weapons, the tongue; never did invaded hen-roost make a more vociferous outcry. It

was all in vain!   The house was sacked and plundered, fire was set to
each room, and in a few moments its blaze shed a baleful light over the
Tappan Sea.   The invaders then pounced upon the blooming Laney Van
Tassel, the beauty of the Roost, and endeavoured to bear her off to the
boat.   But here was the real tug of war.   The mother, the aunt, and the
strapping negro wench, all flew to the rescue.   The struggle continued
down to the very water's edge, when a voice from the armed vessel at
anchor ordered the spoilers to desist; they relinquished their prize,
jumped into their boats, and pulled off, and the heroine of the Roost
escaped with a mere rumpling of the feathers."

CHAPTER XIX.

LOSE by Sunnyside is one of those marvellous villages with which America abounds: it has sprung up like a mushroom, and bears the name of Irvington, in compliment to the late master of Sunnyside. A dozen years ago not a solitary house was there, excepting that of Mr. Dearman, the farmer who owned the land. Piermont, directly opposite, was then the sole eastern terminus of the great New York and Erie Railway, and here seemed to be an eligible place for a village, as the Hudson River Railway was then almost completed. Mr. Dearman had one surveyed upon his lands; streets were marked out, village lots were measured and defined; sales at enormous prices, which enriched the owner, were made, and now upon that farm, in pleasant cottages, surrounded by neat gardens, several hundred inhabitants are dwelling. One of the most picturesque of the station-houses upon the Hudson River Railway is there, and a ferry connects the village with Piermont. Morning and evening, when the trains depart for and arrive from New York, many handsome vehicles may be seen there. This all seems like the work of magic. Over this beautiful slope, where so few years ago the voyager upon the Hudson saw only woodlands and cultivated fields, is now a populous town. The owners are chiefly business men of New York, whose counting rooms and parlours are within less than an hour of each other.

Less than a mile below Irvington, and about half way between that village and Dobbs's Ferry, is the beautiful estate of Nevis, the home and property of the Honourable James A. Hamilton, eldest surviving son of the celebrated General Alexander Hamilton, one of the founders of the republic of the United States.* It stands on the brow of the river slope,

---

* Nevis is the name of one of a group of the Antilles, where General Hamilton was born.

in the midst of a charming lawn, that extends from the highway to the
Hudson, a distance of half a mile, and commands some of the finest and
most extensive views of that portion of the river.   The mansion is large,
and its interior elegant.   It presents many attractions to the lover of
literature and art, aside from the delightful social atmosphere with
which it is filled.   There may be seen the library of General Hamilton,
one of the choicest and most extensive in the country at the time of his
death.   There, too, may be seen a portrait of Washington, by Stuart,

VIEW AT IRVINGTON.*

painted for General Hamilton, in 1798, when, in expectation of a war
with France, the United States organised a provisional government, and
appointed him acting commanding general under the ex-president
(Washington), who consented to be the chief.

On the river bank of the Nevis estate is a charming little cottage,
completely embowered, where Mr. Irving was a frequent and delighted

---

* From this point the traveller southward first obtains a good view of the Palisades on the west side
of the river.

visitor. It is the summer residence of Mr. Schuyler (a grandson of
General Schuyler), Mr. Hamilton's son-in-law. Near it is a more
pretentious residence belonging to Mr. Blatchford, another son-in-law of
the proprietor of " Nevis." Within call of these pleasant retreats is the
superb residence of Mr. Cottinet, a wealthy New York merchant, built in
French style, of Caen stone. This, in point of complete elegance,

NEVIS.

externally and internally, is doubtless superior to any other dwelling on
the banks of the Hudson. The grounds about it are laid out with much
taste, and exhibit many delightful landscape effects.

Dobbs's Ferry, a considerable village, twenty-two miles from New
York, was a place of some note a century ago; but the town has been
mostly built within the last fifteen years. The Indian name was *Weec-*

ques-guck, signifying the place of the Bark Kettle. Its present name is from Dobbs, a Swede from the Delaware, one of the earliest settlers on Philipse's Manor. The village is seated pleasantly on the river front of the Greenburgh Hills, and is the place of summer residence for many New York families. Here active and important military operations occurred during the war for independence. There was no fighting here, but in the movement of armies it was an important point. Upon the high bank, a little south-east from the railway station, a redoubt was built by the

VIEW AT DOBBS'S FERRY.

Americans at an early period of the war. From near that spot our little sketch was taken, which included the long pier at Piermont, the village of Nyack, and the range of hills just below Haverstraw, off which the *Vulture* lay, and at the foot of which Arnold and André met. Several other redoubts were cast up in this vicinity; these commanded the ferry to Paramus, afterwards Sneden's Landing, and now Rockland.

Near Dobbs's Ferry the British rendezvoued, after the battle at White Plains, in October, 1776; and at Hastings, a mile below, a British force of six thousand men, under Lord Cornwallis, crossed the river to Paramus, marched to the attack at Fort Lee, and then pursued the flying Americans under Washington across New Jersey to the Delaware river. Here, in 1777, a division of the American army, under General Lincoln, was encamped; and here was the spot first appointed as the meeting-place of André and Arnold. Circumstances prevented the meeting, and it was postponed, as we have already observed. Here, in the mansion of Van Brugh Livingston, General Greene met the chief of three commissioners from General Sir Henry Clinton, in conference concerning Major André.

VIEW NEAR HASTINGS.

General Robertson was the chief, and he had strong hopes, by imparting information from General Clinton, to save the life of his young friend. Beverly Robinson accompanied them as a witness. They went up in the *Greyhound* schooner, with a flag of truce, but only General Robertson was permitted to land. Greene met Robertson as a private gentleman, by permission of Washington, and not as an officer. He was willing to listen, but the case of an acknowledged spy admitted of no discussion. The subject was freely talked over, and Greene bore from Robertson a verbal message to Washington, and a long explanatory and threatening letter from Arnold. No new facts bearing upon the case were presented, and nothing was offered that changed the minds of the court or the commanding general. So the conference was fruitless.

The Livingston mansion, owned by Stephen Archer, a Quaker, is preserved in its original form; under its roof, in past times, many distinguished men have been sheltered. Washington had his head-

LIVINGSTON MANSION.

quarters there towards the close of the revolution; and there, in November, 1783, Washington, George Clinton, "the civil governor of the State of New York," and Sir Guy Carleton, the British commander, met to confer on the subject of prisoners, the loyalists, and the evacuation of the city of New York by the British forces. The former came down the river from Newburg, with their suites, in barges; the latter, with his suite, came up from New York in a frigate. Four companies of American light infantry performed the duties of a guard of honour on that occasion.

Opposite Dobbs's Ferry and Hastings is the most picturesque portion of

THE PALISADES.

the " Palisades," to which allusion has several times been made. These are portions of a ridge of trap-rocks extending along the western shore of the Hudson from near Haverstraw almost to Hoboken, a distance of about thirty-five miles. Between Piermont and Hoboken, these rocks present, for a considerable distance, an uninterrupted, rude, columnar front, from 300 to 500 feet in height. They form a mural escarpment, columnar in appearance, yet not actually so in form. They have a steep slope of *débris*, which has been crumbling from the cliffs above, during long centuries, by the action of frost and the elements. The ridge is narrow, being in some places not more than three-fourths of a mile in width. It is really an enormous projecting trap-dyke. On the top and among the *débris*, in many places, is a thin growth of trees. On the western and southern sides of the range, the slope is gentle, and composed generally of rich soil covered with trees. Below Tappan it descends to a rich valley, through which a railway now passes.

Viewed from the river this range presents a forbidding aspect; and little does the traveller dream of a fertile, smiling country at the back of this savage front. Several little valleys break through the range, and give glimpses of the hidden landscape beauties behind the great wall. In the bottoms of these the trap-dyke appears; so the valleys are only depressions in the range, not fractures.

Several bluffs in the range exceed 400 feet in height. The most elevated of all is one nearly opposite Sing-Sing, which juts into the river like an enormous buttress, and is a prominent object from every point on the Hudson between New York and the Highlands. It rises 660 feet above tide-water. The Dutch named it *Verdrietigh-Hoeck*—Grievous or Vexatious Point or Angle—because in navigating the river they were apt to meet suddenly, off this point, adverse and sometimes cross winds, that gave them much vexation. The Palisades present a most remarkable feature in the scenery of the Lower Hudson.

Yonkers is the name of a large and rapidly-growing village about four miles below Hastings, and seventeen from New York. Its recent growth and prosperity are almost wholly due to the Hudson River Railway, which furnishes such travelling facilities and accommodations, that hundreds of buiness men in the city of New York have chosen it for their summer residences, and many of them for their permanent dwelling-places. Like Sing-Sing, Tarrytown, Irvington, and Dobbs's Ferry, it has a hilly and exceedingly picturesque country around; and through it the dashing Neperah, or Saw-Mill River, after flowing many miles among the Greenburgh hills, finds its way into the Hudson in a series of rapids and cascades. It forms a merry feature in the scenery of the village.

Yonkers derives its name from *Yonkheer*—Young Master or Lord—the common appellation for the heir of a Dutch family. It is an old settlement, lands having been purchased here from the sachems by some of the Dutch West India Company as early as the beginning of Peter Stuyvesant's administration of the affairs of New Netherland.* Here was the Indian village of *Nap-pe-cha-mak*, a name signifying "the rapid water settlement." This was the name of the stream, afterwards corrupted to Neperah, and changed by the Dutch and English to Saw-Mill River. Those utilitarian fathers have much to answer for, because they expelled from our geographical vocabulary so many of the beautiful and significant Indian names.

To the resident, the visitor, and the tourist, the scenery about Yonkers is most attractive; and the delightful roads in all directions invite equestrian and carriage excursionists to real pleasure. Those fond of boating and bathing, fishing and fowling, may here find gratification at proper seasons, within a half-hour's ride, by railway, from the metropolis.

The chief attraction at Yonkers for the antiquary is the Philipse Manor Hall, a spacious stone edifice, that once belonged to the lords of Philipse Manor. The older portion was built in 1682. The present front, forming an addition, was erected in 1745, when old "Castle Philipse," at Sleepy Hollow, was abandoned, and the Manor Hall became the favourite dwelling of the family. Its interior construction (preserved by the present owner, the Hon. W. W. Woodworth, with scrupulous care) attests the wealth and taste of the lordly proprietor. The great Hall, or passage, is

---

* The domain included in the towns of Yonkers, West Farms, and Morrisania was purchased of the Indians by Adriaen Van der Donck, the "first lawyer in New Netherland," and confirmed to him in 1646 by grant from the Dutch West India Company, with the title and privilege of Patroon. It contained 24,000 acres. He called it *Colen Donck*, or Donck's Colony. Van der Donck, who died in 1655, was an active man in New Amsterdam (now New York), and took part with the people against the governor when disputes arose. He wrote an interesting description of the country. After the English conquest of New Netherland, Frederick Philipse and others purchased a greater portion of his estate on the Hudson and Harlem rivers.

broad, and the staircase capacious and massive. The rooms are large, and the ceilings are lofty; all the rooms are wainscoted, and the chief apartment has beautiful ornamental work upon the ceiling, in high relief, composed of arabesque forms, the figures of birds, dogs, and men, and two medallion portraits. Two of the rooms have carved chimney-pieces of grey Irish marble. The guest-chamber, over the drawing-room, is

PHILIPSE MANOR HALL.

handsomely decorated with ornamental architecture, and some of the fire-places are surrounded with borders of ancient Dutch tiles. The well has a subterranean passage leading from it, nobody knows to where; and the present ice-house, seen on the right of the picture, composed of huge walls and massive arch, was a powder-magazine in the "olden time." Altogether, this old hall—one of the antiquities of the Hudson—is an attractive curiosity, which the obliging proprietor is pleased to show to those who visit it because of their reverence for things of the past. It possesses a bit of romance, too; for here was born, and here lived, Mary Philipse, whose charms captivated the heart of young Washington, but whose hand was given to another, as we shall observe hereafter.

In the river, in front of Yonkers, the *Half-Moon*, Henry Hudson's

THE "HALF-MOON."

exploring vessel, made her second anchorage after leaving New York Bay. It was toward the evening of the 12th of September, 1609; the explorer had then been several days in the vicinity of *Man-na-hat-ta*, as the Indians called the island on which New York stands, and had had some intercourse with the natives. "The twelfth," says "Master Ivet (Juet) of the Lime House," who wrote Hudson's journal, "faire and hot. In the afternoon, at two of the clocke, wee weighed, the winde being variable, betweene the north and the north-west. So we turned into the Riuer two leagues, and anchored. This morning, at ovr first rode in the Riuer, there came eight-and-twentie Canoes full of men, women, and children,.to betray vs; but we saw their intent, and suffered none of them to come abord of vs. At twelue of the clocke they departed; they brought with them Oysters and Beanes, whereof wee bought some. They have great tobacco-pipes of Yellow Copper, and Pots of Earth to dresse their meate in." That night a strong tidal current placed the stern of the *Half-Moon* up stream. That event, and the assurance of the natives that the waters northward, upon which he had gazed with wonder and delight, came from far beyond the mountains, inspired Hudson with great hope, for it must be remembered that his errand was the discovery of a northern passage to India. He now doubted not that the great river upon which he was floating flowed from ocean to ocean, and that his search was nearly over, and would be speedily crowned with success.

A mile and a half below Yonkers, on the bank of the Hudson, is Font Hill, formerly the residence of Edwin Forrest, the eminent American tragedian. The mansion is built of blue granite, in the English castellated form, a style not wholly in keeping with the scenery around it. It would have been peculiarly appropriate and imposing among the rugged hills of the Highlands thirty or forty miles above. The building has six towers, from which very extensive views of the Hudson and the surrounding country may be obtained. The flag, or stair tower, is seventy-one feet in height.

To this delightful residence Mr. Forrest brought his bride, Miss Catherine Sinclair, daughter of the celebrated Scotch vocalist, in 1838, and for six years they enjoyed domestic and professional life in an eminent degree. Unfortunately for his future peace, Mr. Forrest was induced to visit England in 1844. He was accompanied by his wife. There he soon became involved in a bitter dispute with the dramatic critic of the London *Examiner*, and Macready the actor. This quarrel led to the most serious results. Out of it were developed the mob and the bloodshed of what is known, in the social history of the city of New York, as the "Astor Place Riot," and with it commenced Mr. Forrest's domestic troubles, which ended, as all the world knows, in the permanent separation of himself and wife. Font Hill, where he had enjoyed so much happiness, lost its charms, and he sold it to the Roman Catholic Sisters of

FONT HILL.

Charity, of the Convent and Academy of Mount St. Vincent. This institution was founded in 1847, and the academy was in 105th Street, between the Fifth and Sixth Avenues, New York. It is devoted to the instruction of young ladies. The community, numbering about two hundred Sisters at the time of my visit, was scattered. Some were at Font Hill, and others were at different places in the city and neighbourhood. The whole were under the general direction of Mother Superior Mary Angela Hughes. At Font Hill they erected an extensive and elegant pile of buildings, of which they took possession, and wherein they opened a school, on the

MOUNT ST. VINCENT ACADEMY.

1st of September, 1859. It was much enlarged in 1865. They had, in 1860, about one hundred and fifty pupils, all boarders, to whom was offered the opportunity of acquiring a thorough education. The chaplain of the institution occupies the "castle."

Two miles and a-half below Font Hill, or Mount St. Vincent, is Spyt den Duyvel Creek, at the head of York or Manhattan Island. This is a narrow stream, winding through a little tortuous valley for a mile or more, and connecting, at Kingsbridge, with the Harlem River, the first formed by the inflowing of the tide waters of the Hudson, and the last by the waters of the East River. At ebb-tide the currents part at Kingsbridge. The view from the mouth of the Spyt den Duyvel, over which the Hudson River Railway passes, looking either

SPYT DEN DUYVEL CREEK.

across the river to the Palisades, as given in our sketch, or inland, embracing bold Berrian's Neck on the left, and the wooded head of Manhattan Island on the right, with the winding creek, the cultivated ridge on the borders of Harlem River, and the heights of Fordham beyond, present pleasant scenes for the artist's pencil. To these natural scenes, history and romance lend the charm of their associations.

Here, on the 2nd of October, 1608, Henry Hudson had a severe fight with the Indians, who attacked the *Half-Moon* with arrows from canoes and the points of land, as .she lay at anchor in the sheltering mouth of the creek. Here, too, while Governor Stuyvesant was absent on the Delaware, nine hundred of the river Indians encamped, and menaced the little town of New Amsterdam, at the lower extremity of the island, with destruction. Here, according to Diedrick Knickerbocker's "History of New York," Anthony Van Corlear, the trumpeter of Governor Stuyvesant, lost his life in attempting to swim across the creek during a violent storm. "The wind was high," says the chronicler, "the elements were in an uproar, and no Charon could be found to ferry the adventurous sounder of brass across the water. For a short time he vapoured like an impatient ghost upon the brink, and then bethinking himself of the urgency of his errand (to arouse the people to arms), he took a hearty embrace of his stone bottle, swore most valorously that he would swim across in spite of the devil (*en spyt den duyvel*), and daringly plunged into the stream. Luckless Anthony! Scarcely had he buffeted half way over, when he was observed to struggle violently, as if battling with the Spirit of the waters. Instinctively he put his trumpet to his mouth, and giving a vehement blast, sank for ever to the bottom! The clangour of his trumpet, like that of the ivory horn of the renowned Paladin Orlando, when expiring in the glorious field of Roncesvalles, rang far and wide through the country, alarming the neighbours round, who hurried in amazement to the spot. Here an old Dutch burgher, famed for his veracity, and who had been a witness of the fact, related to them the melancholy affair; with the fearful addition (to which I am slow in giving belief), that he saw the Duyvel, in the shape of a huge moss-bonker (a species of inferior fish) seize the sturdy Anthony by the leg, and drag him beneath the waves. Certain it is, the place, with the adjoining promontory, which projects into Hudson, has been called *Spyt den Duyvel* ever since."

During the war for independence, stirring events occurred in the vicinity of the Spyt den Duyvel Creek. Batteries were erected on promontories on each side of it, at its junction with the Hudson; and in Westchester County, in its immediate neighbourhood, many skirmishes took place between Cow Boys and Skinners, Whigs and Tories, British, Hessians, and Indians.

A picturesque road passes along the foot of the Westchester hills that skirt the Spyt den Duyvel Valley, to the mouth of Tippett's Creek, which comes flowing down from the north through a delightful valley, at the back of Yonkers and the neighbouring settlements. This creek was called *Mosh-u-la* by the Indians, and the valley was the favourite residence of a warlike Mohegan tribe. Its lower portion was the scene of almost continual skirmishing during a portion of the war for independence.

THE CENTURY HOUSE.

Tippett's Creek is crossed by a low bridge. A few yards beyond it is Kingsbridge, at the head of the Harlem River, which here suddenly expands into lake-like proportions. The shores on both sides are beautiful, and the view that opens towards Long Island, beyond the East River, is charming.

Kingsbridge has always been a conspicuous point. Land was granted there, in 1693, to Frederick Philipse, with power to erect a toll-bridge, it being specified that it should be called *The King's Bridge*. This was the only bridge that connected Manhattan Island with the Main, and hence all travellers and troops were compelled to cross it, unless they had boats for ferrying. Here, during the war for independence, hostile forces were frequently confronted; and from its northern end to the Croton river, was the famous "Neutral Ground" during the struggle, whereon neither Whig nor Tory could live in peace or safety. Upon the heights each side of the bridge redoubts were thrown up; and here, in January, 1777, a bloody conflict occurred between the Americans, under General Heath, and a large body of Hessian mercenaries, under General Knyphausen. The place was held alternately by the Americans and British; and little more than half a mile below the bridge an ancient story-and-a-half house is yet standing, one hundred and twenty-five years old, which served as head-quarters at different times for the officers of the two armies: it is now a house of public entertainment, and is known as "Post's Century House."

CHAPTER XX.

THE Harlem River (called *Mus-coo-ta* by the Indians), which extends from Kingsbridge to the strait between Long Island Sound and New York Bay, known as the East River, has an average width of nine hundred feet. In most places it is bordered by narrow marshy flats, with high hills immediately behind. The scenery along its whole length, to the villages of Harlem and Mott Haven, is picturesque. The roads on both shores afford pleasant drives, and fine country seats and ornamental pleasure-grounds, add to the landscape beauties of the river. A line of small steamboats, connecting with the city, traverse its waters, the head of navigation being a few yards above Post's Century House. The tourist will find much pleasure in a voyage from the city through the East and Harlem Rivers.

The "High Bridge," or aqueduct over which the waters of the Croton flow from the main land to Manhattan Island, crosses the Island at One Hundred and Seventy-Third Street. It is built of granite. The aqueduct is fourteen hundred and fifty feet in length, and rests upon arches supported by fourteen piers of heavy masonry. Eight of these arches are eighty feet span, and six of them fifty feet. The height of the bridge, above tide water, is one hundred and fourteen feet. The structure originally cost about a million of dollars. Pleasant roads on both sides of the Harlem lead to the High Bridge, where full entertainment for man and horse may be had. The "High Bridge" is a place of great resort in pleasant weather for those who love the road and rural scenery.

A broad, macadamized avenue, called the "Kingsbridge Road," leads from the upper end of York Island to Manhattanville, where it connects with and is continued by the "Bloomingdale Road," in the direction of the city. The drive over this road is very agreeable. The winding avenue passes through a narrow valley, part of the way between rugged hills, only partially divested of the forest, and ascends to the south-eastern slope of Mount Washington (the highest land on the island), on which stands the village of Carmansville. At the upper end of this village, on the high rocky bank of the Harlem River, is a fine old mansion, known

THE HIGH BRIDGE.*

as the "Morris House," the residence, until her death in 1865, of the widow of Aaron Burr, vice-president of the United States, but better known as Madame Jumel, the name of her first husband. The mansion is

---

* This view is from the grounds in front of the dwelling of Richard Carman, Esq., former proprietor of all the land whereon the village of Carmansville stands. He is still owner of a very large estate in that vicinity.

at One Hundred and Sixty-ninth Street. It is surrounded by highly ornamented grounds, and its situation is one of the most desirable on the island. It commands a fine view of the Harlem River at the High Bridge, to the village of Harlem and beyond;* also of Long Island Sound, the villages of Astoria and Flushing, and the green fields of Long Island. Nearer are seen Harlem Plains, and the fine new bridge at Macomb's Dam. This house was built before the old war for independence, by Roger Morris, a fellow-soldier with Washington on the field of Monongohela,

THE HARLEM RIVER, FROM THE MORRIS HOUSE.

where Braddock fell, in the summer of 1755. Morris was also Washington's rival in a suit for the heart and hand of Mary, the heir of the lord of Philipse's Manor. The biographer says that in February, 1756, Colonel Washington went to Boston to confer with Governor Shirley about military affairs in Virginia. He stopped in New York on his return, and

---

* Harlem, situated on the Harlem River, between the Eighth Avenue and East River, was an early settlement on the island of Manhattan, by the Dutch. It was a flourishing village, chiefly bordering the Third Avenue, but is now a part of the great metropolis.

Americans adopted measures early to secure these, by erecting fortifications. Mount Washington (so named at that time) was the most elevated land upon the island, and formidable military works of earth and stone were

VIEW ON WASHINGTON HEIGHTS.

soon erected upon its crown and upon the heights in the vicinity from Manhattanville to Kingsbridge. The principal work was Fort Washington. The citadel was on the crown of Mount Washington, overlooking the country in every direction, and comprising within the scope of vision the Hudson from the Highlands to the harbour of New York. The citadel, with the outworks, covered several acres between One Hundred and Eighty-first and One Hundred and Eighty-sixth Streets.

On the point of the chief promontory of Mount Washington jutting into the Hudson, known as Jeffery's Hook, a strong redoubt was

JEFFERY'S HOOK.

constructed, as a cover to *chevaux-de-frise* and other obstructions placed in the river between that point and Fort Lee, to prevent the British ships going up the Hudson. The remains of this redoubt, in the form of grassy mounds covered with small cedars, are prominent upon the point, as seen in the engraving above. The ruins of Fort Washington, in similar form, were also very conspicuous until within a few years, and a flag staff

marked the place of the citadel. But the ruthless hand of pride, forgetful
of the past, and of all patriotic allegiance to the most cherished traditions
of American citizens, has levelled the mounds, and removed the flag-staff;
and that spot, consecrated to the memory of valorous deeds and courageous
suffering, must now be sought for in the kitchen-garden or ornamental
grounds of some wealthy citizen, whose choice celery or bed of verbenas
has greater charms than the green sward of a hillock beneath which
reposes the dust of a soldier of the old war for independence!

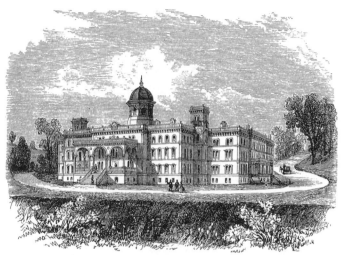

ASYLUM FOR THE DEAF AND DUMB.

"Soldiers buried here?" inquires the startled resident. Yes; your
villa, your garden, your beautiful lawn, are all spread out over the dust
of soldiers, for all over these heights the blood of Americans, English-
men, and Germans flowed freely in the autumn of 1776, when the fort
was taken by the British after one of the hardest struggles of the war.
More than two thousand Americans were captured, and soon filled the
loathsome prisons and prison-ships of New York.

Near the river-bank, on the south-western slope of Mount Washington,
is the New York Institution for the Deaf and Dumb, one of several

retreats for the unfortunate, situated upon the Hudson shore of Manhattan Island. It is one of the oldest institutions of the kind in the United States, the act of the Legislature of New York incorporating it being dated on the day (April 15, 1817) when the Asylum for the Deaf and Dumb at Hartford, Connecticut, was opened. The illustrious De Witt Clinton was the first president of the association. Its progress was slow for several years, when, in 1831, Mr. Harvey P. Peet was installed executive head of the asylum, as principal : he infused life into the institution immediately. Its affairs were administered by his skilful and energetic hand during more than thirty years, and his services were marked by the most gratifying results. In 1845, the title of President was conferred upon Mr. Peet, and three or four years later he received the honorary degree of Doctor of Laws. He was at the head of instruction and of the family in the institution. Under his guidance many of both sexes, shut out from participation in the intellectual blessings which are vouchsafed to well-developed humanity, were newly created, as it were, and made to experience, in a degree, the sensations of Adam, as described by Milton :—

> " Straight towards heaven my wondering eyes I turned,
> And gazed awhile the ample sky, till raised
> By quick instinctive motion, up I sprung,
> As thitherward endeavouring, and upright
> Stood on my feet; about me round I saw
> Hill, dale, and shady woods, and sunny plains,
> And liquid lapse of murmuring streams; by these,
> Creatures that lived, and moved, and walked, or flew;
> Birds on the branches warbling; all things smiled;
> With fragrance and with joy my heart o'erflowed.
> Myself I then perused, and limb by limb
> Surveyed, and sometimes went, and sometimes ran,
> With supple joints, as lively vigour led;
> But who I was, or where, or from what cause,
> Knew not; *to speak I tried, and forthwith spoke :*
> My tongue obeyed, and readily could name
> Whate'er I saw."

The situation of the Institution for the Deaf and Dumb is a delightful one. The lot comprises thirty-seven acres of land, between the Kingsbridge Road and the river, about nine miles from the New York City Hall. The buildings, five in number, form a quadrangle of two hundred

and forty feet front, and more than three hundred feet in depth ; they
are upon a terrace one hundred and twenty-seven feet above the river,
and are surrounded by fine old trees, and shrubbery.   The buildings are
capable of accommodating four hundred and fifty pupils, with their
teachers and superintendents, and the necessary domestics.

In the midst of a delightful grove of forest trees, a short distance below

AUDUBON'S RESIDENCE.

the Asylum for the Deaf and Dumb, is the dwelling of the late
J. J. Audubon, the eminent naturalist, where some of his family still
reside.   Only a few years ago it was as secluded as any rural scene fifty
miles from the city ; now, other dwellings are in the grove, streets have
been cut through it, the suburban village of Carmansville has covered the

adjacent eminence, and a station of the Hudson River Railway is almost in front of the dwelling.

Audubon was one of the most remarkable men of his age, and his work on the "Birds of America" forms one of the noblest monuments ever made in commemoration of true genius. In that great work, pictures of birds, the natural size, are given in four hundred and eighty-eight plates. It was completed in 1844, and at once commanded the highest admiration of scientific men. Baron Cuvier said of it,—"It is the most gigantic and most magnificent monument that has ever been erected to Nature." Audubon was the son of a French admiral, who settled in Louisiana, and his whole life was devoted to his favourite pursuit. The story of that life is a record of acts of highest heroism, and presents a most remarkable illustration of the triumphs of perseverance.

A writer, who visited Mr. Audubon not long before his death, in 1851, has left the following pleasant account of him and his residence near Mount Washington :—

" My walk soon brought a secluded country house into view,—a house not entirely adapted to the nature of the scenery, yet simple and unpretending in its architecture, and beautifully embowered amid elms and oaks. Several graceful fawns, and a noble elk, were stalking in the shade of the trees, apparently unconscious of the presence of a few dogs, and not caring for the numerous turkeys, geese, and other domestic animals that gobbled and screamed around them. Nor did my own approach startle the wild, beautiful creatures that seemed as docile as any of their tame companions.

" ' Is the master at home ?' I asked of a pretty maid-servant who answered my tap at the door, and who, after informing me that he was, led me into a room on the west side of the broad hall. It was not, however, a parlour, or an ordinary reception room that I entered, but evidently a room for work. In one corner stood a painter's easel, with a half-finished sketch of a beaver on the paper; on the other lay the skin of an American panther. The antlers of elks hung upon the walls, stuffed birds of every description of gay plumage ornamented the mantelpiece, and exquisite drawings of field-mice, orioles, and woodpeckers, were scattered promiscuously in other parts of the room, across one end of which a long rude table was stretched, to hold artist's materials, scraps of drawing-paper, and immense folio volumes, filled with delicious paintings of birds taken in their native haunts.

"'This,' said I to myself, 'is the studio of the naturalist,' but hardly had the thought escaped me when the master himself made his appearance. He was a tall, thin man, with a high, arched, and serene forehead, and a bright, penetrating, grey eye; his white locks fell in clusters upon his shoulders, but they were the only signs of age, for his form was erect, and his step as light as that of a deer. The expression of his face was sharp, but noble and commanding, and there was something in it, partly derived from the aquiline nose, and partly from the shutting of the mouth, which made you think of the imperial eagle.

"His greeting, as he entered, was at once frank and cordial, and showed you the sincere, true man. 'How kind it is,' he said, with a slight French accent, and in a pensive tone, 'to come to see me, and how wise, too, to leave that crazy city!' He then shook me warmly by the hand. 'Do you know,' he continued, 'how I wonder that men can consent to swelter and fret their lives away amid those hot bricks and pestilent vapours, when the woods and fields are all so near? It would kill me soon to be confined in such a prison-house, and when I am forced to make an occasional visit there, it fills me with loathing and sadness. Ah! how often, when I have been abroad on the mountains, has my heart risen in grateful praise to God that it was not my destiny to waste and pine among those noisome congregations of the city!'"*

Audubon died at the beginning of 1851, at the age of seventy-one years. His body was laid in a modest tomb in the beautiful Trinity Cemetery, near his dwelling. This burial-place, deeply shaded by original forest trees and varieties that have been planted, affords a most delightful retreat on a warm summer's day. It lies upon the slopes of the river bank. Foot-paths and carriage-roads wind through it in all directions, and pleasant glimpses of the Hudson may be caught through vistas at many points. In the south-western extremity of the grounds,

---

* "Homes of American Authors."

upon a plain granite doorway to a vault, may be seen, in raised letters, the name of AUDUBON.

The drive from Trinity Cemetery to Manhattanville is a delightful one. The road is hard and smooth at all seasons of the year, and is shaded in summer by many ancient trees that graced the forest. From it frequent pleasant views of the river may be obtained. There are some fine

VIEW IN TRINITY CEMETERY.

residences on both sides of the way, and evidences of the sure but stealthy approach of the great city are perceptible.

Manhattanville, situated in the chief of the four valleys that cleave the island from the Hudson to the East River, now a pleasant suburban village, is destined to be soon swallowed by the approaching and rapacious town. Its site on the Hudson was originally called Harlem Cove. It

was considered a place of strategic importance in the war for independence
and the war of 1812, and at both periods fortifications were erected there
to command the pass from the Hudson to Harlem Plains, to whose verge

MANHATTANVILLE FROM CLAREMONT.

the little village extends.   Upon the heights near, the Roman Catholics
have two flourishing literary institutions, namely, the Convent of the
Sacred Heart, for girls, and the Academy of the Holy Infant, for boys.

Upon the high promontory overlooking the Hudson, on the south side of Manhattanville, is Jones's Claremont Hotel, a fashionable place of resort for the pleasure-seekers who frequent the Bloomingdale and Kingsbridge roads on pleasant afternoons. At such times it is often thronged with visitors, and presents a lively appearance. The main, or older portion of the building, was erected, I believe, by the elder Dr. Post,

CLAREMONT.

early in the present century, as a summer residence, and named by him Claremont. It still belongs to the Post family. It was an elegant country mansion, upon a most desirable spot, overlooking many leagues of the Hudson. There, more than fifty years ago, lived Viscount Courtenay, afterwards Earl of Devon. He left England, it was reported, because of political troubles. When the war of 1812 broke out, he returned thither, leaving his furniture and plate, which were sold at auction. The latter is preserved with care by the family of the purchaser. Courtenay was a great "lion" in New York, for he was a handsome bachelor, with title, fortune, and reputation—a combination of excellences calculated to captivate the heart-desires of the opposite sex.

Claremont was the residence, for awhile, of Joseph Buonaparte, ex-king of Spain, when he first took refuge in the United States, after the battle of Waterloo and the downfall of the Napoleon dynasty. Here, too, Francis James Jackson, the successor of Mr. Erskine, the British minister at Washington at the opening of the war of 1812, resided a short time. He was familiarly known as "Copenhagen Jackson," because of his then recent participation in measures for the seizure of the Danish fleet by the British at Copenhagen. He was politically and socially unpopular, and presented a strong contrast to the polished Courtenay.

Manhattanville is the northern termination of the celebrated Bloomingdale Road, which crosses the island diagonally from Union Square ·at Sixteenth Street, to the high bank of the Hudson at One Hundred and Fifteenth Street. It is a continuation of Broadway (the chief retail business street of the city), from Union Square to Harsenville, at Sixty-Eighth Street. In that section it is called Broadway, and is compactly built upon. Beyond Seventieth Street it is still called Bloomingdale Road—a hard, smooth, macadamised highway, broad, devious, and undulating, shaded the greater portion of its length, made attractive by many elegant residences and ornamental grounds, and thronged every fine day with fast horses and light vehicles, bearing the young and the gay of both sexes. The stranger in New York will have the pleasure of his visit greatly enhanced by a drive over this road toward the close of a pleasant day. Its nearest approach to the river is at One Hundred and Fifteenth Street, at which point our little sketch was taken.

Among the places of note on the Bloomingdale Road is the New York Asylum for the Insane, Elm Park, and the New York Orphan Asylum. The former is situated on the east side of the road where it approaches nearest the Hudson, the grounds, containing forty acres, occupying the entire square between Tenth and Eleventh Avenues, and One Hundred and Fifteenth and One Hundred and Twentieth Streets. The institution was opened in the year 1821, for the reception of patients. It may be considered a development of the Lunatic Asylum founded in 1810. Its establishment upon more rational principles is due to the benevolent Thomas Eddy, a Quaker, who proposed to the governors of the old institution a course of *moral treatment* more thorough and extensive than had yet been tried.

The place selected for the asylum, near the village of Bloomingdale, is

VIEW ON BLOOMINGDALE ROAD.

unequalled. The ground is elevated and dry, and affords extensive and delightful views of the Hudson and the adjacent city and country. The buildings are spacious, the grounds beautifully laid out, and ornamented with shrubbery and flowers, and every arrangement is made with a view to soothe and heal the distempers of the mind. The patients are allowed to busy themselves with work or chosen amusements, to walk in the garden or pleasure-grounds, and to ride out on pleasant days, proper discrimination being always observed.

A short distance below the Asylum for the Insane, on the east side of the Bloomingdale Road, is the fine old country seat of the Apthorpe family, called Elm Park. It is now given to the uses of mere devotees of pleasure. Here the Germans of the city congregate in great numbers

ASYLUM FOR THE INSANE.

during hours of leisure, to drink beer, tell stories, smoke, sing, and enjoy themselves in their peculiar way with a zeal that seems to be inspired by Moore's idea that—

"Pleasure's the only noble end,
To which all human powers should tend."

Elm Park was the head-quarters of Sir William Howe, at the time of the battle on Harlem Plains, in the autumn of 1776. Washington had occupied it only the day before, and had there waited anxiously and impatiently for the arrival of the fugitive Americans under General Putnam, who narrowly escaped capture when the British took possession of the city. The Bloomingdale Road, along which they moved, then passed through almost continuous woods in this vicinity. Washington himself had a very narrow escape here, for he left the house only a few minutes before the advanced British column took possession of it.

Elm Park, when the accompanying sketch was made (June, 1861),

ELM PARK IN 1861.

was a sort of camp of instruction for volunteers for the army of the Republic, then engaged in crushing the great rebellion, in favour of human slavery and political and social despotism. When I visited it, companies were actively drilling, and the sounds of the fife and drum were mingled with the voices of mirth and conviviality. It was an hour after a tempest had passed by which had prostrated one or two of the old majestic trees which shade the ground and the broad entrance lane. These trees, composed chiefly of elms and locusts, attest the antiquity of the place, and constitute the lingering dignity of a mansion where wealth and social refinement once dispensed the most generous hospitality. Strong are the contrasts in its earlier and later history.

CHAPTER XXI.

ETWEEN the Bloomingdale Road and the Hudson, and Seventy-third and Seventy-fourth Streets, is the New York Orphan Asylum, one of the noblest charities in the land. It is designed for the care and culture of little children without parents or other protectors. Here a home and refuge are found for little ones who have been cast upon the cold charities of the world. From one hundred and fifty to two hundred of these children of misfortune are there continually, with their physical, moral, intellectual, and spiritual wants supplied. Their home is a beautiful one. The building is of stone, and the grounds around it, sloping to the river, comprise about fifteen acres. This institution is the child of the "Society for the Relief of Poor Widows with Small Children," founded in 1806 by several benevolent ladies, among whom were the sainted Isabella Graham, Mrs. Hamilton, wife of the eminent General Alexander Hamilton, and Mrs. Joanna Bethune, daughter of Mrs. Graham. It is supported by private bequests and annual subscriptions.

There is a similar establishment, called the Leake and Watts Orphan House, situated above the New York Asylum, on One Hundred and Eleventh and One Hundred and Twelfth Streets, between the Ninth and Tenth Avenues. It is surrounded by twenty-six acres of land, owned by the institution. The building, which was first opened for the reception of orphans in 1842, is capable of accommodating about two hundred and fifty children. It was founded by John George Leake, who bequeathed a large sum for the purpose. His executor, John Watts, also made a liberal donation for the same object, and in honour of these benefactors the institution was named.

These comprise the chief public establishments for the unfortunate in the city of New York, near the Hudson river. There are many others in the metropolis, but they do not properly claim a place in these sketches.

Let us here turn towards the interior of the island, drive to the verge of Harlem Plains, and then make a brief tour through the finished portions of the Central Park. Our road will be a little unpleasant a part of the way, for this portion of the island is yet in a state of transition from original roughness to the symmetry produced by art and labour.

Here, on the southern verge of the Plains, we will leave our waggon, and climb to the summit of the rocky bluff, by a winding path up a steep

ORPHAN ASYLUM.

hill covered with bushes, and take our stand by the side of an old square tower of brick, built for a redoubt during the war of 1812, and now used as a powder-house. The view northward, over Harlem Plains, is delightful. From the road at our feet stretch away numerous " truck " gardens, from which the city draws vegetable supplies. On the left is seen Manhattanville and a glimpse of the Palisades beyond the Hudson. In the centre, upon the highest visible point, is the Convent of the Sacred Heart ; and towards the right is the Croton Aqueduct, or High Bridge, over the Harlem river. The trees on the extreme right mark the line of the race-course, a mile in length, beginning at Luff's, the great resort for sportsmen. On this course, the trotting abilities of fast horses are tried by matches every fine day.

In our little view of the Plains and the high ground beyond, is included the theatre of stirring and very important events of the revolution, in the autumn of 1776. Here was fought the battle of Harlem Plains, that saved the American army on Harlem Heights; and yonder, in the distance, was the entrenched camp of the Americans between Manhattanville

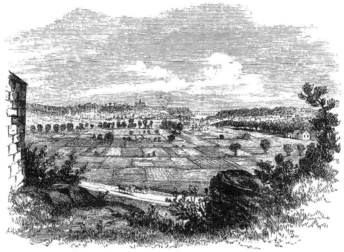

HARLEM PLAINS.

and Mount Washington, within which occurred most of the sanguinary scenes in the capture of Fort Washington by the British and Hessians.

Our rocky observatory, more than a hundred feet above tide-water, overlooking Harlem Plains, is included in the Central Park. Let us descend from it, ride along the verge of the Plain, and go up east of McGowan's Pass at about One Hundred and Ninth Street, where the remains of Forts Fish and Clinton are yet very prominent. These were built on the site of the fortifications of the revolution, during the war of

1812. Here we enter among the hundreds of men employed in fashioning the Central Park. What a chaos is presented! Men, teams, barrows, blasting, trenching, tunnelling, bridging, and every variety of labour needful in the transforming process. We pick our way over an almost impassable road among boulders and blasted rocks, to the great artificial basin of one hundred acres, now nearly completed, which is to be called

VIEW IN CENTRAL PARK.*

the Lake of Man-a-hat-ta. It will really be only an immense tank of Croton water, for the use of the city. We soon reach the finished portions of the park, and are delighted with the promises of future grandeur and beauty.

---

* This is a view of a portion of the Skating-Pond from a high point of the Ramble.

It is impossible, in the brief space allotted to these sketches, to give even a faint appreciative idea of the ultimate appearance of this park, according to the designs of Messrs. Olmstead and Vaux. We may only convey a few hints. The park was suggested by the late A. J. Downing, in 1851, when Kingsland, mayor of the city, gave it his official recommendation. Within a hundred days the Legislature of the State of New York granted the city permission to lay out a park; and in February, 1856, 733 acres of land, in the centre of the island, was in possession of the civic authorities for the purpose. Other purchases for the same end were made, and, finally, the area of the park was extended in the direction of Harlem Plains, so as to include 843 acres. It is more than two and a-half miles long, and half a mile wide, between the Fifth and Eighth Avenues, and Fifty-ninth and One Hundred and Tenth Streets. A great portion of this space was little better than rocky hills and marshy hollows, much of it covered with tangled shrubs and vines. The rocks are chiefly upheavals of *gneiss*, and the soil is composed mostly of alluvial deposits filled with boulders. Already a wonderful change has been wrought. Many acres have been beautified, and the visitor now has a clear idea of the general character of the park, when completed.

The primary purpose of the park is to provide the best practicable means of healthful recreation for the inhabitants of the city, of all classes. Its chief feature will be a Mall, or broad walk of gravel and grass, 208 feet wide, and a fourth of a mile long, planted with four rows of the magnificent American elm trees, with seats and other requisites for resting and lounging. This, as has been suggested, will be New York's great out-of-doors Hall of Re-union. There will be a carriage-way more than nine miles in length, a bridle-path or equestrian road more than five miles long, and walks for pedestrians full twenty-one miles in length. These will never cross each other. There will also be traffic roads, crossing the park in straight lines from east to west, which will pass through trenches and tunnels, and be seldom seen by the pleasure-seekers in the park. The whole length of roads and walks will be almost forty miles.

The Croton water tanks already there, and the new one to be made, will jointly cover 150 acres. There are several other smaller bodies of water, in their natural basins. The principal of these is a beautiful, irregular lake, known as the Skating-Pond. Pleasure-boats glide over it in summer, and in winter it is thronged with skaters.* One portion of the Skating-Pond is devoted exclusively to the gentler sex. These, of nearly all ages and conditions, throng the ice whenever the skating is good.

Open spaces are to be left for military parades, and large plats of turf for games, such as ball and cricket, will be laid down—about twenty acres for the former, and ten for the latter; and it is intended to have a beautiful meadow in the centre of the park.

There will be arches of cut stone, and numerous bridges of iron and stone (the latter handsomely ornamented and fashioned in the most costly style), spanning the traffic-roads, ravines, and ponds. One of the most remarkable of these, forming a central architectural feature, is the Terrace Bridge, at the north end of the Mall, already approaching completion. This bridge covers a broad arcade, where, in alternate niches, will be statues and fountains. Below will be a platform, 170 feet wide, extending to the border of the Skating-Pond. It will embrace a spacious basin, with a fine fountain jet in its centre. This structure will be composed of exquisitely wrought light brown freestone, and granite.

Such is a general idea of the park, the construction of which was begun at the beginning of 1858; it is expected to be completed in 1864—a period of only about six years. The entire cost will not fall much short of 12,000,000 dollars. As many as four thousand men and several hundred horses have been at work upon it at one time.†

From the Central Park—where beauty and symmetry in the hands of Nature and Art already performed noble æsthetic service for the citizens of New York—let us ride to "Jones's Woods," on the eastern borders of the island, where, until recently, the silence of the country forest might have been enjoyed almost within sound of the hum of the busy town.

* The New York *Spirit of the Times*, referring to this lake, said:—"From the commencement of skating to the 24th day of February (1861) was sixty-three days; there was skating on forty-five days, and no skating on eighteen days. Of visitors to the pond, the least number on any one day was one hundred; the largest number on one day (Christmas) estimated at 100,000; aggregate number during the season, 540,000; average number on skating days, 12,000."

† This brief description was written, and the accompanying sketches were made, in 1861. The great work of fashioning this Park, leaving Nature, in the growth of trees and shrubbery, to enrich and beautify it, is now (1866) nearly completed.

But here, as everywhere else, on the upper part of Manhattan Island, the early footprints in the march of improvement are seen. As we leave the beautiful arrangement of the park, the eye immediately encounters scenes of perfect chaos, where animated and inanimated nature combine in making pictures upon memory, never to be forgotten. The opening and grading of new streets produce many rugged bluffs of earth and rock; and upon these, whole villages of squatters, who are chiefly Irish, may

THE TERRACE BRIDGE AND MALL.

be seen. These inhabitants have the most supreme disregard for law or custom in planting their dwellings. To them the land seems to "lie out of doors," without visible owners, bare and unproductive. Without inquiry they take full possession, erect cheap cabins upon the "public domains," and exercise "squatter sovereignty" in an eminent degree, until some innovating owner disturbs their repose and their title, by undermining their castles—for in New York, as in England, "every man's house is his *castle*." These form the advanced guard of the growing metropolis; and so eccentric is Fortune in the distribution of her favours in this land of general equality, that a dweller in thése "suburban cottages," where swine and goats are seen instead of deer and blood-cattle, may, not many years in the future, occupy a palace upon Central Park—perhaps, upon the very spot where he now uses a pig for a pillow, and breakfasts upon the milk of she-goats. In a superb mansion of his own,

A SQUATTER VILLAGE.

within an arrow's flight of Madison Park, lived a middle-aged man in 1861, whose childhood was thus spent among the former squatters in that quarter.

"Jones's Woods," formerly occupying the space between the Third Avenue and the East River, and Sixtieth and Eightieth Streets, are rapidly disappearing. Streets have been cut through them, clearings for buildings have been made, and that splendid grove of old forest trees a few years ago, has been changed to clumps, giving shade to large numbers of pleasure-seekers during the hot months of summer, and the delightful weeks of early autumn. There, in profound retirement, in an elegant mansion on the bank of the East River, lived David Provoost, better

PROVOOST'S TOMB—JONES'S WOODS.

known to the inhabitants of New York—more than a hundred years ago— as "Ready-money Provoost." This title he acquired because of the sudden increase of his wealth by the illicit trade in which some of the

and the latter nursery schools for poor children, and a penal house of refuge for juvenile delinquents. This is a delightful portion of the East River, and here the lover of sport may find good fishing at proper seasons.

Ward's Island contains about 200 acres, and lies in the East River, from One Hundred and First to One Hundred and Fifteenth Streets inclusive. The Indians called it *Ten-ken-as*. It was purchased from them by First Director Van Twilles, in 1637. A portion of the island is a potter's field, where about 2,500 of the poor and strangers are buried annually. The island is supplied with Croton water. A ferry connects it with the city at One Hundred and Sixth Street. Randall's Island, nearly north from Ward's, close by the Westchester shore, was the residence of Jonathan Randall for almost fifty years; he purchased it in 1754. It has been called, at different times, Little Barn Island, Belle Isle, Talbot's Island, and Montressor's Island. The city purchased it, in 1835, for 50,000 dollars. The House of Refuge is on the southern part of the island, opposite One Hundred and Seventeenth Street. There youthful criminals are kept free from the contaminating influence of old offenders, are taught useful trades, and are continually subjected to reforming influences. Good homes are furnished them when they leave the institution, and in this way the children of depraved parents who have entered upon a career of crime, have their feet set in the paths of virtue, usefulness, and honour.'

Near the southern border of "Jones's Woods" is "The Coloured Home," where the indigent, sick, and infirm of African blood have their physical, moral, and religious wants supplied. It is managed by an association of women, and is sustained by the willing hands of the benevolent.

A little farther south, on the high bank of the East River, at Fifty-first Street, is the ancient family mansion of a branch of the Beekman family, whose ancestor accompanied Governor Stuyvesant to New Amsterdam, now New York. There General Howe made his headquarters after the battle on Long Island and his invasion of New York, in 1776; and there he was made *Sir* William Howe, because of those events, by knightly ceremonies performed by brother officers, at the command of the king. Captain Nathan Hale, the spy, whose case and Major

André's have been compared, was brought before General Howe at this place soon after his arrest. He was confined during the night in the conservatory, and the next morning, without even the form of a trial, was handed over to Cunningham, the inhuman provost marshal, who hanged him upon an apple-tree, under circumstances of peculiar cruelty. The act was intended to strike the minds of the Americans with terror; it only served to exasperate and strengthen them.*

The old Beekman mansion, with its rural surroundings, remained uninvaded by the Commissioner of Streets until about ten years ago. I remember with pleasure a part of the day that I spent there with the hospitable owner. Then there were fine lawns, with grand old trees, blooming gardens, the spacious conservatory in which Hale was confined, and an ancient sun-dial that had marked the hours for a century. Over the elaborately-wrought chimney-pieces in the drawing-room were the arms of the Beekman family; and in an outhouse was a coach bearing the same arms, that belonged to the first proprietor of the mansion. It was a fine old relic of New York aristocracy a hundred years ago, and one of only three or four coaches owned in the city at that time. Such was the prejudice against the name of coach—a sure sign of aristocracy—that Robert Murray, a wealthy Quaker merchant, called his "a leathern conveniency." But the beauty of the Beekman homestead has departed; the ground is reticulated by streets and avenues, and the mansion is left alone in its glory.

Directly opposite to the Beekman mansion is the lower end of Blackwell's Island, a narrow strip of land in the East River, extending to Eighty-eighth Street, and containing 120 acres. Beyond it is seen the pretty village of Ravenswood, on the Long Island shore. The Indians called Blackwell's Island *Min-na-han-nock*. It was also named Manning Island, having been owned by Captain John Manning, who, in 1672, betrayed

---

* Nathan Hale was an exemplary young man, of a good Connecticut family. Washington was anxious to ascertain the exact position and condition of the British army on Long Island, and Hale volunteered to obtain it. He was arrested, and consigned to Cunningham for execution. He was refused the services of a clergyman and the use of a Bible, and letters that he wrote during the night to his mother and sisters were destroyed by the inhuman marshal. His last words were,—"I only regret that I have but one life to give to my country."

the fort at New York into the hands of the Dutch.*   In 1828 it was purchased by the city of New York, of Joseph Blackwell, and appropriated to public uses.   Upon it are situated the almshouse, almshouse hospital, penitentiary hospital, New York city small-pox hospital, workhouse, city penitentiary, and New York lunatic asylum.   These are under the super-

THE BEEKMAN MANSION.

vision of a board of ten governors.   There is a free ferry to the island, at the foot of Sixty-first Street.

Turtle Bay, at Forty-seventh Street—from the southern border of

* Manning was bribed to commit the treason. He escaped punishment through the intervention of his king, Charles II., who, it was believed, shared in the bribe.

which our sketch of Blackwell's Island was taken—was a theatre of some stirring scenes during the revolution. Until within a few years it remained in its primitive condition—a sheltered cove with a gravelly beach, and high rocky shores covered with trees and shrubbery. Here the British government had a magazine of military stores, and these the *Sons of Liberty*, as the early Republicans were called, determined to seize, in

TURTLE BAY AND BLACKWELL'S ISLAND.

July, 1775. A party, under the direction of active members of that association, proceeded stealthily by water, in the evening, from Greenwich, Connecticut, passed the dangerous vortex of Hell-gate at twilight, and at midnight surprised and captured the guard, and seized the stores. The old storehouse in which they were deposited was yet standing, in 1861, a venerable relic of the past among the busy scenes of the present.

At Turtle Bay we fairly meet the city in its gradual movement along the shores of the East River. Below this point almost every relic of the past, in Nature and Art, has been swept away by pick and powder; and wharves, store-houses, manufactories, and dwellings, are occupying places where, only a few years ago, were pleasant country seats, far away from the noise of the town. Our ride in this direction will, therefore, have no special attractions, so let us turn towards the Hudson again, and visit some points of interest in the central and lower portions of the island within the limits of the regulated streets. The allotted space allows us to take only glimpses at some of the most prominent points and objects.

THE RESERVOIR, FIFTH AVENUE.

The great distributing reservoir of the Croton water, upon Murray Hill, between Fortieth and Forty-second Streets, and Fifth and Sixth Avenues, challenges our attention and admiration. Up to and beyond this point the Fifth Avenue—the street of magnificent palatial residences —is completed, scarcely a vacant lot remaining upon its borders. The reservoir stands in solemn and marked contrast to these ornamental structures, and rich and gay accompaniments. Its walls, in Egyptian style, are of dark granite, and average forty-four feet in height above the adjacent streets. Upon the top of the wall, which is reached by massive steps, is a broad promenade, from which may be obtained very extensive views of the city and the surrounding country. This is made secure by a

FIFTH AVENUE HOTEL, MADISON PARK.

strong battlement of granite on the outside, and next to the water by an iron fence.

The reservoir covers an area of two acres, and its tank capacity is over twenty millions of gallons. The water was first let into it on the 4th of July, 1842. On the 14th of October following it was distributed over the town, and the event was celebrated on that day by an immense

military and civic procession. Such a display had never been seen in
New York since the mingling of the waters of the Great Lake and the
Hudson River, through the Erie Canal, was celebrated in 1825.

At the request of the Corporation of the City of New York, George P.
Morris wrote the following Ode, which was sung near the fountain then
playing in the City Hall Park, by the members of the New York Sacred
Music Society :—

THE CROTON ODE.

I.

Gushing from this living fountain,
  Music pours a falling strain,
As the goddess of the mountain
  Comes with all her sparkling train.
From her grotto springs advancing,
  Glittering in her feathery spray,
Woodland fays beside her dancing,
  She pursues her winding way.

II.

Gently o'er the rippling water,
  In her coral shallop bright,
Glides the rock-king's dove-eyed daughter,
  Decked in robes of virgin white.
Nymphs and Naiads sweetly smiling,
  Urge her bark with pearly hand,
Merrily the sylph beguiling
  From the nooks of fairy-land.

III.

Swimming on the snow-curled billow,
  See the river spirits fair
Lay their cheeks, as on a pillow,
  With the foam-beads in their hair.
Thus attended, hither wending,
  Floats the lovely Oread now,
Eden's arch of promise bending
  Over her translucent brow.

IV.

Hail the wanderer from a far land !
  Bind her flowing tresses up !
Crown her with a fadeless garland,
  And with crystal brim the cup ;
From her haunts of deep seclusion,
  Let Intemperance greet her too,
And the heat of his delusion
  Sprinkle with this mountain-dew.

V.

Water leaps as if delighted,
  While her conquered foes retire !
Pale Contagion flies affrighted
  With the baffled demon Fire !
Safety dwells in her dominions,
  Health and Beauty with her move,
And entwine their circling pinions
  In a sisterhood of love.

VI.

Water shouts a glad hosanna !
  Bubbles up the earth to bless !
Cheers it like the precious manna
  In the barren wilderness.
Here we wondering gaze, assembled
  Like the grateful Hebrew band,
When the hidden fountain trembled,
  And obeyed the prophet's wand.

VII.

Round the aqueducts of story,
  As the mists of Lethe throng,
Croton's waves in all their glory
  Troop in melody along.
Ever sparkling, bright, and single,
  Will this rock-ribbed stream appear,
When posterity shall mingle
  Like the gathered waters here.

The waters of the Croton flow from the dam to the distributing reservoir, forty miles and a half, through a covered canal, made of stone and brick, at an average depth of $2\frac{1}{2}$ feet. The usual flow is about 30,000,000 of gallons a day; its capacity is 60,000,000. It passes through sixteen tunnels in rock, varying from 160 to 1,263 feet. In Westchester county it crosses twenty-five streams, from 12 to 70 feet below the line of grade, besides numerous small brooks furnished with culverts. After crossing the Harlem River over the high bridge already described, it passes the Manhattan valley by an inverted siphon of iron pipes, 4,180 feet in length, and the Clendening valley on an aqueduct 1,900 feet. It then enters the first receiving reservoir, now in the Central Park, which has a capacity of 150,000,000 gallons. In a hygienic and economic view, the importance of this great work cannot be estimated; in insurance alone it caused the reduction of 40 cents on every 100 dollars in the annual rates. It is estimated that the capacity of the Croton River is sufficient to supply the

city with a population of 5,000,000. The ridge line, or water-shed, enclosing the Croton valley above the dam, is 101 miles in length. The
stream is 39 miles in length, and its tributaries 136 miles.* The total
area of the valley is 352 square miles; within it are thirty-one natural
lakes and ponds.

From the reservoir we ride down Fifth Avenue, the chief fashionable

WORTH'S MONUMENT.

quarter of the metropolis. For two miles we may pass between houses
of the most costly description, built chiefly of brown freestone, some of it

---

* The principal one of the remote sources of the Croton River is a spring near the road side, not far
from the house of William Hoag, on Quaker Hill, in the town of Pawling. The spring is by the side of
a stone fence, with a barrel-curb, and is 1,300 feet above tide water.

elaborately carved. Travellers agree that in no city in the world can be found an equal number of really splendid mansions in a single street; they are furnished, also, in princely style. The side-walks are flagged with heavy blue stone, or granite, and the street is paved with blocks of the latter material. At Madison Square, between Twenty-third and Twenty-sixth Streets, it is crossed diagonally by Broadway, and there, as an exception, are a few business establishments. At the intersection, and fronting Madison Park, is the magnificent Fifth Avenue Hotel, built of white marble, and said to be the largest and most elegant in the world. As we look up from near the St. Germain, this immense house, six stories in height, is seen on the left, and the trees of Madison Park on the right. In the middle distance is the Worth House, a large private boarding establishment, and near it the granite monument erected by the city of New York to the memory of the late General William J. Worth, of the United States army.

This is the only public monument in the city of New York, except a mural one to the memory of General Montgomery, in the front wall of St. Paul's Church. It is of Quincy granite; the apex is fifty-one feet from the ground, and the smooth surface of the shaft is broken by raised bands, on which are the names of the battles in which General Worth had been engaged. On the lower section of the shaft are representations of military trophies in relief. General Worth was an *aide-de-camp* of General Scott in the battles of Chippewa and Niagara, in the summer of 1814, and went through the war with Mexico with distinction. His name holds an honourable place among the military heroes of his country. The monument was erected in 1858.

CHAPTER XXII.

OWN Broadway, a few streets below the Fifth Avenue Hotel, is Union Park, whose form is an ellipse. It is at the head of Old Broadway, at Fourteenth Street, and is at such an elevation that the Hudson and East Rivers may both be seen by a spectator on its Fourteenth Street front. It is a small enclosure, with a large fountain, and pleasantly shaded with young trees. Only a few years ago this vicinity was an open common, and where Union Park is was a high hill. On its northern side is the Everett House, a large, first-class hotel, named in honour of Edward Everett, the American scholar and statesman, who represented his country at the Court of St. James's a few years ago. On its southern side is the Union Park Hotel, and around it are houses that were first-class a dozen years ago. In one of the four triangles outside the square is a bronze equestrian statue of Washington, by H. K. Brown, an American sculptor, standing upon a high granite pedestal, surrounded by heavy iron railings. This is the only public statue in the city of New York, if we except a small sandstone one in the City Hall Park, and a marble one of William Pitt, at the corner of Franklin Street and West Broadway, which stood at the junction of Wall and William Streets, when the old war for independence broke out. The latter is only a *torso*, the head and arms having been broken off by the British soldiery after Sir William Howe took possession of the city in the autumn of 1776.* In our little picture we look up the Fourth Avenue, which extends to Harlem, and from which proceed two great railways, namely, the Harlem, leading to Albany, and the New Haven, that connects with all the railways in New England. On the left, by the side of Union Park, is seen a marquee, the head-quarters of

---

* This broken statue has disappeared since the above was written.

a regiment of Zouave volunteers for the United States army. These signs of war might then be seen in all parts of the city.

Let us turn here and ride through broad Fourteenth Street, towards the East River, passing the Opera House on the way. We are going to visit the oldest living thing in the city of New York,—an ancient pear-tree, at the corner of Thirteenth Street and Third Avenue. It was

UNION PARK.

brought from Holland by Peter Stuyvesant, the last and most renowned of the governors of New Netherland (New York) while it belonged to the Dutch. Stuyvesant brought the tree from Holland, and planted it in his garden in the year 1647. I believe it was never known to fail in bearing fruit. Many of the pears have been preserved in liquor as curiosities,

In a cluster, a short distance from St. Mark's, are the Bible House, Cooper Institute, Clinton Hall, and Astor Library,* places which intelligent strangers in the city should not pass by. The first three are seen

ST. MARK'S CHURCH AND HISTORICAL SOCIETY HOUSE.

in our sketch, the Bible House on the right, the Cooper Institute on

* The New York Society Library, in University Place, is the oldest public library in the United States. It was incorporated in the year 1700, under the title of "The Public Library of New York." Its name was changed to its present one in 1754. It contains almost 50,000 volumes.

the left, and Clinton Hall in the distance. The open area is Astor Place.

The Bible House occupies a whole block or square. It belongs to the American Bible Society. A large portion of the building is devoted to the business of the association. Blank paper is delivered to the presses in the sixth story, and proceeds downwards through regular stages of

BIBLE HOUSE, COOPER INSTITUTE, AND CLINTON HALL.

manufacture, until it reaches the depository for distribution on the ground floor, in the form of finished books. A large number of religious and kindred societies have offices in this building.

The Cooper Institute is the pride of New York, for it is the creation of a single New York merchant, Peter Cooper, Esq. The building, of brown freestone, occupies an entire block or square, and cost over

300,000 dollars. The primary object of the founder is the advancement of science, and knowledge of the useful arts, and to this end all the interior arrangements of the edifice were made. When it was completed, Mr. Cooper formally conveyed the whole property to trustees, to be devoted to the public good.* By his munificence, benevolence, and wisdom displayed in this gift to his countrymen, Mr. Cooper takes rank among the great benefactors of mankind.

Clinton Hall belongs to the Mercantile Library Association, which is composed chiefly of merchants and merchants' clerks. It has a membership of between four and five thousand persons, and a library of nearly seventy thousand volumes. The building was formerly the Astor Place Opera House, and in the open space around it occurred the memorable riot occasioned by the quarrel between Forrest and Macready, to which allusion has been made.

Near Astor Place, on Lafayette Place, is the Astor Library, created by the munificence of the American Crœsus, John Jacob Astor, who bequeathed for the purpose 400,000 dollars. The building (made larger than at first designed, by the liberality of the son of the founder, and chief inheritor of his property) is capable of holding 200,000 volumes. More than half that number are there now. The building occupies a portion of the once celebrated Vauxhall Gardens, a place of amusement thirty years ago.

Let us now ride down the Bowery, the broadest street in the city, and lined almost wholly with small retail shops. It leads us to Franklin Square, a small triangular space at the junction of Pearl and Cherry Streets. This, in the "olden time," was the fashionable quarter of the city, and was remarkable first for the great Walton House, and a little later as the vicinity of the residence of Washington during the first year of his administration as first President of the United States. That building was No. 10, Cherry Street. By the demolition of some houses

---

* The chief operations of the Institute (which Mr. Cooper calls "The Union") are free instruction of classes in science and the useful arts, and free lectures. The first and second stories are rented, the proceeds of which are devoted to defraying the expenses of the establishment. In the basement is a lecture-room 125 feet by 82 feet, and 21 feet in height. The three upper stories are arranged for purposes of instruction. There is a large hall, with a gallery, designed for a free Public Exchange.

between it and Franklin Square, it formed a front on that open space. In 1856, the Bowery was continued from Chatham Square to Franklin Square, when this and adjacent buildings were demolished, and larger edifices erected on their sites. There Washington held his first *levees*, and there Mr. Hammond, the first resident minister from England sent to the new Republic, was received by the chief magistrate of the Republic.

WASHINGTON'S RESIDENCE AS IT APPEARED IN 1850.

The chief attraction to the stranger at Franklin Square at the present time, is the extensive printing and publishing house of HARPER and BROTHERS.

The Walton House, now essentially changed in appearance, was by far the finest specimen of domestic architecture in the city or its suburbs.

It stood alone, in the midst of trees and shrubbery, with a beautiful garden covering the slope between it and the East river. It was built by a wealthy shipowner, a brother of Admiral Walton, of the British navy, in pure English style. It attracted great attention. A lately-deceased resident of New York once informed me, that when he was a schoolboy and lived in Wall Street, he was frequently rewarded for good behaviour, by permission to "go out on Saturday afternoon to see Master Walton's grand house." The family arms, carved in wood, remained over the street door until 1850. It was a place of great resort for the British officers during the war for independence; and there William IV., then a midshipman under Admiral Digby, was entertained with the courtesy due to a prince.

On the site of the residence of Walter Franklin, a Quaker and wealthy merchant, whose name the locality commemorates, stand the Harpers' magnificent structures of brick and iron (the front all iron), which soon arose from the ashes of their old establishment, consumed near the close of 1853. There are two buildings, the rear one fronting on Cliff Street. The latter is seven stories in height, and the one on Franklin Square six stories, exclusive of the basements and sub-cellars. Between them is a court, in which is a lofty brick tower, with an interior spiral staircase. From this iron bridges extend to the different stories. The buildings are almost perfectly fire-proof. It is the largest establishment of its kind in the United States. Over six hundred persons are usually employed in it. It was founded nearly fifty years ago, by two of the four brothers who compose the firm. They are all yet (1866) actively engaged in the management of the affairs of the house, with several of their sons, and may be found during business hours, ever ready to extend the hand of cordial welcome to strangers, and to give them the opportunity to see the operation of book-making in all its departments, and in the greatest perfection.

On our way from Franklin Square to the Hudson, by the most direct route, we cross the City Hall Park, which was known a century ago as "The Fields." It was then an open common on the northern border of the city, at "the Forks of the Broadway." It is triangular in form. The great thoroughfare of Broadway is on its western side, and the City

Hall, a spacious edifice of white marble, stands in its centre. Near its southern end is a large fountain of Croton water. On its eastern side was a declivity overlooking "Beekman's Swamp." That section of the city is still known as "The Swamp"—the great leather mart of the metropolis. On the brow of that declivity, where Tammany Hall now stands, Jacob Leisler, "the people's governor," when James II. left the

FRANKLIN SQUARE.

English throne and William of Orange ascended it, was hanged, having been convicted on the false accusation of being a disloyal usurper. He was the victim of a jealous and corrupt aristocracy, and was the first and last man ever put to death for treason alone within the domain of the United States down to the close of the Civil War in 1865.

When the war for independence was kindling, the Field became the theatre of many stirring scenes. There the inhabitants assembled to hear the harangues of political leaders and pass resolves: there "liberty poles" were erected and prostrated; and there soldiers and people had collisions. There obnoxious men were hung in effigy; and there at six o'clock in the

BROADWAY AT ST. PAUL'S.

evening of a sultry day in July, 1776, the Declaration of Independence was read to one of the brigades of the Continental Army, then in the city under the command of Washington.

The vicinity of the lower or southern end of the park has ever been a point of much interest. On the site of Barnum's Museum,* the "Sons of Liberty" in New York—the ultra-republicans before the revolution—had a meeting-place, called "Hampden Hall." Opposite was St. Paul's Church, a chapel of Trinity Church; where, in after years, when the objects for which the "Sons of Liberty" had been organised were accomplished, namely, the independence of the colonies, the *Te Deum Laudamus* was sung by a vast multitude, on the occasion of the inauguration of Washington (who was present), as the first chief magistrate of the United States. There it yet stands, on the most crowded portion of Broadway (where various omnibus lines meet), a venerable relic of the past, clustered with important and interesting associations. Around it are the graves of the dead of several generations. Under its great front window is a mural monument erected to the memory of General Montgomery, who fell at the siege of Quebec, in 1775: and a few feet from its venerable walls is a marble obelisk, standing at the grave of Thomas Addis Emmet, brother of, and co-worker with the eminent Robert Emmet, who perished on the scaffold during the uprising of the Irish people against the British government, in 1798.

Passing down Broadway, we soon reach Trinity Church, founded at the close of the seventeenth century. The present is the fourth edifice, on the same site. Soon after the British army took possession of New York, in September, 1776, a fire broke out in the lower part of the town. Five hundred edifices were consumed—an eighth of all that were in the city. Trinity Church (the second edifice) was among the number destroyed. It was rebuilt in 1788, and taken down in 1839. The present fine building was then commenced, and was completed in 1843. Within the burial-ground around the church, and the most conspicuous object there, is the magnificent brown freestone monument, erected by order of the vestry, in 1852, and dedicated as "Sacred to the Memory," as an inscription upon it says, "of those brave and good men who died, whilst imprisoned in the city, for their devotion to the cause of American Independence." Hereby is indicated a great change, wrought by time.

---

* The Museum building (seen opposite St. Paul's in the picture), with all its contents, was destroyed by fire in 1865.

When these "brave and good men" were in prison, one of their most unrelenting foes was Dr. Inglis, the Rector of Trinity, because they were "devoted to the cause of American Independence."*   The church fronts Wall Street, the site of the wooden palisades or wall that extended from the Hudson to the East River, across the island, when it belonged to the

SOLDIERS' MONUMENT IN TRINITY CHURCHYARD.

Dutch.   Here we enter the ancient domain of New Amsterdam, a city around which the mayor was required to walk every morning at sunrise,

---

* When Washington arrived in New York with troops from Boston, in the spring of 1776, he occupied a house in Pearl Street, near Liberty, not far from Trinity Church. Being a communicant of the Church of England, he attended Divine service there.   On Sunday morning, one of Washington's generals called on Dr. Inglis, and requested him to omit the violent prayer for the king and royal family. He paid no regard to it.   He afterwards said to that officer, "It is in your power to shut up the churches, but you cannot make the clergy depart from their duty."   The prisoners alluded to in the inscription on the monument, were those who died in the old Sugar-houses of the city, which were used for hospitals. Many of them were buried in the north part of Trinity Churchyard.

unlock all the gates, and give the key to the commander of the fort. Such was New York two hundred years ago.*

According to early accounts, New Amsterdam must have been a quaint old town in Stuyvesant's time, at about the middle of the seventeenth century. It was, in style, a reproduction of a Dutch village of that period, when modest brick mansions, with terraced gables fronting the street, were mingled with steep-roofed cottages with dormer windows in sides and gables. It was then compactly built. The area within the palisades was not large; settlers in abundance came; and for several years few ventured to dwell remote from the town, because of the hostile Indians, who swarmed in the surrounding forests. The toleration that had made Holland an asylum for the oppressed, was practised here to its fullest extent. "Do you wish to buy a lot, build a house, and become a citizen?" was the usual question put to a stranger. His affirmative answer, with proofs of its sincerity, was a sufficient passport. They pryed not into private opinion or belief; and bigotry could not take root and flourish in a soil so inimical to its growth. The inhabitants were industrious, thrifty, simple in manners and living, hospitable, neighbourly, and honest; and all enjoyed as full a share of human happiness as a mild despotism would allow, until the interloping "Yankees" from the Puritan settlements, and the conquering, overbearing English,

---

* The harbour of New York was discovered by Hudson in September, 1609. It is supposed to have been entered twenty-five years earlier, by Verrazani, a Florentine. Traders speedily came after the discovery was proclaimed, and established a trading-house at Albany. In 1613, Captain Block built a ship near the Bowling Green, to replace the one in which he sailed from Holland, and which was accidentally burnt. A Dutch West India Company was formed in 1621, with all the elementary powers of government. Their charter gave them territorial dominion, and the country, called New Netherland, was made a county of Holland. The seal bore the representation of a beaver rampant—an animal very valuable for its fur, and then abundant. The seal of the city of New York (seen in the engraving) has the beaver in one of its quarterings. New Amsterdam remained in the possession of the Dutch until 1664, when it was surrendered into the hands of the English, on demand being made, in the presence of numerous ships of war, laden with land troops. Then the name was changed from New Amsterdam to New York, in honour of James, Duke of York, afterwards James II., to whom the whole domain had been granted by his profligate brother, King Charles.

SEALS OF NEW AMSTERDAM AND NEW YORK.

disturbed their repose, and made society alarmingly cosmopolitan. This feature increased with the lapse of time; and now that little Dutch trading village two hundred years ago—grown into a vast commercial metropolis, and ranking among the most populous cities of the world—contains representatives of almost every nation on the face of the earth.

Broadway, the famous street of commercial palaces, terminates at a

DUTCH MANSION AND COTTAGE IN NEW AMSTERDAM.

shaded mall and green, called "The Battery," a name derived from fortifications that once existed there. The first fort erected on Manhattan Island, by the Dutch, was on the banks of the Hudson, at its mouth, in the rear of Trinity Church. The next was built upon the site of the Bowling Green, at the foot of Broadway. These were on eminences overlooking the bay. The latter was a stronger work, and became permanent. It was called Fort Amsterdam. The palisades on the line of Wall Street (and which suggested its name) were of cedar, and were planted in 1653, when an English invading force was expected. In 1692, the English, apprehensive of a French invasion, built a strong battery on a rocky point at the eastern end of the present Battery, at the foot of White Hall Street. Finally a stone fort, with four bastions, was erected. It covered a portion of the ground occupied by the Battery of to-day. It was called Fort

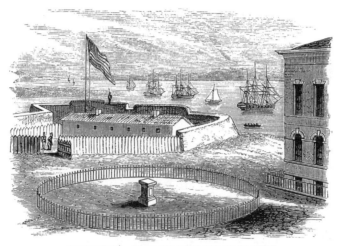

THE BOWLING GREEN AND FORT GEORGE IN 1783.*

George, in honour of the then reigning sovereign of England. Within its walls were the governor's house and most of the government offices.

In the vicinity of the fort many stirring scenes were enacted when the old war for independence was kindling. Hostile demonstrations of the opponents of the famous Stamp Act of 1766 were made there. In front

---

* This little picture shows the appearance of the Bowling Green and its vicinity, soon after the close of the war for independence. Within the enclosure is seen the pedestal on which stood the statue of the king. Near it, the Kennedy House, mentioned in the text, and beyond it, Fort George, the Bay of New York, Governor's Island, and the Narrows, on the left, and Staten Island bounding most of the horizon, in the distance.

of the fort, Lieutenant-Governor Colden's fine coach, his effigy, and the wooden railing around the Bowling Green, were made materials for a great bonfire by the mob.

At the beginning of the war for independence, Fort George and its dependencies had three batteries,—one of four guns, near the Bowling Green ; another (the Grand Battery) of twenty guns, where the flag-staff on the Battery now stands ; and a third of two heavy guns at the foot of White Hall Street, called the White Hall Battery. Here the boldness of the Sons of Liberty was displayed at the opening of the revolution, by the removal of guns from the battery in the face of a cannonade from a British ship of war in the harbour. From here was witnessed, by a vast and jubilant crowd, the final departure of the British army, after the peace of 1783, and the unfurling of the banner of the Republic from the flag-staff of Fort George, over which the British ensign had floated more than six years. The anniversary of that day—"Evacuation Day"—(the 25th of November) is always celebrated in the city of New York by a military parade and *feu de joie*.

Fort George and its dependencies have long ago disappeared, but the ancient Bowling Green remains. An equestrian statue of George the Third, made of lead, and gilded, was placed upon a high pedestal, in the centre of it, in 1770. It was ordered by the Assembly of the province in 1766, in token of gratitude for the repeal of the odious Stamp Act. The Green was then enclosed with an iron paling.* Only six years later, on the evening when the Declaration of Independence was read to Washington's army in New York, soldiers and citizens joined in pulling down the statue of the king. The round heads of the iron fence-posts were knocked off for the use of the artillery, and the leaden statue of his Majesty was made into bullets for the use of the republican army. "His troops," said a writer of the day, referring to the king, "will probably have melted majesty fired at them." The pedestal of the statue, seen in the engraving, remained in the Bowling Green some time after the war ;

* This work of art was by Wilton, of London, and was the first equestrian statue of his Majesty ever erected. Wilton made a curious omission—stirrups were wanting. It was a common remark of the Continental soldiers, that it was proper for "the tyrant" to ride a hard trotting horse without stirrups.

and the old iron railing, with its decapitated posts, is still there. A fountain of Croton water occupies the site of the statue; and the surrounding disc of green sward, where the citizens amused themselves with bowling, is now shaded by magnificent trees.

Near the Bowling Green, across Broadway (No. 1), is the Kennedy

THE BOWLING GREEN IN 1861.

House, where Washington and General Lee, and afterwards Sir Henry Clinton, Generals Robertson and Carleton, and other British officers, had their head-quarters. It has been recently altered by an addition to its height.*

---

* This house was built by Captain Kennedy, of the Royal Navy, at about the time of his marriage with the daughter of Peter Schuyler, of New Jersey, in 1765.

The present Battery or park, looking out upon the bay of New York, was formed early in the present century; and a castle, pierced for heavy guns, was erected near its western extremity. For many years, the Battery was the chief and fashionable promenade for the citizens in summer weather; and State Street, along its town border, was a very desirable place of residence. The castle was dismantled, and became a place of

THE BATTERY AND CASTLE GARDEN.

public amusement. For a long time it was known as Castle Garden; but both are now deserted by fashion and the Muses. All of old New York has been converted into one vast business mart, and there are very few respectable residences within a mile of the Battery. At the present time (September, 1861), it exhibits a martial display. Its green sward is covered with tents and barracks for the recruits of the Grand National Army of Volunteers, and its fine old trees give grateful shade to the newly-fledged soldiers preparing for the war for the Union.

At White Hall, on the eastern border of the Battery, there was a great civic and military display, at the close of April, 1789, when Washington,

OLD FEDERAL HALL.

coming to the seat of government to be inaugurated first President of the United States, landed there. He was received by officers and people with shouts of welcome, the strains of martial music, and the roar of cannon. He was then conducted to his residence on Franklin Square, and afterwards to the Old Federal Hall in Wall Street, where Congress held its sessions. It was at the corner of Wall and Nassau Streets, the site on which a fine marble building was erected for a Custom House, and which is now used for the purposes of a branch Mint. In the gallery, in front of the hall, the President took the oath of office, administered by Chancellor Livingston, in the presence of a great assemblage of people who filled the street.

The Hudson from the Battery, northward, is lined with continuous piers and slips, and exhibits the most animated scenes of commercial life. The same may be said of the East River for about an equal distance from

HUDSON RIVER STEAMERS LEAVING NEW YORK.

the Battery. Huge steam ferry-boats, magnificent passenger steamers, and freight barges, ocean steamships, and every variety of sailing vessel and other water craft may be seen in the Hudson River slips, or out upon the bosom of the stream, fairly jostling each other near the wharves because of a lack of room. Upon every deck is seen busy men; and the *yo-heave-o !* is heard at the capstan on all sides. But the most animated scene of all is the departure of steamboats for places on the Hudson, from four to six o'clock each afternoon. The piers are filled with coaches, drays, carts, barrows, every kind of vehicle for passengers and light freight. Orange-women and news-boys assail you at every step with the cries of "Five nice oranges for a shilling!"—"'Ere's the Evening Post and Express, third edition!" whilst the hoarse voices of escaping waste-steam, and the discordant tintinnabulation of a score of bells, hurry on the laggards by warnings of the near approach of the hour of departure. Several bells suddenly cease, when from different slips, steamboats covered with passengers will shoot out like race-horses from their grooms, and turning their prows northward, begin the voyage with wonderful speed, some for the head of tide-water at Troy, others for intermediate towns, and others still for places so near that the vessels may be ranked as ferryboats. The latter are usually of inferior size, but well appointed ; and at several stated hours of the day carry excursionists or country residents to the neighbouring villages. Let us consider a few of these places, on the western shore of the Hudson, which the stranger would find pleasant to visit because of the beauty or grandeur of the natural scenery, and historic associations.

The most remote of the villages to which excursionists go is Nyack, opposite Tarrytown, nearly thirty miles from New York. It lies on the bank of the Hudson at the foot of the Nyack Hills, which are broken ridges, extending several miles northward from the Palisades. Back of the village, and along the river shore, are fertile and well-cultivated slopes, where fruit is raised in abundance. On account of the salubrity of the climate, beautiful and romantic scenery, and good society, it is a very delightful place for a summer residence. From every point of view interesting landscapes meet the eye. The broad Tappan Sea is before it, and stretching along its shores for several miles are seen the towns, and villas, and rich farms of Westchester County. In its immediate vicinity the huntsman and fisherman may enjoy his favourite sport. In its southern suburbs is the spacious building of the Rockland Female Institute, seen in our sketch, in the midst of ten acres of land, and affording accommodation for one hundred pupils. During the ten weeks' summer vacation, it is used as a first-class boarding-house, under the title of the Tappan Zee House.

About four miles below Nyack is Piermont, at which is the terminus of

the middle branch of the New York and Erie Railway. The village is
the child of that road, and its life depends mainly upon the sustenance it
receives from it. The company has an iron foundry and extensive
repairing shops there; and it is the chief freight depôt of the road. Its
name is derived from a pier which juts a mile into the river. From it

VIEW NEAR NYACK.

freight is transferred to cars and barges. Tappantown, where Major
André was executed, is about two miles from Piermont.

A short distance below Piermont is Rockland, a post village of about
three hundred inhabitants, pleasantly situated on the river, and flanked
by high hills. Here the Palisades proper have their northern termination;
and from here to Fort Lee the columnar range is almost unbroken. This
place is better known as Sneeden's Landing. Here Cornwallis and six

thousand British troops landed, and marched upon Fort Lee, on the top of the Palisades, a few miles below, after the fall of Fort Washington, in the autumn of 1776.

One of the most interesting points on the west shore of the Hudson, near New York, and most resorted to, except Hoboken and its vicinity, is Fort Lee. It is within the domain of New Jersey. The dividing line between that State and New York is a short distance below Rockland or Sneeden's Landing; and it is only the distance between there and its mouth (about twenty miles) that the Hudson washes any soil but that of the State of New York.

The village of Fort Lee is situated at the foot of the Palisades. A winding road passes from it to the top of the declivity, through a deep, wooded ravine. The site of the fort is on the left of the head of the ravine, in the ascent, and is now marked by only a few mounds and a venerable pine-tree just south of them, which tradition avers once sheltered the tent of Washington. As the great patriot never pitched his tent there, tradition is in error. Washington was at the fort a short time at the middle of November, 1776, while the combined British and Hessian forces were attacking Fort Washington on the opposite shore. He saw the struggle of the garrison and its assailants, without ability to aid his friends. When the combat had continued a long time, he sent word to the commandant of the fort, that if he could hold out until night, he could bring the garrison off. The assailants were too powerful; and Washington, with Generals Greene, Mercer, and Putnam, and Thomas Paine, the influential political pamphleteer of the day, was a witness of the slaughter, and saw the red cross of St. George floating over the lost fortress, instead of the Union stripes which had been unfurled there a few months before. The title of Fort Washington was changed to that of Fort Knyphausen, in honour of the Hessian general who was engaged in its capture. Fort Lee was speedily approached by the British under Cornwallis, and as speedily abandoned by the Americans. The latter fled to the Republican camp at Hackensack, when Washington commenced his famous retreat through New Jersey, from the Hudson to the Delaware, for the purpose of saving the menaced federal capital, Philadelphia.

The view from the high point north of Fort Lee is extensive and interesting, up and down the river. Across are seen the villages of Carmansville and Manhattanville, and fine country seats near; while southward, on the left, the city of New York stretches into the dim

VIEW FROM FORT LEE.

distance, with Staten Island and the Narrows still beyond. On the right are the wooded cliffs extending to Hoboken, with the little villages of Pleasant Valley, Bull's Ferry, Weehawk, and Hoboken, along the shore.

CHAPTER XXIII.

BOUT three miles below Fort Lee is Bull's Ferry, a village of a few houses, and a great resort for the working-people of New York, when spending a leisure day. The steep, wooded bank rises abruptly in the rear, to an altitude of about two hundred feet. There, as at Weehawk, are many pleasant paths through the woods leading to vistas through which glimpses of the city and adjacent waters are obtained. Hither pic-nic parties come to spend warm summer days, where—

> " Overhead
> The branches arch, and shape a pleasant bower,
> Breaking white cloud, blue sky, and sunshine bright,
> Into pure ivory and sapphire spots,
> And flocks of gold; a soft, cool emerald tint
> Colours the air, as though the delicate leaves
> Emitted self-born light."

Our little sketch of Bull's Ferry is taken from Weehawk Wharf, and shows the point on which was a block-house during the revolution; from that circumstance it has always been called Block-house Point. Its history has a melancholy interest, as it is connected with that of the unfortunate Major André. In the summer of 1780, a few weeks before the discovery of Arnold's treason, that block-house was occupied by a British picket, for the protection of some woodcutters, and the neighbouring New Jersey loyalists. On Bergen Neck below was a large number of cattle and horses, belonging to the Americans, within reach of the foragers who might go out from the British post at Paulus's Hook, now Jersey City. Washington's head-quarters were then inland, near Ramapo. He sent General Wayne, with some Pennsylvanian and Maryland troops, horse and foot, to storm the block-house, and to drive the cattle within the American lines. Wayne sent the cavalry, under Major Henry Lee, to perform the latter duty, whilst he and three Pennsylvanian regiments marched against the block-house with four pieces of cannon. They made a spirited attack, but their cannon were too light to be effective, and, after a skirmish, the Americans were repulsed with a loss of sixty men, killed and wounded. After burning some wood-boats near,

BULL'S FERRY.

and capturing those who had them in charge, Wayne returned to camp with a large number of cattle driven by the dragoons.

This event was the theme of a satirical poem, in three cantos, in the ballad style, written by Major André, and published in Rivington's *Royal Gazette*, in the city of New York. The following is a correct copy, made by the writer for his PICTORIAL FIELD BOOK OF THE REVOLUTION, in 1850, from an original in the hand-writing of Major André. It was written upon small folio paper. The poem is entitled

THE COW CHASE.

CANTO I.

To drive the kine one summer's morn,
　The tanner* took his way;
The calf shall rue, that is unborn,
　The yumbling of that day.

And Wayne descending steers shall know
　And tauntingly deride,
And call to mind, in every low,
　The tanning of his hide.

Yet Bergen cows still ruminate
　Unconscious in the stall,
What mighty means were used to get
　And lose them after all.

For many heroes bold and brave
　From New Bridge and Tapaan,
And those that drink Passaic's wave,
　And those that eat soupaan; †

And sons of distant Delaware,
　And still remoter Shannon,
And Major Lee with horses rare,
　And Proctor with his cannon; ‡

All wondrous proud in arms they came—
　What hero could refuse,
To tread the rugged path to fame,
　Who had a pair of shoes?

At six the host, with sweating buff,
　Arrived at Freedom's Pole,
When Wayne, who thought he'd time enough,
　Thus speechified the whole:

'O ye whom glory doth unite,
　Who Freedom's cause espouse,
Whether the wing that's doomed to fight,
　Or that to drive the cows;

---

* This is in allusion to the supposed business of General Wayne, in early life, who, it was said, was a tanner. He was a surveyor.

† A common name for hasty-pudding, made of the meal of maize or Indian corn.

‡ Major Harry Lee was commander of a corps of light horseman, and Colonel Proctor was at the head of a corps of artillery.

" Ere yet you tempt your further way,
    Or into action come,
Hear, soldiers, what I have to say,
    And take a pint of rum.

",Intemp'rate valour then will string
    Each nervous arm the better,
So all the land shall IO! sing,
    And read the gen'ral's letter.

" Know that some paltry refugees,
    Whom I've a mind to fight,
Are playing h—l among the trees
    That grow on yonder height.

" Their fort and block-house we'll level,
    And deal a horrid slaughter ;
We'll drive the scoundrels to the devil,
    And ravish wife and daughter.

" I under cover of th' attack,
    Whilst you are all at blows,
From English Neighb'rhood and Tinack
    Will drive away the cows.

" For well you know the latter is
    The serious operation,
And fighting with the refugees
    Is only demonstration."

His daring words from all the crowd
    Such great applause did gain,
That every man declared aloud
    For serious work with Wayne.

Then from the cask of rum once more
    They took a heady gill,
When one and all they loudly swore
    They'd fight upon the hill.

But here—the muse has not a strain
    Befitting such great deeds,
" Hurra," they cried, " hurra for Wayne ! "
    And, shouting—did their needs.

CANTO II.

Near his meridian pomp, the sun
    Had journey'd from the horizon,
When fierce the dusky tribe moved on,
    Of heroes drunk as poison.

The sounds confused of boasting oaths,
    Re-echoed through the wood,
Some vow'd to sleep in dead men's clothes,
    And some to swim in blood.

At Irvine's nod,* 'twas fine to see
    The left prepared to fight,
The while the drovers, Wayne and Lee,
    Drew off upon the right.

Which Irvine 'twas Fame don't relate,
    Nor can the Muse assist her,
Whether 'twas he that cocks a hat,
    Or he that gives a glister.

For greatly one was signalised,
    That fought at Chestnut Hill,
And Canada immortalised
    The vendor of the pill.

Yet the attendance upon Proctor
    They both might have to boast of ;
For there was business for the doctor,
    And hats to be disposed of.

Let none uncandidly infer
    That Stirling wanted spunk,
The self-made peer had sure been there,
    But that the peer was drunk.†

But turn we to the Hudson's banks,
    Where stood the modest train,
With purpose firm, though slender ranks,
    Nor cared a pin for Wayne.

For then the unrelenting hand
    Of rebel fury drove,
And tore from ev'ry genial band
    Of friendship and of love.

And some within a dungeon's gloom,
    By mock tribunals laid,
Had waited long a cruel doom,
    Impending o'er their heads.

Here one bewails a brother's fate,
    There one a sire demands,
Cut off, alas! before their date,
    By ignominious hands.

And silver'd grandsires here appear'd
    In deep distress serene,
Of reverend manners that declared
    The better days they'd seen.

Oh! cursed rebellion, these are thine,
    Thine are these tales of woe ;
Shall at thy dire insatiate shrine
    Blood never cease to flow ?

* General William Irvine, of Pennsylvania.

† William Alexander, who unsuccessfully claimed the title of the Scotch Earl of Stirling. It was believed that his claim was just, and he was generally called "Lord Stirling."

And now the foe began to lead
  His forces to th' attack ;
Balls whistling unto balls succeed,
  And make the block-house crack.

No shot could pass, if you will take
  The gen'ral's word for true ;
But 'tis a d—ble mistake,
  For ev'ry shot went through.

The firmer as the rebels pressed,
  The loyal heroes stand ;
Virtue had nerved each honest breast,
  And Industry each hand.

In valour's frenzy, Hamilton
  Rode like a soldier big,
And secretary Harrison,
  With pen stuck in his wig.*

But, lest chieftain Washington
  Should mourn them in the mumps,†
The fate of Withrington to shun,
  They fought behind the stumps.

But ah! Thaddeus Posset, why
  Should thy poor soul elope?
And why should Titus Hooper die,
  Ah! die—without a rope?

Apostate Murphy, thou to whom
  Fair Shela ne'er was cruel ;
In death shalt hear her mourn thy doom,
  Och! would ye die, my jewel?

Thee, Nathan Pumpkin, I lament,
  Of melancholy fate,
The gray goose, stolen as he went,
  In his heart's blood was wet.

Now as the fight was further fought,
  And balls began to thicken,
The fray assumed, the gen'rals thought,
  The colour of a licking.

Yet undismay'd the chiefs command,
  And, to redeem the day,
Cry, " Soldiers, charge!" they hear, they stand,
  They turn and run away.

CANTO III.

Not all delights the bloody spear,
  Or horrid din of battle,
There are, I'm sure, who'd like to hear
  A word about the rattle.

---

* Colonels Hamilton and Harrison, of Washington's staff.
† A painful swelling of the glands, then prevalent in the Republican army.

The chief whom we beheld of late,
  Near Schralenberg haranguing,
At Yan Van Poop's unconscious sat
  Of Irvine's hearty banging.

While valiant Lee, with courage wild,
  Most bravely did oppose
The tears of women and of child,
  Who begg'd he'd leave the cows.

But Wayne, of sympathising heart,
  Required a relief,
Not all the blessings could impart
  Of battle or of beef.

For now a prey to female charms,
  His soul took more delight in
A lovely Hamadryad's arms
  Than cow driving or fighting.

A nymph, the refugees had drove
  Far from her native tree,
Just happen'd to be on the move,
  When up came Wayne and Lee.

She in mad Anthony's fierce eye
  The hero saw portray'd,
And, all in tears, she took him by
  —The bridle of his jade.

"Hear," said the nymph, "O great commander,
  No human lamentations,
The trees you see them cutting yonder
  Are all my near relations.

"And I, forlorn, implore thine aid
  To free the sacred grove:
So shall thy prowess be repaid
  With an immortal's love."

Now some, to prove she was a goddess!
  Said this enchanting fair
Had late retired from the *Bodies*,*
  In all the pomp of war.

That drums and merry fifes had play'd
  To honour her retreat,
And Cunningham himself convey'd
  The lady through the street.

Great Wayne, by soft compassion sway'd,
  To no inquiry stoops,
But takes the fair, afflicted maid
  Right into Yan Van Poop's.

* A cant appellation given among the soldiery to the corps that had the honour to guard his majesty's person.

So Roman Anthony, they say,
    Disgraced th' imperial banner,
And for a gipsy lost a day,
    Like Anthony the tanner.

The Hamadryad had but half
    Received redress from Wayne,
When drums and colours, cow and calf,
    Came down the road amain.

All in a cloud of dust were seen,
    The sheep, the horse, the goat,
The gentle heifer, ass obscene,
    The yearling and the shoat.

And pack-horses with fowls came by,
    Befeathered on each side,
Like Pegasus, the horse that I
    And other poets ride.

Sublime upon the stirrups rose
    The mighty Lee behind,
And drove the terror-smitten cows,
    Like chaff before the wind.

But sudden see the woods above
    Pour down another corps,
All helter skelter in a drove,
    Like that I sung before.

Irvine and terror in the van,
    Came flying all abroad,
And cannon, colours, horse, and man,
    Ran tumbling to the road.

Still as he fled, 'twas Irvine's cry,
    And his example too,
" Run on, my merry men all—for why ? "
    The shot will not go through.*

As when two kennels in the street,
    Swell'd with a recent rain,
In gushing streams together meet,
    And seek the neighbouring drain ;

So meet these dung-born tribes in one,
    As swift in their career,
And so to New Bridge they ran on—
    But all the cows got clear.

---

* Five refugees ('tis true) were found
    Stiff on the block-house floor,
But then 'tis thought the shot went round,
    And in at the back door.

Poor Parson Caldwell,* all in wonder,
  Saw the returning train,
And mourn'd to Wayne the lack of plunder,
  For them to steal again.

For 'twas his right to seize the spoil, and
  To share with each commander,
As he had done at Staten Island
  With frost-bit Alexander.†

In his dismay, the frantic priest
  Began to grow prophetic,
You had swore, to see his lab'ring breast,
  He'd taken an emetic.

"I view a future day," said he,
  "Brighter than this day dark is,
And you shall see what you shall see,
  Ha! ha! one pretty marquis ;‡

" And he shall come to Paulus' Hook, §
  And great achievements think on,
And make a bow and take a look,
  Like Satan over Lincoln.

" And all the land around shall glory
  To see the Frenchman caper,
And pretty Susan tell the story
  In the next Chatham paper."

This solemn prophecy, of course,
  Gave all much consolation,
Except to Wayne, who lost his horse,
  Upon the great occasion :

His horse that carried all his prog,
  His military speeches,
His corn-stalk whisky for his grog—
  Blue stockings and brown breeches.

And now I've closed my epic strain,
  I tremble as I show it,
Lest this same warrio-drover, Wayne,
  Should ever catc the poet.

It has been remarked as a curious coincidence, that on the day when the last canto of the above poem was published in Rivington's *Gazette*, Major André was arrested ; and that General Wayne, so ridiculed in it, and who is so peculiarly alluded to in the last stanza, was the commander of the military force from which was detailed the guard that accompanied

* A patriotic preacher of the Gospel, at Elizabethtown, New Jersey, who was afterwards murdered.
† William Alexander, Lord Stirling.   ‡ The Marquis de Lafayette.   § New Jersey city.

the gifted young officer to the scaffold.   On the autograph copy from which I copied the poem, and which André dated " Elizabethtown [New Jersey], August 1, 1780," were the following lines :—

> " When this epic strain was sung,
>   The poet by the neck was hung ;
>   And to his cost he finds too late,
>   The ' *dung-born tribe* ' decides his fate."

The next village below Bull's Ferry is Weehawk,* a place of great

DUELLING GROUND—WEEHAWK.

resort in summer by pleasure seekers from the metropolis.   It is made

---

* This is an Indian word, and is thus spelt in its purity.   The Dutch spelt it Wiehachan, and it is now common'y written Weehawken; I have adopted the orthography that expresses the pure Indian pronunciation.

famous by its connection with the duelling ground where General Alexander Hamilton, one of the founders of the Republic, was mortally wounded in single combat, by Aaron Burr, then Vice-President of the United States. They were bitter political foes. Without just provocation, in the summer preceding an important election, Burr, anxious to have Hamilton out of his way, challenged him to fight. The latter, out of unnecessary respect for a barbarous public opinion, accepted the challenge; and early in the morning of the 11th of July, 1804, they and friends crossed the Hudson to Weehawk, and stood as foes upon the duelling ground. Hamilton was opposed to duelling; and, pursuant to his previous resolution, did not fire his pistol. The malignant Burr took deliberate aim, and fired with fatal precision. Hamilton lived little more than thirty hours. His death produced the most profound grief throughout the nation. Burr lived more than thirty years, a fugitive, like Cain, and suffering the bitter scorn of his countrymen. This crime, added to his known vices, made him thoroughly detested, and few men had the courage to avow themselves his friend. A monument was erected to the memory of Hamilton, on the spot where he fell. It was afterwards destroyed by some marauder. The place is now a rough one, on the margin of the river, and is marked by a rude arm-chair or sofa (seen in our sketch, in which we are looking up the river) made of stones. On one of them the half-effaced names of Hamilton and Burr may be seen.

The next place of interest below Weehawk is that known in former times as the Elysian Fields. I remember it as a delightful retreat at "high noon," or by moonlight, for those who loved Nature in her quiet and simple forms. Then there were stately trees near the bank of the river, and from their shades the eye rested upon the busy surface of the stream, or the busier city beyond. There, on a warm summer afternoon, or a moonlit evening, might be seen scores of both sexes strolling upon the soft grass, or sitting upon the green sward, recalling to memory many beautiful sketches of life in the early periods of the world, given in the volumes of the old poets. All is now changed; the trips of Charon to the Elysian Fields are suspended, and the grounds, stripped of many of the noble trees, have become "private," and subjected to the manipulations of the "real estate agent." Even the Sibyl's Cave, under Castle

Point, at the southern boundary of the Elysian Fields—a cool, rocky cavern containing a spring—has been spoiled by the clumsy hand of Art. The low promontory below Castle Point was the site of the large

VIEW AT THE ELYSIAN FIELDS.

Indian village of *Hobock*. There the pleasant little city of Hoboken now stands, and few of its quiet denizens are aware of the dreadful tragedy performed in that vicinity more than two hundred years ago. The story may be related in few words. A fierce feud had existed for some time between the New Jersey Indians and the Dutch on Manhattan. Several of the latter had been murdered by the former, and the Hollanders had resolved on vengeance. At length the fierce Mohawks, bent on procuring tribute from the weaker tribes westward of the Hudson, came sweeping down like a gale from the north, driving great numbers of fugitives upon the Hackensacks at Hobock. Now was the opportunity for the Dutch. A strong body of them, with some Mohawks, crossed the Hudson at midnight, in February, 1643, fell upon the unsuspecting Indians, and before morning murdered almost one hundred men, women, and children. Many were driven from the cliffs of Castle Point, and perished in the freezing

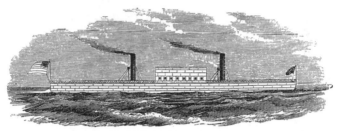

STEVENS'S FLOATING BATTERY.

flood. At sunrise the murderers returned to New Amsterdam, with prisoners and the heads of several Indians.

A large proportion of the land at Hoboken is owned by the Stevens family, who have been identified with steam navigation from its earliest triumphs. The head of the family laid out a village on Hoboken Point, in 1804. It has become a considerable city. Members of the same family had large manufacturing establishments there; and for several years before the Civil War had been constructing, upon a novel plan, a huge floating battery for harbour defences, for the government of the United States, and more than a million of dollars had already been spent in its construction, when the war broke out. It had been utterly shut in from the public eye, until a very short time before that event. Our space will allow nothing more than an outline description of it. It is a vessel seven hundred feet long (length of the *Great Eastern*), covered with plates of iron so as to be absolutely bomb and round shot proof. It is to be moved by steam engines of sufficient power to give it a momentum that will cause it to cut a man-of-war in two, when it strikes it at the waists. It will mount a battery of sixteen heavy rifled cannon in bomb-proof casemates, and two heavy columbiads for throwing shells will be on deck, one forward and one aft. The smoke-pipe is constructed in sliding sections, like a telescope, for obvious purposes; and the huge vessel may be sunk so that its decks alone will be above the water. It is to be rated at six thousand tons. The war was productive of a variety of iron-clad vessels far more effective than this promises to be, and it is probable that it will never be completed.

Opposite the lower part of the city of New York, and separated from Hoboken by a bay and marsh, is Jersey City, on a point at the mouth of the Hudson, known in early times as Paulus's or Pauw's Hook, it having been originally obtained from the Indians by Michael Pauw. This was an important strategic point in the revolution. Here the British esta-blished a military post after taking possession of the city of New York in 1776, and held it until August, 1779, when the active Major Henry Lee, mentioned in André's satire of "The Cow Chase," with his legion, sur-prised the garrison, killed a number, and captured the fort, just before the dawn. Now a flourishing city—a suburb of New York—covers that point. Immense numbers of travellers pass through it daily, it being the terminus of several important railways that connect with New York by powerful steam ferry-boats. Here, too, are the wharves of the Cunard line of ocean steamers. Before it is the broad and animated bay of New York, forming its harbour, and, stretching away to the south-west, nine miles or more, is Newark Bay, that receives the Passaic River.

Here we leave the Hudson proper, and after visiting some prominent places in the vicinity of the metropolis, will accompany the reader to the sea.

Adjacent to Manhattan Island, and separated from it by the narrow East River, is Long Island, which stretches along the coast from West to East, about one hundred and forty miles. It is rich in traditional, legendary, and historical reminiscences. Near its western extremity, and opposite the city of New York, is the large and beautiful city of Brooklyn,* whose intimate social and business relations with the metropolis, and connection by numerous ferries, render it a sort of suburban town. Its growth has been wonderful. Less than sixty years ago, it contained only a ferry-house, a few scattered dwellings, and a church. Now it comprises an area of 16,000 acres, with an exterior line of twenty-two miles. Like New York, it has absorbed several villages. It was incorporated a village in 1816, and a city in 1834. Its central portion is

JERSEY CITY AND CUNARD DOCK.

upon a range of irregular hills, fortified during the revolution. The bluff on which Fort Stirling stood—now known as "The Heights"—is covered with fine edifices, and affords extensive views of New York and its harbour. Williamsburgh, which had become quite a large city, was annexed to Brooklyn in 1854. Between the two cities is Wallabout Bay, the scene of great suffering among the American prisoners, in British prison-ships, during the revolution. Eleven thousand men perished

* From the Dutch *Breuck-landt*—broken land.

,there, and their remains were buried in shallow graves on the shore. Near its banks was born Sarah Rapelje, the first child of European parents that drew its earliest breath within the limits of the State of New York.* Upon that *aceldama* of the old war for independence in the vicinity of the Hudson, is now a dockyard of the United States Government, which covers about forty-five acres of land. Within the enclosure is a depository of curious things, brought home by officers and seamen of the navy, and is called the Naval Lyceum. It contains a fine geological

BROOKLYN FERRY AND HEIGHTS.

cabinet, and a library of several thousand volumes. Upon a gentle hill back of the Navy Yard is a United States Marine Hospital, seen in our sketch.

The southern portion of Brooklyn lies upon low ground, with an extensive water front. There, immense commercial works have been

---

* In April, 1623, thirty families, chiefly Walloons (French Protestants who had taken refuge in Holland), arrived at Manhattan, in charge of the first Governor of New Netherland. Eight of these families went up the Hudson, and settled at Albany; the remainder chose their place of abode across the channel of the East River, upon lands now covered by a portion of the city of Brooklyn and the United States Navy Yard.

constructed, known as the Atlantic Docks, covering forty acres, and affording within the "slips" water of sufficient depth for vessels of largest size. There is an outside pier, three thousand feet in length, and on the wharves are extensive warehouses of granite. These wharves afford perfect security from depredators to vessels loading and unloading.

A little below Brooklyn, and occupying a portion of the ground whereon the conflict between the British and American armies, known as the battle of Long Island, was fought, at the close of the summer of

NAVY YARD, BROOKLYN.

1776, is Greenwood Cemetery, one of the most noted burial-places in the country. A greater portion of it is within the limits of the city of Brooklyn. It comprises four hundred acres of finely diversified land. The present population of that "city of the dead" is probably not less than 70,000. One of the most delightful places within its borders is Sylvan Water, near the shores of which may be seen a monument, over the grave of an Indian princess, of the tribe of *Min-ne-ha-ha*, the bride of Longfellow's *Hi-a-wat-ha*, who died in New York a few years ago. Also the grave of M'Donald Clarke, known in New York, twenty years ago, as the "Mad Poet." His monument is seen upon a little hillock in our sketch of Sylvan Water. Clarke was an eccentric child of genius. He

SYLVAN WATER, GREENWOOD.

became, in his latter years, an unhappy wanderer, with reason half dethroned, a companion of want, and the victim of the world's neglect. His proud spirit disdained to ask food, and he famished. Society, of

whom his necessities asked bread, "gave him a stone"—a monument of
white marble, with his profile in *bas-relief*. He died in March, 1842.
"He was a poet," says his biographer, "of the order of Nat Lee ; one of
those wits, in whose heads, according to Dryden, genius is divided from
madness by a thin partition." *

From two or three prominent points in Greenwood Cemetery fine
views of New York city and bay may be obtained, but a better comprehension of the scenery of the harbour, and adjacent shores, may be had
in a voyage down the Bay to Staten Island.† This may be accomplished

GOVERNOR'S AND BEDLOE'S ISLANDS.

many times a day, on steam ferry-boats, from the foot of Whitehall
Street, near "The Battery." As we go out from the "slip," we soon
obtain a general view of the harbour. On the left is Governor's Island,
with Castle Williams upon its western extremity, and Fort Columbus

---

* Duyckinck's "Cyclopædia of American Literature."

† This island was purchased from the Indians in 1630, by the proprietor of the land on which Jersey
city now stands, and all of that vicinity. It reverted to the Dutch West India Company, when it was
called Status Eylandt, or the State's Island. A considerable number of French Protestants (Huguenots),
who fled to America after the revocation of the Edict of Nantes, settled on Staten Island. The British
troops took possession of the island in 1776, and held it until the autumn of 1783.

lying upon its crown, shaded with old Lombardy poplars. On the right is Bedloe's Island,* mostly occupied by Fort Wood, a heavy fortification, erected in 1841. Near it is Ellis's Island, with a small military work, called Fort Gibson. This was formerly named Gibbet Island, it being then, as now, the place for the execution of pirates. These islands belong to the United States. The forts upon them were used as prisons for captured soldiers of the armies in rebellion during the Civil War.

Before the voyager down the bay lies Staten Island, which, with the western end of Long Island, presents a great barrier to the ocean winds

THE NARROWS, FROM QUARANTINE.

and waves, and affords a shelter to vessels in the harbour of New York from the tempest outside. It is nearly oval-shaped, fourteen miles in length, and eight in breadth. It was heavily wooded, and sparsely settled, when the British army occupied it, in the summer of 1776. Now, the hand of cultivation is everywhere visible. Its shores bordering on New York Bay are dotted with lively villages, and all over the broad range of hills that extend from the Narrows, across the island, are superb

* So named from Isaac Bedloe, the *patentee* under Governor Nicholson.

country-seats, and neat farmhouses. It is a favourite place of summer residence for the wealthy and business men of New York—easy of access, and salubrious. These country-seats usually overlook the bay. The tourist will find an excursion over this island a delightful one.

On the northern extremity of Staten Island, the State of New York established a quarantine as early as 1799, and maintained it until the beginning of September, 1858, when the inhabitants of the village that had grown up there, and of the adjacent country, who had long petitioned for its removal as a dangerous nuisance, destroyed all the buildings by fire. There had been more than five hundred cases of yellow fever there

FORT LAFAYETTE.

two years before, and the distress and alarm created by that contagion made the people determine to rid themselves of the cause. Since the destruction of the establishment, a hospital-ship, to serve quarantine purposes, has been anchored in the lower bay, preparatory to some permanent arrangement.

From the Quarantine Dock may be obtained an excellent view of the Narrows, the ship channel between Long and Staten Islands through which vessels pass to and from the sea. Our little sketch gives a comprehensive view of that broad gate to the harbour of New York. On the right is seen Staten Island, with the new and substantial battery on the water's edge, just below the unfinished Fort Wadsworth (formerly Fort Richmond). On the left is the Long Island shore, with Fort Hamilton on its high bank, and Fort Lafayette, formerly Fort Diamond, in the stream below. The latter fort is upon Hendrick's Reef, two hundred yards from the Long Island shore. It was commenced in 1812, but had not been thoroughly completed when the Civil War commenced, although 350,000 dollars had been spent upon it. It was then capable of having mounted seventy-five heavy guns. It soon became famous as a

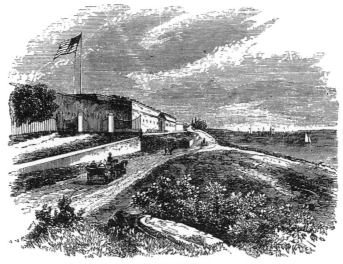

FORT HAMILTON.

political state prison in which many citizens, charged with disloyal, seditious, and treasonable acts toward the Government, were confined. Among them was Mr. Faulkner, of Virginia, who was the United States minister to the French Court during Mr. Buchanan's administration; the mayor and chief of police of Baltimore; members of the Maryland legislature, and the mayor of Washington city. The latter was released after a short confinement, on taking the oath of allegiance.

On the eastern border of the Narrows stands Fort Hamilton, a strong fortification completed in 1832, when a war with France seemed to be impending. It was enlarged and strengthened during the Civil War. At the beginning of the rebellion it mounted sixty heavy guns (a portion of them *en barbette*), forty-eight of which bore upon the ship channel. The fort is elevated, and commands the Lower Bay from the Narrows towards Sandy Hook. This work, with the fortifications on the opposite shore of Staten Island, and the water battery of Fort Lafayette in the channel, render the position, at the entrance to New York Bay, almost impregnable.

A delightful voyage of fifteen minutes in a steamer, or half an hour

SURF BATHING, CONEY ISLAND.

in a sail-boat, will take us to Coney Island, once a peninsula of Long Island at the lower end of Gravesend Bay. It is now connected with the main, by a good road, a causeway, and a bridge. The island is about five miles in length, and one in width, and contains about sixty acres of arable land. The remainder is made up of sand dunes, formed by the

action of the winds. These resemble snow-drifts, and are from five to
thirty feet in height. It is a favourite summer resort for bathers, its
beach being unsurpassed. Near the Pavilion, at its western end, the
scene of our little sketch, the beach is very flat, and surf bathing is
perfectly safe. There crowds of bathers of both sexes, in their sometimes
grotesque dresses, may be seen every pleasant day in summer, especially
at evening, enjoying the water. Refreshments are served at the Pavilion
near, and a day may be spent there pleasantly and profitably. There are
two or three summer boarding-houses at the other end of the island,
which may be reached from Brooklyn in the space of forty-five minutes,
by railways.

Between Coney Island and Sandy Hook, is an expanse of water, several

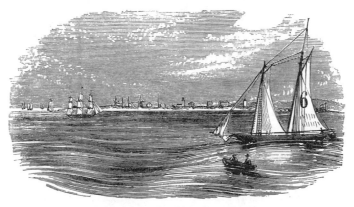

SANDY HOOK, FROM THE SHIP CHANNEL.

miles across, in which is the sinuous channel followed by large vessels
in their entrance to and exit from the harbour of New York in charge of
the pilots. To the right, beyond Raritan Bay, is seen the New Jersey
shore; while southward, in the blue distance, loom up the Navesink
Highlands, on which stand the lighthouses first seen by the voyager from
Europe, when approaching the port of New York.

Sandy Hook is a long, low, narrow strip of sandy land, much of it covered with shrubs and dwarf trees. It is about five miles in length, from the Navesink Lights to its northern extremity, whereon are two lighthouses. It is the southern cape of Raritan Bay, and has twice been an island, within less than a century. An inlet was cut through by the sea during a gale in 1778, but closed again in the year 1800. Another

SANDY HOOK, FROM THE LIGHTHOUSES.

inlet was cut in 1830, and for several years it was so deep and broad that steamboats passed through it. That is now closed.

At the northern extremity of Sandy Hook, the United States are now erecting strong fortifications. These will materially strengthen the defences of the harbour of New York, as this fort will command the ship channel.   About a mile below the pier, near the lighthouse, on the inner shore of the Hook, once stood an elegant monument, erected to the memory of a son of the Earl of Morton, and thirteen others, who were cast away near there, in a snow-storm, during the revolution, and perished.   All but one were officers of a British man-of-war, wrecked there.   They were discovered, and buried in one grave.   The mother of the young nobleman erected the monument, and it remained, respected even by the roughest men of the coast, until 1808, when some vandals, from a French vessel-of-war, landed there, and destroyed that beautiful memorial of a mother's love.

Here, reader, on the borders of the great sea, we will part company for a season.   We have had a pleasant and memorable journey from the Wilderness, three hundred miles away to the northward, where the forest shadows eternally brood, and the wild beasts yet dispute for dominion with man.   We have looked upon almost every prominent object of Nature and Art along the borders of the Hudson, and have communed profitably, I hope, with History and Tradition on the way.   We have seen every phase of material progress, from Nature in her wildest forms, to Civilisation in its highest development.   Our journey is finished—our observations have ceased—and here, with the yielding sand beneath our feet, a cloudless sky bending over us, and the heaving ocean before us—

> "The sea! the sea! the open sea!
> The blue, the fresh, the ever free!"—

we will say FAREWELL!

THE END.